Presentism, Gender, and Sexuality in Shakespeare

Also by Evelyn Gajowski

THE ART OF LOVING: Female Subjectivity and Male Discursive Traditions in Shakespeare's Tragedies

RE-VISIONS OF SHAKESPEARE: Essays in Honor of Robert Ornstein *(editor)*

Presentism, Gender, and Sexuality in Shakespeare

Edited by

Evelyn Gajowski

palgrave
macmillan

First published 2009 by
PALGRAVE MACMILLAN

Palgrave Macmillan in the UK is an imprint of Macmillan Publishers Limited, registered in England, company number 785998, of Houndmills, Basingstoke, Hampshire RG21 6XS.

Palgrave Macmillan in the US is a division of St Martin's Press LLC, 175 Fifth Avenue, New York, NY 10010.

Palgrave Macmillan is the global academic imprint of the above companies and has companies and representatives throughout the world.

Palgrave® and Macmillan® are registered trademarks in the United States, the United Kingdom, Europe and other countries.

ISBN-13: 978–0–230–22383–7 hardback
ISBN-10: 0–230–22383–4 hardback

This book is printed on paper suitable for recycling and made from fully managed and sustained forest sources. Logging, pulping and manufacturing processes are expected to conform to the environmental regulations of the country of origin.

A catalogue record for this book is available from the British Library.

Library of Congress Cataloging-in-Publication Data

Gajowski, Evelyn.
Presentism, gender, and sexuality in Shakespeare / Evelyn Gajowski.
p. cm.
Includes bibliographical references and index.
ISBN-13: 978–0–230–22383–7 (alk. paper)
ISBN-10: 0–230–22383–4 (alk. paper)
1. Shakespeare, William, 1564–1616 – Criticism and interpretation. 2. Sex role in literature. 3. Gender identity in literature. 4. Sexual orientation in literature. 5. Homosexuality in literature. 6. Women in literature. 7. Presentism (Literary analysis) 8. Feminist literary criticism. I. Title.

PR3069.S45G35 2009
822.3′3—dc22 2008029929

10 9 8 7 6 5 4 3 2 1
18 17 16 15 14 13 12 11 10 09

Printed and bound in Great Britain by
CPI Antony Rowe, Chippenham and Eastbourne

For my mother and the memory of my father

We don't see things as they are; we see them as we are.

Anias Nin

Contents

Illustrations

Acknowledgments

As always, my greatest debt is to my husband, Harvey Berenberg – *sine qua non.*

I am grateful to the contributors to this volume for their willingness and their ability to think through the implications of presentism for sexuality and gender issues in Shakespeare studies and in so doing to explore genuinely new theoretical terrain.

The intellectual labor behind this collection is, of course, indebted to the intellectual labor of other Shakespeare scholars who have gone before.

The pioneering work on presentism of Terry Hawkes, Hugh Grady, and Linda Charnes has provided inspiration for this collection of essays. Terry's book-length studies include (in reverse chronological order) *Presentist Shakespeares; Shakespeare in the Present; Meaning by Shakespeare;* and *That Shakespeherian Rag.* Hugh's book-length studies include (in reverse chronological order) *Presentist Shakespeares; Shakespeare, Machiavelli, and Montaigne: Power and Subjectivity from* Richard II *to* Hamlet; *Shakespeare's Universal Wolf: Postmodernist Studies in Early Modern Reification;* and *The Modernist Shakespeare: Critical Texts in a Material World.* Linda has been instrumental in developing presentist thinking in a series of important books and articles, culminating, most recently, in *Hamlet's Heirs* and 'Reading for the Wormholes: Micro-periods from the Future'.

Without self-consciously labeling herself and her work 'presentist', Phyllis Rackin, in books such as *Shakespeare and Women* and articles such as 'Misogyny Is Everywhere' nonetheless has recently raised crucial questions about the vexed relationship of historicism and feminism, with particular emphasis on the negative implications of the former for the latter.

This collection of essays is indebted, as well, to the feminist and queer scholars working in Shakespeare studies in recent years. In many ways, the present collection builds on and hopes to contribute to the pioneering research they have conducted.

I am grateful to Hugh Grady for generously sharing his work in progress with me at several junctures and for several scholarly discussions on the subject of presentism, especially his off-hand comment at the Seventh World Shakespeare Congress in Valencia, Spain, in April 2001, that the implications of presentism for feminism were a subject worthy of investigation.

New developments in Shakespeare studies are often enabled by those hothouse environments known as professional conferences, where new ideas are first tried out in public and where unexpected collaborations can sometimes occur. For the opportunity to co-lead or lead several research seminars that examined the implications of presentism for the subjects of sexuality, gender, and war, I am appreciative of the Trustees of the Shakespeare Association of America and the Executive Board of the International Shakespeare Association. Adrian Kiernander co-chaired two research seminars with me: 'Shakespeare, Gender, and Sexual Orientation in the Present', at the 33rd annual meeting of the Shakespeare Association of America in Bermuda in March 2005 and 'Performing Shakespeare and Gender in the Present', at the eighth World Shakespeare Congress in Brisbane, Australia, in July 2006. I am grateful to Adrian for sharing the responsibility of guiding and leading these deliberations (in each case, over a period of several months) in such a thoroughly collaborative and gracious manner and for coming up with the insane idea that seminar leaders should also contribute papers to their own seminars. I also chaired a third research seminar, 'The Presence of Shakespeare and War', at the 35th annual meeting of the Shakespeare Association of America in San Diego, California, in April 2007. I am grateful to Hugh Grady and Jean Howard for assisting me in responding to seminar participants' papers on that occasion.

Students in my Shakespeare and gender courses at the University of Nevada, Las Vegas, and particularly in my graduate seminars, have invigorated me with their excitement and curiosity about presentism as a newly evolving theoretical paradigm.

A few ideas in my introductory chapter were originally published by Routledge in somewhat different form in my contribution, 'Lavinia as "blank page" and the presence of feminist critical practices', to the collection, *Presentist Shakespeares*, edited by Hugh Grady and Terence Hawkes for the Accents on Shakespeare series.

An earlier version of Michael Mangan's essay originally appeared in *Ilha do Desterro*, no. 49 (2005), pp. 195–213.

Every effort has been made to trace rights holders, but if any have been inadvertently overlooked the publishers would be pleased to make the necessary arrangements at the first opportunity.

Contributors

Linda Charnes is Professor of English and West European Studies at Indiana University, Bloomington. She is the author of *Hamlet's Heirs: Shakespeare and the Politics of a New Millennium* and *Notorious Identity: Materializing the Subject in Shakespeare*. She is currently working on a book about Shakespeare and the cultural logic of the 'fourth wall'.

Evelyn Gajowski has published two books on Shakespeare: *Re-Visions of Shakespeare: Essays in Honor of Robert Ornstein* and *The Art of Loving: Female Subjectivity and Male Discursive Traditions in Shakespeare's Tragedies*. She is Professor of English at the University of Nevada, Las Vegas.

Douglas E. Green is Professor of English and Women's Studies at Augsburg College in Minneapolis. His most recent article, 'Branagh's *Love's Labour's Lost* and the Return of the Hollywood Musical: Song of the Living Dead', appears in *Shakespeare Bulletin*. He writes on Shakespeare in light of performance, gender and sexuality, and pedagogy.

Adrian Kiernander is Professor of Theatre Studies at the University of New England in New South Wales, Australia. He is the author of *Ariane Mnouchkine and the Théâtre du Soleil* and has published extensively on issues of gender and sexuality in theatre. Together with Jonathan Bollen and Bruce Parr, he has co-edited a collection of essays on gender and performance entitled, *What a Man's Gotta Do?*, and has co-authored a book on masculinity in Australia theatre, *Men at Play*.

Arthur L. Little, Jr is Associate Professor of English at the University of California, Los Angeles, with affiliations in Women Studies, LGBTS, and African American Studies. The author of *Shakespeare Jungle Fever: National-Imperial Re-Visions of Race, Rape, and Sacrifice* and articles on Shakespeare and other writers, he is a General Co-Editor of Palgrave's Race and Early Modern Series. He is currently working on a cultural study of *Hamlet*.

Michael Mangan is Professor of Drama at Exeter University. He has also worked as a playwright, a director, a literary manager, a dramaturg and an actor. He has published books, articles, and papers on the subjects of theatre and gender, Shakespeare and Renaissance theatre, the cultural history of popular performance, applied theatre and contemporary

British theatre. His most recent book is *Performing Dark Arts: A Cultural History of Conjuring.*

Kathleen McLuskie is Director of the Shakespeare Institute in Stratford upon Avon. She has written numerous articles on the plays of Shakespeare and his contemporary playwrights and is author of *Feminist Readings of Renaissance Dramatists* and *Dekker and Heywood: Professional Dramatists.* She has edited Webster's *The Duchess of Malfi* and a collection of *Plays on Women* and co-edited a collection of essays, *Shakespeare and the Modern Theatre.* She is currently working on an AHRC-funded project, 'Interrogating Cultural Value in the 21st Century: The Case of Shakespeare'.

Anthony Guy Patricia is a PhD student at the University of Nevada, Las Vegas. His primary areas of specialization include Shakespeare, Renaissance drama, and queer theory. He is working on a dissertation that analyzes the male homoerotics of Shakespeare's dramatic texts and sonnets. He has recently published book reviews of critical texts dealing with Milton and Shakespeare in *Popular Culture Review.*

Phyllis Rackin is Professor of English Emerita at the University of Pennsylvania. A former President of the Shakespeare Association of America, she has published four books on Shakespeare: *Shakespeare and Women*; *Engendering a Nation: A Feminist Account of Shakespeare's English Histories*, which she wrote in collaboration with Professor Jean Howard of Columbia University; *Stages of History: Shakespeare's English Chronicles*; and *Shakespeare's Tragedies.*

Kathryn Schwarz is Associate Professor of English at Vanderbilt University. She is the author of *Tough Love: Amazon Encounters in the English Renaissance* and is currently completing a book on women and will in early modern England.

Bruce R. Smith is College Distinguished Professor of English at the University of Southern California. A former President of the Shakespeare Association of America, he is the author of *Shakespeare and Masculinity* and *Homosexual Desire in Shakespeare's England*, in addition to four other books, most recently, *The Key of Green: Passion and Perception in Renaissance Culture.*

Kay Stanton is a Shakespeare specialist and Professor of English at California State University at Fullerton. She is currently completing a book, *Shakespeare's Whores: Erotics, Politics, and Poetics.* She has published more than twenty scholarly articles, including work on Marlowe, Milton, and Arthur Miller, as well as Shakespeare.

The Presence of the Past

Evelyn Gajowski

> For every image of the past that is not recognized by the present as one of its own concerns threatens to disappear irretrievably...
>
> History is the subject of a structure whose site is not homogeneous, empty time, but time filled by the presence of the now [*Jetztzeit*].
>
> –Walter Benjamin, 'Theses on the Philosophy of History'

'You're talking about my body!' I said, pointing to my abdomen. I didn't realize what I'd said till the words escaped my lips.

The room was getting hot and stuffy. Every seat was filled. People leaned against the walls and spilled out the doorway into the hall.

I was terrified. Maybe one of the patriarchs would contact the chair of my department at my home institution and say something that would be used against me at tenure.

Near the rear of the packed room, one of them rose to respond.

'You have dropped decorum!' he scolded, going on to speak at length about how supportive he was of his daughters and his wife.

The occasion was an open forum on the relationship between literature and politics, organized by the Executive Board at the annual convention of the Rocky Mountain Modern Language Association. It was trying to compensate for having voted to hold the convention in a state notorious for its anti-choice legislation – a vote that proved to be controversial. Unable to reverse the Board's decision, members of the Women's Caucus were protesting by organizing sessions and making a fuss about women's body issues or else boycotting the convention altogether.

That was October, 1992, Ogden, Utah.

> 'There is help available for child abusers, wife beaters, alcoholics, drug addicts, and homosexuals', he said. 'Those people should find cures for their diseases'.
>
> Same patriarch. Same session. Same professional organization. One year later.
>
> 'I cannot tell you how embarrassed I am', I responded as I rose to my feet. 'I have invited the incoming President of the Shakespeare Association of America to participate in our proceedings, and he has honored us with his presence, only to be subjected to insult'.

Once again, the Executive Board had convened an open forum devoted to discussing the relationship between literature and politics. It had voted to hold the annual convention of the RMMLA not only once but two years in a row in a state that had recently passed anti-gay legislation known as Amendment 2. Two more controversial decisions. Once again, unable to reverse the Board's decision, members of the GLBT Caucus and the Women's Caucus jointly protested by organizing sessions on queer issues.

That was October, 1993, Denver, Colorado.

Events such as these suggest how interpenetrating and inseparable academia and politics can be, animating the 1960s motto, 'the personal is political', with new vitality. They also suggest how conservative political, religious, and social developments can serve to galvanize opposition to oppression and spur the growth of progressive movements and activism. Even as these events suggest the ways in which academic and political developments are mutually constitutive, so too, do they point to the origins of feminist studies in the women's liberation movement of the late twentieth century and the origins of queer studies in the Stonewall Inn riots at Sheridan Square in Greenwich Village beginning on 28 June, 1969, the watershed event that precipitated the gay liberation movement.

Insofar as feminist and queer literary theory and criticism are discursive practices that are rooted in and are informed by early twenty-first century political, economic, and social practices, they are inevitably presentist in nature. Put another way – more succinctly, perhaps, and appropriating the useful formulation of Jacques Derrida (and, after him, Stephen Greenblatt) – feminist and queer studies are *always already* (1972, 1988) presentist. Foregrounding gender and sexual orientation in Shakespeare's texts and culture constitutes theoretical and critical strategies that are inherently presentist. These issues have been, and continue to be, of urgency on the intellectual, political and social agendas of the late twentieth and early twenty-first centuries, and the questions they raise are of genuine, felt significance in our lives. In recent decades, gender and queer theory have challenged the essentialism of ideological constructions; emphasized previously neglected, suppressed, or repressed aspects of performances and texts; re-evaluated gendered experiences; and rethought canons. Beginning in the mid-1970s, ground-breaking book-length feminist and queer studies – Juliet Dusinberre's *Shakespeare and the Nature of Women*; Carolyn Ruth Swift Lenz's, Gayle Greene's, and Carol Thomas Neely's *The Woman's Part: Feminist Criticism of Shakespeare*; Alan Bray's *Homosexuality in Renaissance England*; Joseph Pequigney's *Such Is My Love: A Study of Shakespeare's Sonnets* – opened up new meanings in Shakespeare's texts and culture that had been repressed for nearly four centuries.

In the first collection of feminist essays on Shakespeare, *The Woman's Part*, editors Lenz, Greene, and Neely spelled out four aims: to liberate female characters from the stereotypes to which traditional liberal humanist criticism had confined them; to examine female characters' relations to each other; to analyze the nature and effects of patriarchal structures; and to explore the implications of genre for the representation of females (1980, 4).[1] The first feminist monograph on Shakespeare, Juliet Dusinberre's book constructed Shakespeare as a proto-feminist and appropriated him as a political ally of contemporary feminist scholars. Within a decade, however, under the influence of feminist historian Joan Kelly's groundbreaking article – 'Did Women Have a Renaissance?' – to which the answer was a resounding 'No', Lisa Jardine and Kathleen McLuskie offered a counter-argument that Shakespeare was a 'patriarchal bard'. A third phase of feminist criticism attempted to transcend the 'Shakespeare as proto-feminist' or 'Shakespeare as patriarchal bard' stalemate by examining early modern English documents that had given rise to it. Under the influence of historicism, feminism became preoccupied with the relationship between text and context, exploring the position of women in early modern English society. After all, if the object of feminist inquiry is women, as Dympna Callaghan pointed out, then the heavily mediated representations of femininity in Shakespeare's texts offer only an oblique bearing on the subject (2000, xii).

In the last decades of the twentieth century, feminism took its place among cultural materialism, deconstruction, psychoanalysis, and historicism as one of the dominant approaches to interpreting Shakespeare anew. By the mid-1990s, however, a profound change had occurred. Historicism had developed into the dominant theoretical approach, as Hugh Grady observes, to the extent of deprivileging all the others:

> At present, the trend toward historicizing Shakespeare appears to have become so dominant in the field and therefore so highly valued that more 'presentist' approaches – that is, those oriented towards the text's meaning in the present, as opposed to 'historicist' approaches oriented to meanings in the past – are in danger of eclipse. (1996, 4–5)

Eventually, under the influence of historicism, feminism lost its voice. It became naïve to analyze female agency and unfashionable to analyze female subversion; it became fashionable, instead, to underscore how any subversion, including female subversion, was inevitably contained by power structures, including patriarchal structures. 'Chaste, silent, and obedient', the message that was endlessly repeated in early modern English household manuals, conduct books, and marriage sermons, became a refrain repeated more often in contemporary scholarship, as Lena Cowen Orlin shrewdly pointed out, than it may have been in early modern England (1998, quoted in Rackin 2000, 54). The most recent developments in feminist studies have focused on the intersections of gender with sexual orientation, nationality, post-colonialism, race, and class. At the millennium, Dympna Callaghan enunciated the aims of her collection, *The Feminist Companion to Shakespeare*, as follows:

> to demonstrate feminist visibility – even to the point of conspicuousness – *and* its integration into the broader field of Shakespeare studies via a series of overlapping categories: the history of feminist Shakespeare criticism, text and language, social economies, sexuality, race, and religion. (2000, xv)[2]

Theory and criticism that was informed by an awareness of sexual orientation in the early 1980s initially intersected with feminist interrogations of gender identity and sexuality.[3] To the extent that heterosexist, patriarchal power structures objectified and oppressed both women and gays, ideological and political alliances between the two groups seemed possible, and advantageous. As GLBT studies evolved into gender studies, however, its focus broadened to include constructions of masculinity, as well as constructions of femininity. Historians Michel Foucault, in volume one of *The History of Sexuality*, and David Halperin, in *One Hundred Years of Sexuality*, pointed out that our contemporary understanding of homosexuality as a matter of identity was an invention of the nineteenth century. A profound shift in sexual sensibility occurred after the seventeenth century that constructed the category of 'homosexuality' as deviant from the 'norm' of heterosexual identity. Sexual practices that were later understood as emanating from a (deviant) homosexual identity were instead understood in early modern England as isolated, deviant acts – that is, 'sodomy' and 'buggery'. In the first book in early modern studies written by a gay-identified author, historian Alan Bray followed Foucault's formulation and, in turn, anticipated Halperin. These theories set off a debate about the possibility, or impossibility, of homosexual identity in early modern England, something Jonathan Dollimore addressed in his article, 'Shakespeare Understudies: The Sodomite, the Prostitute, the Transvestite and Their Critics' (1994). Likewise, Alan Sinfield disputed Foucault's and Bray's theories in his article, 'How to read *The Merchant of Venice* without being heterosexist' (1996). More recently, Sinfield argues that 'the intriguing parts of the unfinished business of cultural materialism' are those points at which 'poetic and dramatic texts appear to undermine the hegemony' of heteronormativity (2006a, 29).

Queer theory developed in tandem with and at least in part as a response to the AIDs epidemic in the late 1980s. Queer studies and queer theory provided a rallying point that called attention to the crisis by appropriating the derogatory term, 'queer', and deliberately transvaluing it into a source of pride. Under the influence of post-structuralist thought – particularly that of Foucault as mediated by Eve Kosofsky Sedgwick and Judith Butler – queer theory has been concerned with deconstructing static, fixed ideologies of identity and the binary oppositions of male/female, hetero/homo, past/present. In their article, 'Queering History', Jonathan Goldberg and Madhavi Menon pose the question, 'Why has historicism constructed the early modern period and homosexuality alike as alterity?' They call the entire historicist project into question from a queer standpoint, particularly its mapping of sexual difference onto chronological difference – when, as they put it, 'the difference between past and present becomes also the difference between sexual regimes' (2005, 1609). They urge resistance to this collapsing of categories. Instead of historicism's construction of a relationship between past and present that is fixed, knowable and different, they theorize that history is insufficient to house the queer project – what they call *unhistoricism*. Instead of historicism's construction of history based on heterosexual difference, they theorize suspending ideologies of 'determinate sexual and chronological difference' and expanding non-heterosexual possibilities – a gesture they call *homohistory* (2005, 1609). These theoretical gestures resonate with earlier ones, such as theorizing 'her' story in opposition to 'his' story on the part of feminist scholars of a prior generation. At the same time, Goldberg and Menon exemplify what Terence Hawkes gets at when he speaks of the never-ending dialog between past and present in which scholars of Shakespeare and early modern English culture are continually engaged. They echo his call for a 'principled and self-inventing betrayal' of an oppressive scholarly tradition – one that expands the interventionist possibilities of criticism into history (2002, 20).

It is true that to respond to a Shakespeare text is to enter into a dialog with the past, whether or not we are prompted, as Greenblatt is, by a desire 'to speak with the dead' (1988, 1). Entering into such a conversation means entering into a dialog not only with Shakespeare and his contemporaries, I would add, but also with the tradition of theatrical and critical responses to Shakespeare's texts that has accumulated over the course of four centuries. And these themselves constitute not merely passive responses but also active constructions of meaning in their own right. Yet we are also compelled 'to talk with the living', as Terence Hawkes puts it (2002, 4). Enmeshed in the early twenty-first century as we are, we cannot help but be influenced in our apprehension of Shakespeare's texts by contemporary discursive practices, ideologies, and events that constitute us, even as we, in turn, constitute Shakespeare's texts. In a chain of mutually constitutive relationships, these discursive practices, ideologies, and events construct meanings in us, even as we, in turn, construct meanings in texts.

Situated in the liminal present moment, we occupy a position analogous to that of the classical Janus figure at the doorway – simultaneously looking backward into the past and looking forward into the future. This is nothing new, of course. We have inevitably had to view the past from the perspective of the present, as twentieth-century philosophers of history such as Benedetto Croce emphasize when theorizing that 'all history is contemporary history' (1941, 19–22, 1960, 11–15). In fact, we cannot help but do so, in Hawkes's formulation: 'None of us can step beyond time. It can't be drained out of our experience' (2002, 3). At the outset of the twenty-first century, literary theoretical and critical practices are on the threshold of recognizing this crucial factor and deliberately focusing on it more self-consciously than in recent decades – more fully, perhaps, than ever before. Realizing that we view the past through the lens of our present, even as those in the future will inevitably view us through the lens of their present, enables us, I believe, to gain a heightened awareness of the narrative of human history as an ongoing, imbricated (and imbricating) process. To re-write history is to write the future. Feminism is about creating the future differently, as Dympna Callaghan observes, by looking at history differently (2000, xv). Yet the future will write our epitaph. Questions that naturally come to mind are the following: 'What will those in the future see?' 'How will they regard us?' 'Will it be in the way we would hope or wish to be regarded?' Of course, we can never know the answers. We cannot foresee the future, Callaghan notes, or what the world beyond patriarchy – and, I would add, heterosexism – might be (2000, xv).

Yet the ethical implications of our actions in the present enter into the equation in a way not possible under the regime of those theoretical approaches that privilege the past at the expense of the present. Nearly two decades ago, Don Wayne discerned an ethos 'struggling to emerge' through historicism – a postmodern ethics 'based on the acknowledgment of difference, but also on the principle of relationship' (1990, 802). Amidst recent critical practices of fetishizing early modern material objects, or indulging in 'antiquarianism', as Hugh Grady puts it (2005, 112), piling up historical anecdotes, and constructing thick descriptions, the present moment has been obliterated, in Grady's view, or repressed, in Ewan Fernie's view. 'As what must be excluded from critical awareness to sustain historical contact, the present may be considered the unconscious of new historicism', Fernie observes. So desperately has historicism repressed the present in recent years, he notes, that it suggests 'an imminent theoretical crisis' (2005b, 8). Regardless of whether historicism has obliterated or repressed the present in its quest for the past, the present has gone undertheorized, or untheorized.

And I would go further, pointing out that the present as well as the past has been unpoliticized or, more accurately, drained of the political content that originally animated new historicism, cultural materialism, and feminism alike. A quarter-century ago, historicism and materialism tended to exhibit an awareness of themselves as theoretical frameworks and critical practices firmly anchored in the late twentieth-century. Their practitioners recognized the influence of the present on the meanings they constructed in early modern English texts and culture. In

Renaissance Self-Fashioning, Stephen Greenblatt's groundbreaking book that ushered in historicism, for example, he owns up to the impossibility of 'leaving behind one's own situation' – of fully 'reconstructing and re-entering the culture of the sixteenth-century' and admits that 'the questions I ask of my material are shaped by the questions I ask of myself' (1980, 5). And in her classic article, 'The New Historicism in Renaissance Studies', Jean Howard argues for abandoning the myth of objectivity – 'there is no transcendent space from which one can perceive the past "objectively" ' – and emphasizes the 'groundedness' in the present of historicists' investigations of the past: 'our view is always informed by our present position', as she puts it (1986, 22). Positioned within the present social formation, she goes on to observe, critics are motivated by 'quite different senses of the *present* needs and *present* problems which, it is hoped, will be clarified or reconfigured through the study of the past' (emphasis hers, 1986, 23). Indeed, historicism conceived of history itself as 'a contemporary activity of narrating or representing the past', as Graham Holderness notes (1988, 2).

Yet historicism remained powerfully under the influence of Foucault, particularly his theorization of radical breaks between historical epistemes to counter naïve narratives of continuity that project the present into the past. What was to become more characteristic on the part of historicists was a smokescreen, as Don Wayne puts it, of 'ingenious and agile rhetoric' that avoids articulating 'the cultural economy of their relation to the past' (1990, 802). Eventually, historicists came to represent as subversive in early modern England that which was drained of any subversive power in the present. Their work thereby came to embody the belief that 'there is subversion, no end of subversion', in Greenblatt's infamous formulation, 'only not for us' (1988, 39, 65). Or, as Carol Thomas Neely puts it in 'Constructing the Subject', her critique of historicism from a feminist standpoint, 'there can be no subversion – and certainly not for us!' (1988, 12).

Feminist and queer critical practices are inextricably rooted in the political, economic, and social forces of the late twentieth and early twenty-first centuries. Feminist scholars cannot help but be aware of this connection, as Dympna Callaghan notes:

> questions about both scholarly and political relevance are of course also questions that feminist Shakespeareans ask themselves all the time because we necessarily also belong to broader intellectual and political communities, whose critiques not only pressure but also shape feminist studies of Shakespeare. (2000, xii)

Because of their rootedness in the present, feminist and queer critical practices have a particular responsibility to acknowledge that connection. More explicitly than any other Shakespeare scholar, perhaps, Phyllis Rackin has recently appreciated and articulated the inherently presentist nature of the feminist project:

> Our own experience of Shakespeare's women is conditioned not only by the accumulated tradition of Shakespeare scholarship and reception but also by the present history of the world in which we live: both of these histories help to shape our experience of the plays, whether we study them in an academic setting, see them on stage or screen, or read them in the privacy of our own rooms. Both of these histories will need feminist intervention in the twenty-first-century. (2005, 5–6)

It is worth noting that Rackin invokes the same kind of interventionary critical practice into history from a feminist standpoint that Hawkes calls for from a presentist standpoint (2002, 20). In her most recent work, she develops her critique of historicism (2000), interrogates feminism's rootedness in the present (2005), and, in her contribution to the present collection, explicitly considers its relationship to presentism. By no means do I intend to suggest, however, that she is the first or the only scholar to critique historicism's marginalization or erasure of gender issues, particularly female subjectivity and agency. More than two decades ago, Peter Erickson simultaneously critiqued historicism and argued for the inherently presentist nature of feminism:

> while new historicism has been seen, incorrectly, as synonymous with, or included in, the 'new politics', the main line of new historicism is more accurately characterized as apolitical because its attention to the politics of the Renaissance period is accompanied by neglect of politics in our period. (1987, 336)

The strengths of feminist criticism, in Erickson's view, are twofold: its belief that 'the present has a valid, positive role in historical studies' and its commitment to 'cultural and social change' (1987, 336). The same year, in her article – 'The Family in Shakespeare Studies; or – Studies in the Family of Shakespeareans; or – The Politics of Politics' – Lynda Boose condemned the shared indifference to feminism and gender on the part of both historicism and materialism:

> When gender is not being simply ignored in the materialist critiques, it repeatedly ends up getting displaced into some other issue – usually race or class – and women are silently eradicated from the text, leaving only one gender for consideration. This kind of displacement and erasure ... is, in effect, a modern day re-silencing taking place even as Renaissance strategies of silencing are being discussed ... (1987, 728–29)

She goes on to call Greenblatt out on his infamous statement in his chapter, 'Fiction and Friction', that 'on stage there is in fact but a single gender' (1986, 52): 'Suddenly, there is one gender and there are no more women in Shakespeare's plays', she notes (1987, 730). Further, she memorably historicizes historicists, placing them *vis-a-vis* feminists amidst the political and social turmoil in the US during the 1960s and 1970s. She points out that (the largely male) historicists' theoretical pessimism (its emphasis on inevitable containment rather than the possibility of subversion) has its roots in the emasculating process of having come of age during the Vietnam War draft. Feminists' optimism, on the other hand, was rooted in the potentialities of the women's liberation movement during the same years (1987, 738–41).

The year after Boose's article appeared, Carol Thomas Neely's article, 'Constructing the Subject: Feminist Practice and the New Renaissance Discourses', excoriates both historicists and materialists for remarginalizing, if not completely erasing (in a way uncannily similar to that of traditional liberal humanists before them) the female subject in early modern literature and society that feminists had long been laboring to bring to life:

> The denial of subjectivity and identity are pleasurable ... especially to those who have had the luxury of indulging in and benefiting from them. But for feminist criticism, this decentering is a decapitation. If feminist criticism abandons the notion of the subject, replacing it with the much more slippery concept of subject positions, and by doing so calls into question the notion of gendered subjects, gendered authors, gendered texts, the ground for its critique is eliminated. Denying the unitary subject, declaring the end of difference, does not do away with the difference between men and women or with the subordination of women; it merely conceals it. (1988)[4]

More recently, the historicist construction of the relationship between the subject and the power structures within which that subject is situated has been scrutinized by Hugh Grady, who finds the conception of the subject as 'monolithically determined by all-containing structures of ideology and power' to be an inescapable 'straitjacket'. This view of the subject has its origins in the structuralist phase of Althusserian and Foucaultian theory. By shifting emphasis to different theoretical sources and taking into consideration some of the issues of the Frankfurt School – Derrida, the late Foucault, Habermas, and Lacan – however, Grady discerns the possibility of a much less straitjacketed subjectivity, one that is 'an active agent', not merely 'a passive effect'. He explains the relationship between power structures and subjectivity that emerges as follows:

> Rather than seeing power as in-forming individual subjectivities through the mediation of ideology-like discursive formations, I traced a process in which subjectivity reacted to (reified) power not by being interpellated by it but by distinct kinds of compensatory reaction-formations *against* (Foucault, of course, would say *within*) it. (1996, 216–17)

Grady thus theorized from a presentist standpoint a decade ago the necessity for a kind of subjectivity that Neely theorized from a feminist standpoint two decades ago. Like her, he finds the 'consolidation/subversion/containment' paradigm inadequate, particularly historicism's privileging of power structures' containment of any possibility of subversion on the part of a subject. He is concerned to spell out an alternative materialist approach to subjectivity that possesses 'the potential of resistance to power', as well as 'a potential for complicity with it' (1996, 14). Like historicists and materialists, but unlike traditional liberal humanists, the understanding of subjectivity he is working toward is 'historically produced' rather than 'timeless'. Yet, I would underscore, in arguing for a concept of subjectivity that possesses a potentially *critical* rather than a merely *complicit* relation to emerging forms of early modern English power (1996, 14, 219), Grady is gesturing importantly toward an understanding of subjectivity that accommodates the concerns of feminist and queer theorists alike.

None of us can step beyond time, Terence Hawkes argues. It can't be drained out of our experience: 'As a result, the critic's own "situatedness" does not – cannot – contaminate the past. In effect, it constitutes the only means by which it's possible to see the past and perhaps comprehend it' (2002, 3). And since we can view the past only through the eyes of the present, we might add, few of us would deny that the present has a major influence on our view of the past. While granting that we should read Shakespeare historically, presentism asks, given that history results from an endless dialog between present and past, how we determine whose historical circumstances should have priority – Shakespeare's, or ours.

Insisting that facts and texts are not transparent, neutral artifacts that speak for themselves, presentism instead asks us to own up to our subjectivity – the crucial role that we play in choosing literary texts and constructing meanings in those texts. In deliberately beginning with the material present and using it to set an interrogative agenda, presentism reverses, to some degree, the strategies of historicism. Rather than an obstacle to be avoided or a prison to be escaped from,[5] the present is acknowledged as an experience with which we inevitably engage. Instead of contaminating our view of the past, the present fundamentally invigorates, and shapes, our view of it. A heightened degree of awareness of ourselves, alive in the early twenty-first century, defines us as theorists, critics, and scholars. Overtly owning up to a heightened degree of critical self-awareness in this way, furthermore, constitutes a theoretical stance – one that enables us to put into practice the intervention of that awareness on the past. Presentist work is based on the understanding that all our knowledge of Shakespeare, including that of his historical context, is shaped by the ideologies and discourses of our cultural present. Far from being an impediment to our knowledge, this understanding is its enabling foundation.[6]

Indeed, in deliberately beginning with the material present and using it to set an interrogative agenda, feminist and queer studies reverse the strategies of historicism. Their theoretical and critical practices intervene on the past with a heightened awareness of the ways that the present influences the very questions we pose. Inviting us to own up to our situatedness in the 'here and now' and base our critical practice on an active engagement with that situatedness, they do not view the present as a contaminating force. Instead, feminist and queer critical practices are capable of constructing transformative readings of early modern English texts, such as those of Shakespeare, by exploring, for example, how they represent the conflict between subjectivity on the one hand, and patriarchal, heterosexist power structures on the other – conceiving, furthermore, of the power of the former as opposed to the latter.

What the contributions to *Presentism, Gender, and Sexuality in Shakespeare* aim to do is map out, in an exploratory way, the implications of presentism for twenty-first century studies of transgendered, feminine and masculine subjectivities, and bi-, homo-, and hetero-sexualities in Shakespeare's texts and early modern English society. Doing so seeks to interrogate what would happen if we were to reverse traditional prejudices and, as Gilles Deleuze puts it, 'think difference'. Degrees of difference might come to be seen to exist everywhere – as central rather than marginal to experience. Traditional liberal humanism privileged masculinity over femininity, heterosexuality over homosexuality, public over private, power over gender. Historicism, in turn, re-inscribed these binary oppositions. Feminist and queer theoretical strategies challenge these binaries, however, seeking not so much to reverse them as to deconstruct them altogether. In the process, these strategies sophisticate our notions of how the early modern English performed, or played, gender and sexual orientation. For in society, as on the stage, as Judith Butler (following Foucault) reminds us, both are profoundly a matter of performance (1990, 140–41).

The contributions to *Presentism, Gender, and Sexuality in Shakespeare* attempt to put into practice the kind of heightened degree of contemporary critical self-awareness I have suggested, allowing that awareness to intervene on problems and questions such as the following:

- What have the implications of historicism been for feminist and queer theory and criticism? What directions have these theoretical strategies and critical practices taken under its influence?
- What might the implications of presentism be for feminist and queer theory and criticism? What new directions might these theoretical strategies and critical practices profitably take under its influence?
- How might insisting upon a heightened awareness of our situatedness in the twenty-first century fundamentally shape our attempts at constructing the past? In what ways might presentism help us construct transgendered, feminine, and masculine subjectivities and bi-, homo-, and hetero-sexualities in Shakespeare's texts and early modern English society?
- What kinds of constructions of meaning in Shakespeare's texts and early modern English society emerge from a theoretical strategy that insists upon a heightened awareness of our situatedness in the twenty-first century?
- How does the fact that we are situated in a post-women's-liberation world, for example, influence the performance of gender that we

construct in Shakespearean dramatic texts such as *The Taming of the Shrew?*
- How does the fact that we are situated in a post-Holocaust world influence the performance of religious and cultural difference that we construct in dramatic texts such as *The Merchant of Venice?*
- How does the fact that we are situated in a postcolonial world influence the performance of racial and ethnic difference that we construct in dramatic texts such as *Othello, Antony and Cleopatra,* and *The Tempest?*

Presentism, Gender, and Sexuality in Shakespeare opens with a section that establishes "Theoretical and Political Frameworks" for the essays that follow. Among Shakespeare's strong female protagonists, the most astonishing transgression into maleness is Lady Macbeth's, as Bruce Smith contends in his essay, 'Resexing Lady Macbeth's Gender – and Ours'. News that Duncan comes to lodge in her house prompts this murderous resolve to act as a man would act: 'Come, you spirits / That tend on human thoughts, unsex me here' (1.5.39–40). At least, that's what she said in 1606. What she would say in an updated production today would be something like, 'Come, you ideologies / That dictate thoughts of the social subject, / *Ungender* me here'. One of the most decisive moves – perhaps *the* decisive move – in feminism, queer theory, and masculinity studies has been an insistence on the distinction between sex and gender as conceptual categories. Yet Lady Macbeth experiences gender in totally biological terms and the images she uses have specifically physical meanings in Galenic physiology. The separation of sex from gender in late twentieth-century criticism has been politically useful and personally liberating for many people, but the case of Lady Macbeth suggests that if we wish to be rigorously historical in studying early modern gender we must find a way of putting sex and gender back together in historically specific ways.

As recent philosophers of history have repeatedly argued, there is a very important sense in which all history is present history. Any attempt to write about the past is inevitably shaped by the personal and professional interests of the historian – interests that are themselves shaped by the pressures of the time and place in which the historian writes. These pressures are everywhere apparent in the history of feminist Shakespeare criticism, as Phyllis Rackin points out in her essay, 'Dated and Outdated: The Present Tense of Feminist Shakespeare Criticism', although the protocols of academic discourse, with its demand for scientific objectivity, have typically rendered them unacknowledged and unrecognized. For feminist critics and scholars, the recognition and analysis of these factors is necessary because their work is inevitably implicated in the political. Accordingly, Rackin examines the political implications of recent feminist Shakespeare criticism – both the impact they reveal of the political pressures that produced them and the likely political consequences of their circulation.

One historicist who gets at the contemporary political implications of understanding the dual nature of our relationship to the past as different, yet connected, is Don Wayne: 'By recognizing that our construction of the past is a function of our relation to the present', he observes, 'we can participate in producing alternatives to the present' (1990, 802–03). Encountering the otherness of an early modern text has the potential of engendering an awareness in us that the future will be different yet again, as Fernie notes (2005b, 18–19). Wayne understands the transformative nature of the past – that it is simultaneously distant from us yet ours to employ in transforming our lives, our society. Accordingly, 'Making War/Making Histories', the second group of essays in *Presentism, Gender, and Sexuality in Shakespeare,* foregrounds the political and military dimension he gestures toward, explicitly addressing the significance of these issues for us – as for Shakespeare's time.

My contribution to the volume, '"Mirror[s] of all Christian kings": Hank Cinq and George Deux', comparatively analyzes Shakespeare's Henry 5 and US President George W. Bush. Both are reformed prodigal sons of national political leaders who inherit the mantles of their fathers. Both conduct imperialistic invasions of foreign countries, recruiting soldiers from the working classes to do so. Both violate war etiquette and international agreements regarding the treatment of prisoners of war, prompting the charge, 'war criminal', to be lodged against them. Both believe in the absolute power of their respective offices – power that is, moreover, divinely inspired. Negotiating between fictional and historical records, as well as between past and present, I attempt to read Shakespeare's *Henry 5*, the historical Battle of Agincourt, and the 2003 US invasion and subsequent occupation of Iraq intertextually. Focusing on the ways in which military invasion is gendered masculine while the vanquished country and war critics alike are gendered feminine, I interrogate the implications of such a reading for the construction of meaning in the contemporary political climate in which we find ourselves enmeshed, as in Shakespeare's dramatic texts.

In her essay, 'Ventriloquized Sentimentality, or, The Theory and Practice of Women in War', Kathryn Schwarz takes up the processes through which masculine subjects appropriate a feminized rhetoric to motivate and at the same time sanitize the violence of war. Beginning with a consideration of the rhetorical gestures that represent language as a feminine subject, and particularly with the ubiquitous yet problematic term, 'mother tongue', she pursues the ways in which deployments of the maternal, intended to authorize an agent by way of an idealized genealogy, instead complicate that agent's claims to mastery and autonomy. The sentimental language of filial piety that enables men to invoke a mother country and to fight in that maternal name risks a more literal evocation: feminine subjects, material and immanent rather than abstract and distant, often appear in the narratives that deploy them as a figure. The tension that inheres in the term 'figure' preoccupies the discourse of war, disrupting the masculine exclusivity of chauvinist violence. Schwarz concludes with a reading of the scene in *King John* in which Constance breaks the truce, arguing that her intervention, as an actual mother advocating the rights of a particular son, unravels homosocial consolidations of national identity.

Few females, historical or fictional, offer as many and as diverse interpretive challenges, past and present, as does Joan of Arc, Kay Stanton contends in her contribution, 'A Presentist Analysis of Joan, la Pucelle: "What's past and what's to come she can descry"'. As cross-dressing warrior-hero of France, Joan professed virginity, divine agency, and prophecy, yet she was regarded by the English as a whore, blasphemer, and witch. Using the ambiguous epithet, 'La Pucelle', for her in *1 Henry 6*, Shakespeare keeps an eye on cultural prejudices of his own present time while simultaneously addressing conflicting and shifting French and English attitudes toward Joan in her time and anticipating a time which did indeed come, in the twentieth century, when she would become the Patron Saint of France. Stanton focuses on the commanding presence of Joan as a locus of sexual, religious, and cultural ambiguities and anxieties that disrupt the patriarchal narratives of history.

'I am in the present and only the present matters to me', the credo of the contemporary French theatre director, Ariane Mnouchkine, emphasizes the contemporaneity of each and every performance of a dramatic text. Where traditional liberal humanism privileged literature over criticism and text over performance, presentism underscores the performative function of dramatic texts, as Terence Hawkes points out, connecting with the current realignment of critical responses that stresses 'the *performance* of a play as much as its "reference"'. In other words, presentism considers 'what the play *does*, here and now in the theatre' in addition to 'what it *says* in the world to which its written text refers' (2002, 5). The kind of realignment that Hawkes is getting at results in a more sophisticated, expanded idea of performance, refocusing attention on what the early modern English theatre meant by the activity it labeled 'playing' – something closer to what we understand as improvisation.[7] '"A kiss is just a kiss"/Performativities', the third group of essays in *Presentism, Gender, and Sexuality in Shakespeare,* accordingly focuses on contemporary theatrical and cinematic productions of Shakespeare's dramatic texts with the performative nature of sexuality and gender in mind.

Adrian Kiernander's essay, '"You'll be the man!": Homophobia and the Present in Performances of *Twelfth Night* and *Romeo and Juliet*', considers evidence of changes in the social acceptance of sexual desire between men. He focuses on how a presentist critical practice enables two significant concerns for contemporary society and scholarship: the role of Shakespeare as a privileged site from which to comment on society in the late twentieth and early twenty-first centuries, on the one hand, and the rapidly changing attitudes towards non-heterosexual and non-monogamous relationships, on the other. Kiernander analyzes the implications of the live act of a male-to-male kiss in Ariane Mnouchkine's 1981 production of *Twelfth Night* at a time when the act was illegal in many parts of the Western world and how this moment is indicative of changing ways of staging the play, especially the character of Antonio, throughout its performance history. He also analyzes the performance of masculinity in the role of Romeo by Australian directors John Bell, in a 1979 theatrical production featuring Mel Gibson, and Baz Luhrmann, in a 1990 stage production and a 1996 cinematic text with Leonardo di Caprio.

In his essay, '"My hand is ready, may it do him ease": Shakespeare and the Theatre of Display', Michael Mangan analyzes the Katharina/Petruchio relationship in *The Taming of the Shrew* through the lens of Marjorie Garber's provocative, playful, and serious essay, 'Fetish Envy'. Arguing that 'fetishism is a kind of theatre of display – and indeed that theatre represents an enactment of the fetishistic scenario', Garber concludes with the judgment that fetishism is foundational to theatre itself. Her use of the term 'fetishism' derives from the discourse of Freudian/Lacanian theory and is rooted in a complex set of equations concerning the terms 'p' ('penis'), 'P' ('Phallus'), and 'f' ('fetish'). The term has infiltrated the mainstream of Western capitalist culture, becoming in the process both more complex and less clearly defined. In view of this transvaluation of the term 'fetishism', Mangan explores its implications for *The Taming of the Shrew* to raise questions both about fetishism as a 'theatre of display' and about the strategies of presentism itself as an approach to Shakespeare.

If one of the aims of presentist literary criticism is 'scrupulously to seek out salient aspects of the present as a crucial trigger for its investigations', as Terence Hawkes puts it (2002, 22), then the trigger for Anthony Patricia's essay, '"Through the Eyes of the Present": Screening the Male Homoerotics of Shakespearean Drama', is a concern with interactions between male characters. Considering Michael Radford's *The Merchant of Venice*, Trevor Nunn's *Twelfth Night*, and Oliver Parker's *Othello*, he analyzes how these three directors use cinema to bridge the gap between 'the here and now' and the dramatic texts' original moments of conception and production in the late fifteenth and early sixteenth centuries. As different as these three cinematic texts are from one another, he argues, all three directors are compelled by a contemporary understanding of early modern English sexuality that continues to acquire depth, nuance, and significance to render the male homoerotic visible and integral, bringing to light in the present male same-sex relations that have been buried or overlooked for centuries with a force that leaves no room for further avoidance, equivocation, or rationalization.

Doug Green analyzes the representations of the willow song scene in the Laurence Olivier and the Oliver Parker cinematic texts of *Othello* in his essay, 'Estranging Bedfellows: Early Modern Cinema Today'. Each cinematic text functions as a palimpsest of past and present texts. The two representations of this crucial scene raise issues – or can be used to raise them – of current and enduring interest about the play's performance history, especially the shift from boy-player to adult woman actor, and about the history of gender and sexuality. Consideration of the two cinematic texts intertextually also shifts perspective to the changing conventions of cinema, the ways in which those conventions have constructed gender and sexuality, and the ways in which Shakespearean constructions and inscriptions of gender and sexuality interact with cinematic conventions. The conjunction of Shakespeare and cinema provides a nearly perfect instance of intersection between present(s) and past(s) that allows us to question our assumptions about both.

The penultimate group of essays in *Presentism, Sexuality, and Gender in Shakespeare* foregrounds the subject of 'Uncivil Unions'. The anti-gay, pro-heterosexual marriage amendments that the religious right in the US deployed on state ballots as a wedge issue during the 2004 Presidential election, in particular, were premised on the belief that civil unions and same-sex marriage are recent social developments that disrupt an institution that has been historically defined as heterosexual. Contrary to these right-wing premises, however, the historical research of Alan Bray (1982, 1995) and John Boswell (1994) has demonstrated that precedents exist for non-heterosexual family structures, including the contemporary civil union, that are centuries old. More recently, Alan Tulchin published a groundbreaking article on the existence of same-sex unions in medieval France. These marriage contracts, or *affrèrement* (literally, 'brother-making'), typically included two conditions that were concerned with the disposition of property. First, partners no longer owned property individually – that is, all individually owned property became the joint property of the couple. Second, partners agreed to name each other as their heirs – that is, whoever died second (rather than nearest relatives) inherited the joint property. Same-sex partners were tightly bound to each other by *affrèrement,* agreeing to share one common household, *'un pain, un vin, un bourse'* ('one bread, one wine, one purse'), and mentioning affection or love for each other (using the French verb, *aimer*) as the rationale for entering into the marriage contract.

Despite the contemporary argument against same-sex marriage on the part of the religious right in the US on the grounds that it violates both nature and culture – that marriage is for the procreation of children – many heterosexual married partners remain childless, many by choice, as Linda Charnes points out in her essay, 'Uncivil Unions'. Contemporary medical technologies enable heterosexual couples who wish to have children and are unable to conceive 'naturally', moreover, to have children that are not necessarily biologically their own. The insistence that marriage is a sanctified union between a man and a woman for the purpose of procreating and raising children, Charnes argues, is not only obsolete but increasingly cynical – a perfect example of what philosopher Peter Sloterdijk labels 'cynical idealism'. While early modern English marriage was defined as a heterosexual institution because of the indefeasible linkage of property transmission and patrimony, many couples in Shakespeare's dramatic texts do not conform either to the model of companionate marriage or to standard ideologies of gender complementarity – evincing a more reasonable and flexible attitude about what constitutes companionability and attraction than even our own post-Enlightenment culture admits.

In his essay, '"A local habitation and a name": Presence, Witnessing, and Queer Marriage in Shakespeare's Romantic Comedies', Arthur Little takes up Terence Hawkes's invitation to consider presentism in view of the lessons that have been learned from decades of historicism. Exploring the distinction Hawkes draws between acting and playing – particularly the latter's dependence on a symbiotic, unpredictable relationship between actor and audience – Little considers *As You Like It* and *Twelfth Night* before focusing on *A Midsummer Night's Dream,* analyzing how each is apparently governed by a heterosexual marriage plot, yet is marked with anxieties about the possibility of queer marriage. He suggests that Bottom links the performative in the story of Shakespeare's dramatic text with the actual material world and the realities of the playhouse itself. The specter of queer marriage remains an elusive yet serious challenge to the heterosexual marriage plot that not only governs the characters in *A Midsummer Night's Dream* but regulates and adjudicates the ideological underpinnings of the theater itself.

Presentism, Gender, and Sexuality in Shakespeare concludes with an explicit interrogation of the issue of 'Temporalities'. 'The Future in the Instant' by Kathleen McLuskie examines how Lady Macbeth's formulation resonates with the issues of temporality that are crucial to presentist thinking. Interrogating the imbricated and imbricating nexus of past, present, and future, McLuskie considers how the early modern moment of the production of a Shakespearean dramatic text is of necessity performed and read at ever-changing contemporary moments that inevitably carry the further implication of interpretations that occur at yet other moments – in the future. Pointing out Shakespeare's omnipresent, metaphoric use of time in *Macbeth*, McLuskie argues that this trope refers to both the passage of time and the conditions in which Macbeth has to act. Shakespeare's use of this trope, furthermore, opens up the possibility of deeper resonances at crucial moments in the dramatic action – resonances that can be made visible through a reading that presents *Macbeth* as an enactment of existential questions about the relationship between action and time.

Notes

1. After Juliet Dusinberre's 1976 monograph and Carolyn Ruth Swift Lenz, Gayle Greene, and Carol Thomas Neely's 1980 collection of essays, book-length studies of Shakespeare and early modern England from a feminist perspective include, in chronological order, the following: Irene Dash, *Wooing, Wedding, and Power: Women in Shakespeare's Plays* (1981); Coppelia Kahn, *Man's Estate: Masculine Identity in Shakespeare* (1981); Linda Bamber, *Comic Women, Tragic Men* (1982); Lisa Jardine, *Still Harping on Daughters: Women and Drama in the Age of Shakespeare* (1983); Marianne Novy, *Love's Argument: Gender Relations in Shakespeare* (1984); Linda Woodbridge, *Women and the English Renaissance: Literature and the Nature of Womankind, 1540–1620* (1984); Carol Thomas Neely, *Broken Nuptials in Shakespeare's Plays* (1985); Dympna Callaghan, *Woman and Gender in Renaissance Tragedy: A Study of* King Lear, Othello, The Duchess of Malfi, *and* The White Devil (1989); Valerie Wayne, ed., *The Matter of Difference: Materialist Feminist Criticism of Shakespeare* (1991); Evelyn Gajowski, *The Art of Loving: Female Subjectivity and Male*

Discursive Traditions in Shakespeare's Tragedies (1992); Ania Loomba, *Gender, Race, Renaissance Drama* (1992); Margo Hendricks and Patricia Parker, eds, *Women, 'Race', and Writing in the Early Modern Period* (1994); Deborah Barker and Ivo Kamps, eds, *Shakespeare and Gender: A History* (1995); Shirley Nelson Garner and Madelon Sprengnether, eds, *Shakespearean Tragedy and Gender* (1996), Jean Howard and Phyllis Rackin, *Engendering a Nation: A Feminist Account of Shakespeare's English Histories* (1997); Coppelia Kahn, *Roman Shakespeare: Warriors, Wounds, and Women* (1997); Dympna Callaghan, *Shakespeare Without Women: Representing Gender and Race on the Renaissance Stage* (2000); Dympna Callaghan, ed., *A Feminist Companion to Shakespeare* (2000); Naomi Liebler, ed., *The Female Tragic Hero in English Renaissance Drama* (2002); Joyce MacDonald, *Women and Race in Early Modern Texts* (2002).

2. See Phyllis Rackin's contribution to the present collection in the following pages for a fuller analysis of feminism *vis-à-vis* historicism, on the one hand, and feminism's relationship to contemporary political, social, and economic developments in the US, on the other.
3. After Alan Bray's 1982 and Joseph Pequigney's 1985 monographs, book-length studies of Shakespeare and early modern England from a GLBT/queer perspective include, in chronological order, the following: Greg Bredbeck, *Sodomy and Interpretation: Marlowe to Milton* (1991); Jonathan Dollimore, *Sexual Dissidence: Augustine to Wilde, Freud to Foucault* (1991); Bruce R. Smith, *Homosexual Desire in Shakespeare's England: A Cultural Poetics* (1991); Jonathan Goldberg, *Sodometries: Renaissance Texts, Modern Sexualities* (1992); Valerie Traub, *Desire and Anxiety in Shakespeare: Circulations of Sexuality in Shakespearean Drama* (1992); Jonathan Goldberg, ed., *Queering the Renaissance* (1994); Mario DiGangi, *The Homoerotics of Early Modern Drama* (1997); Jeffrey Masten, *Textual Intercourse: Collaboration, Authorship, and Sexualities in Renaissance Drama* (1997); Theodora Jankowski, *Pure Resistance: Queer Virginity in Early Modern English Drama* (2000); Valerie Traub, *The Renaissance of Lesbianism in Early Modern England* (2002); Alan Sinfield, *Shakespeare, Authority, Sexuality: Unfinished Business in Cultural Materialism* (2006b).
4. In addition to Peter Erickson, Lynda Boose, and Carol Thomas Neely, other scholars who have offered critiques of historicism from a feminist standpoint, particularly in the late 1980s and early 1990s, include, in chronological order, the following: Marguerite Waller (1987), Carolyn Porter (1988, 1990), Sarah Eaton (1991), Ann Thompson (1991), Valerie Wayne (1991a), Evelyn Gajowski (1992), and Lisa Jardine (1996). This list is intended to be suggestive, rather than exhaustive.
5. The historicist configuration of the present as an impediment is, perhaps, put forth most emphatically by Leonard Tennenhouse and David Scott Kastan. Tennenhouse views the present as an undesirably 'tight-fitting turtleneck' from which the contemporary critic must disentangle himself (1986, 11). Kastan (presumably under the influence of Foucault) disregards the power of the present in shaping the past, arguing instead that we need to guarantee 'that what we hear are [Shakespeare's] concerns rather than the projections of our own' and that we 'restore his works to the specific imaginative and material circumstances in which they were written and engaged' (1999, 16–17).
6. Pioneers of presentist thinking include, foremost (and in chronological order), Terence Hawkes (1986, 1992, 2002, 2007), Hugh Grady (1991, 1996,

2002, 2004, 2005, 2007), and Linda Charnes (2000a, 2000b, 2006, 2007a, 2007b). Grady is concerned to resituate history in the present, noting that it is within its discourses that our views of the past are formed. Under the influence of reader response theory, Hawkes is concerned to emphasize the presence of the interpretive act, arguing that it is *we* who construct meanings in texts. Other theorists, practitioners, and advocates of presentism include, in chronological order, Michael D. Bristol (1996, 2001, 2007), Christy Desmet (1999), Robert Sawyer (1999), Kathleen McLuskie (2001), Ewan Fernie (2005a, 2005b, 2007), Catherine Belsey (2007), Cary DiPietro (2007), John Drakakis (2007), Evelyn Gajowski (2007), and Kiernan Ryan (2007). Early modern English scholars whose work is presentist in nature even though they may not explicitly use the label 'presentist', include Graham Holderness (1988), Richard Halpern (1997), Barbara Hodgdon (1998), Ania Loomba (1998), Martin Orkin (1998), and Gabriel Egan (2006). As the latter list suggests, arguments could be made for including performance, postcolonial, and ecocritical studies, as well as studies of Shakespeare as an icon of contemporary culture and appropriation studies, in the list of inherently presentist theoretical strategies. For early critical responses to presentism, see, for example, Robin Headlam Wells (2000) and Helen Moore (2003).

7. For Terence Hawkes, the concept of 'playing' gets at the unscripted, extra-verbal, and spontaneous components implied by Shakespeare's dramatic texts that may be riffed in a jazz-like improvisation (2002, 126).

Part I

Theoretical and Political Frameworks

1

Resexing Lady Macbeth's Gender – and Ours

Bruce R. Smith

'Come, you spirits / That tend on human thoughts, unsex me here': that's what the actor playing Lady Macbeth said in 1606.[1] What she would say today in an updated production would be something like 'Come, you ideologies / That dictate thoughts of the social subject, / *Ungender* me here'. One of the most decisive moves – perhaps *the* decisive move – in feminism, queer theory, and masculinity studies over the past 25 years has been an insistence on the distinction between sex and gender as conceptual categories. Myra Jehlen's entry for 'Gender' in *Critical Terms for Literary Study* exemplifies what now passes for dogma. The term 'gender', Jehlen explains, points up

> the way the sexed nature of both women and men is not natural but cultural. In this sense, gender may be opposed to sex as culture is to nature so that its relation to sexual nature is unknown and probably unknowable: how, after all, do we speak of human beings outside of culture? From the perspective of gender, identity is a role, character traits are not autonomous qualities but functions and ways of relating. Actions define actors rather than vice versa. Connoting history and not nature, gender is not a category of human nature. (1995, 265)

A category of human nature is, of course, just what most social codes of gender claim to be. Because men and women possess different sorts of bodies, so goes the logic, it is only natural that men should behave one way and women another. Culture-specific ideology thus tries to pass itself off as universal common sense (Williams 1983, 219–24, Dollimore 1991, 113–16).

Etymology is on the side of feminism, queer theory and masculinity studies: the words *sex* and *gender* have different origins. *Sex*, 'the two divisions of organic beings distinguished as male and female' (*Oxford English Dictionary* 1989: 'sex' *n.* 1.a) is a biological concept, quite specific in its application; *gender,* 'kind, sort, class' (*OED* 'gender', *n.* 1), is an ontological concept, broadly applicable to all sorts of phenomena. Yet as early as the 1520s *sex* had become something more elusive than body parts, '*quality* in respect of being male or female' (*OED* 'sex' *n.* 2, emphasis added), and by 1630 had acquired even more abstract status as 'the distinction between male and female in general' (3.a). The attempt to undo this conflation, to separate gender from sex, is dated by the *OED* to the 1960s. *Gender,* according to this definition, is 'a euphemism for the sex of a human being, often intended to emphasize the social and cultural, as opposed to the biological, distinctions between the sexes' (3.b). Lady Macbeth, that it is to say, could have unsexed herself with impunity from 1606 until 1966.

Audiences at the Globe in 1606 heard Lady Macbeth say one thing; audiences 400 years later would like for her to have said something else entirely. How to negotiate this dilemma?[2] Historicism would let Lady Macbeth have her say. Medical and legal discourses about gender and sexuality in early modern England, historicist critics would insist, determined what someone in Lady Macbeth's position *could* say about herself.[3] If she has breasts capable of giving milk, she has no choice in 1606 but to speak of her female gender in biological terms. Giving milk is one of the things women *do*: it is a marker of womanliness (Rackin 1999). Historicist criticism might also stress the material circumstances of the play's performance at the Globe in 1606. *The Tragedy of Macbeth* includes a particular fiction about female behavior, a fiction offered for sale as a commodity that cost one penny, two pennies, three pennies, or a shilling and more, depending on where one stood or sat while consuming that commodity (Gurr 1992, 214). Unavoidable in those particular material circumstances is the physical, physiological, and psychological fact that it was a boy actor who dressed as Lady Macbeth and spoke her lines in 1606 (Stallybrass 1991a). *Macbeth* figures as the first in a sequence of scripts by Shakespeare that feature strong female protagonists. Lady Macbeth, Cleopatra, Volumnia in *Coriolanus,* Innogen in *Cymbeline,* Paulina in *The Winter's Tale*: each of these 'persons' (to use the early modern term for the characters in the fiction) commands a proportionately large number of lines.[4] It is tempting to conclude that in about 1605 a boy actor with particularly remarkable skills joined the King's Men or that a boy actor already in the company came into his own about then, working the same effect on Shakespeare's female roles that Robert Armin's entry into the company in 1599 or 1600 worked on

Shakespeare's clown parts (Wiles 1987). Finally, historicism would inquire about the kind of 'social work' Lady Macbeth's speech was doing in 1606 – how, for example, it confirmed models of acceptable female behavior by representing one particularly horrific counter-example (Sinfield 1992, 95–108). Such a reading would find containment in what might seem to be a subversion of behavioral norms (Levin 2002). In sum, historicism would maintain a rigorous focus on 1606 and use that reference point to make observations about externally available 'facts' concerning the culture of early modern England, facts that can be verified by reference to other written texts of the period.

A presentist interpretation would, by contrast, make no apologies for insisting that 'gender' be detached from 'sex'. Where historicism found containment, presentism would find subversion. It would exploit the subversive potential in Lady Macbeth's speech, in particular her refusal of child-bearing as a female obligation and her embrace of political ambition as a male prerogative. What the script shows happening to Lady Macbeth later in the play – her sleeplessness, her obsession with washing away her guilt, her hopeless physical condition at the hands of her male physician – would not just be explained away; it would be excoriated. With respect to material circumstances, a presentist investigation would seize on the deconstructive potential in the boy actor's performance, its queerness in the larger sense of that term as an interrogation of 'the binaristic thinking that has traditionally characterized sexual politics, in particular such familiar oppositions as heterosexuality/homosexuality, masculine/feminine, sex/gender, closeted/out, center/margin, conscious/unconscious, nature/culture, and normal/pathological, to name a few' (Hanson 2005, 418–19). Historical support for such a move, if any were needed, can be found in the range of comments made by sixteenth- and seventeenth-century writers who actually saw boy actors playing female parts. Those comments range from homosexual panic in Philip Stubbes's 'sodomy or worse' in *The Anatomy of Abuses* to Henry Jackson's straightforward description of the boy actor playing Desdemona at Oxford in 1610 as if he *were* Desdemona to George Sandys's opinion that the women's parts he saw being performed by women players at Messina in 1611 were 'too naturally passionated' to Lady Mary Wroth's ridicule of 'play boys' as failed women (Shapiro; extracts from Stubbes, Sandys, *et al.* reprinted in Shakespeare 2001, 273–78). Sandys offers a particularly sharp challenge to strict historicism. Is it really possible for a spectator of 2006 to devote her attention to the artifice of boy actors and 'unthink' the problematics of gender and sexuality that 30 years of criticism have set in place? Would she even *want* to? In sum, a presentist approach would search out the untypical, the counter-example, the subversive, the queer. It would take as a starting point the critic's interestedness in Lady Macbeth's speech, the critic's own psychological investment in what happens in the play – and in so doing it would accept the impossibility of ever attaining the objectivity to which historicism aspires.

Lyotard in *Phenomenology* argues that such a position of objectivity can never actually be achieved, even when the objects being studied are chronologically distant from the investigator. According to Lyotard, all objects of historical inquiry are never really objects. The analyst is connected with what he analyzes along a continuum of time: the past is both 'now' and 'no longer' as the future is both 'now' and 'not yet'. As a result, no fixed, final meaning can be assigned to a given historical event like the boy actor's declamation of Lady Macbeth's 'unsex me here' speech in London in 1606. The meaning of such an event, Lyotard argues,

> is ambiguous precisely because it is in the process of becoming. Just as we cannot assign some definitive meaning to a subjectivity, since this subjectivity is cast forward toward a future whose open possibilities will define it further, so the full meaning (the direction) of a historical situation is not assignable once and for all – since the society being affected cannot be viewed as an object evolving according to mechanical laws, and one stage of this complex system is not succeeded by another, but by an array of possibilities. These possibilities are not innumerable, and this is why there is meaning in history, but they are numerous, and this is why the meaning cannot be read off effortlessly. Ultimately this open future, as open, belongs to the present situation itself. It is not superadded, it is extended within it by is very essence. (1991, 121)

Note the parenthesis and the appositive: 'the full meaning' of an historical situation is the same thing as the 'direction' of that situation. To name something – 'female gender in early modern England' for example – is to turn that something into an object with an assignable meaning, to position the analyst here and *it* over there so that *it* can be seen, known, mastered. In effect, Lyotard abolishes such acts of naming. In place of this configuration of knowledge,

1 | 0,

Lyotard substitutes this configuration of knowledge:

I ---------- O ---------- ∞.

Instead of 'one is not zero' we have 'function-I is continuous with function-O is continuous with infinity'. Where is the first-person observer in Derrida's 1 | 0 binary? Somewhere else, in a third dimension, 18 inches or more from the page on which 1 | 0 is inscribed. Marks of *différance* are made in passive voice; the marker is marked even as he marks. In Lyotard's scheme, by contrast, the first-person observer is embedded in the act of knowing: I is the starting point. Lyotard's observer accepts her first-personhood. The observer (I) and the object being observed (O) do not stand in a fixed relationship to each other but vary in their 'distance', now closer to each other, now farther away. I can exist in close proximity to O, as I does (and as I do) in presentism, or at a greater distance, as I purports (and I purport) to do in historicism, usually in the guise of a third-person 'one' or, worse, an ill-defined first-person-plural 'we'. The horizontal line implied in Lyotard's model of knowledge offers much more flexibility and much more subtlety than Derrida's vertical bar. The horizontal line signals that the past is never a fixed object. Considered from left to right, the past exists in a state of infinite regress. Considered from right to left, the past is always coming at us.

The bi-directionality opened up by presentism makes it possible to address not just *one* past moment (1606, for example) but *multiple* pasts, all at the same time. With respect to gender and sexuality, presentism can take the long view. It can entertain models of gender and sexuality that existed *before* Shakespeare's time as well as *after* and not be particularly worried about the currency of those models in 1606. The result is, or can be, a back-and-forth movement between present and past, a dialectic in which a synthesis between I and O stands as a critique, not only of past 'facts', but of presentist presumptions. Lady Macbeth's 'unsex me here' speech is a case in point. Taking the long view makes it possible to discern in her speech two competing models of how gender is related to sexuality, one that is located in the material human body, the other in acts of marking made by the mind. Both models were current in Shakespeare's time, and both still carry force, as witness the stand-off between 'gender' (mind) and 'sexuality' (body). Early modern notions of the gender-sexuality connection suggest a third model, grounded not in bodies or binary markings but in acts of imagination that combine bodies and markings. That third model, a synthesis of the material and the mental, assumes the shape of a continuum and offers a way out from under the tyranny of 1 | 0. Let us consider these three models one by one.

Matter

In Western thinking, the conviction that gender is rooted in biology finds its earliest, smartest, and most influential spokesman in Aristotle. In the *History of Animals,* Aristotle starts with the concept of gender as 'kind, sort, class', but quickly moves to position sex as a subset of gender in this more general sense. In Aristotle's scheme, humankind is a *genus* that is subdivided into male and female *sexes*. 'In all genera in which the distinction of male and female is found', he begins, 'nature makes a similar differentiation in the characteristics of the two sexes'. The distinction is most obvious in larger animals, quadrupeds – and humans.

> In all cases, excepting those of the bear and leopard, the female is less spirited than the male; in regard to the two exceptional cases, the superiority in courage rests with the female. With all other animals the female is softer in disposition, is more mischievous, less simple, more impulsive, and more attentive to the nurture of the young; the male, on the other hand, is more spirited, more savage, more simple and less cunning. The traces of these characteristics are more or less visible everywhere, but they are especially visible where character is the more developed, and most of all in man. (608.a.10–608.b.7, 1: 948–49)[5]

Aristotle is insistent that the differences here are *material* differences. In the *Metaphysics,* he considers the question of why, if male and female are so different, they don't constitute different species. The reason turns on 'formula' versus 'matter'. Male and female are products of the same human formula in just the way that all horses are products of the same horse formula. The differences between male and female are accidents of the matter in which the human formula is realized (1058.a.30–1058.b.1). Accidents, perhaps, but with huge consequences. The practical result of this deterministic line of thinking is spelled out in the *Politics*, where Aristotle asserts, 'the male is by nature superior, and the female inferior; and the one rules, and the other is ruled; this principle, of necessity, extends to all mankind' (1254.b.13–15).

Galenic medicine elaborated the material differences between male and female, identifying maleness with the hot, dry properties of blood and the hot, moist qualities of choler, and femaleness with the cold, moist properties of phlegm and the cold, dry properties of earth (Siraisi 1990, 97–113). Partly as a result of their comparative wetness, female bodies were imagined to be more volatile than male bodies – with consequences for male and female behavior. Levinus Lemnius, whose works on health and physiology enjoyed wide circulation in Latin and in English translation for nearly a hundred years, provides an extreme example. My quotations are taken from an English translation published in 1658, long after, one might have supposed, modern empiricism had supplanted scholastic dogma. 'A womans mind is not so strong as a man's', Lemnius claims, 'nor is she so full of understanding and reason and judgement, and upon every small occasion she casts off the bridle of reason, and like a mad dogg, forgetting all decency, and her selfe, without choice, she sets uppon all, be they known or unknown' (1658, 274).[6] If a man wants 'a natural reason' why this should be so, Lemnius would point him to biology. It is noteworthy that the anatomy of the female body that ensues does *not* include the vagina:

> a womans flesh is loose, soft and tender, so that the choler being kindled, presently spreads all the body over, and causeth a sudden boyling of the blood about the heart. For as fire soonest takes hold of light straw, and makes a great flame, but it is soon at an end, and quiet; so a woman is quickly angry and flaming hot, and rageth strangely; but this rage and crying out, is soon abated, and grows calm in a body that is not so strong and valiant, and that is more moyst; and all her heat and fury is quenched by her shedding of teares, as if you should throw water upon fire to put it out. (1658, 274)

The key words here are 'flesh', 'choler', 'blood', and 'tears'. It is the nature of soft, tender flesh to be susceptible to the boiling up of blood and choler – and just as susceptible, because of its moistness, to cooling off.

For an example of choler taking over moist flesh, one could hardly find one better than Lady Macbeth. The images in her imperative 'unsex me here' demonstrate how solidly grounded her ideas of gendered behavior are in Galenic physiology. 'Make thick my blood' (1.5.42) she commands, appropriating the bodily fluid most closely associated with maleness. 'Take my milk for gall' (1.5.47) confirms, even for listeners unfamiliar with early modern physiology, how Lady Macbeth assumes behavior to be a function of biology. In Galenic medicine, the body's four elemental fluids – blood, gall, black bile and phlegm – were imagined to be fungible, convertible into one another according to what was happening to a person outside and inside. The results of those biochemical changes were the psycho-physical states that early modern men and women knew as 'passions' (Paster 1993, 64–112; Paster 2004,

1–24; Paster, Rowe, and Floyd-Wilson 2004, 1–20; Schoenfeldt 1999, 1–39; Siraisi 1990, 97–113). Male as well as female bodies were subject to these changes. After identifying femaleness with soft, moist flesh, Lemnius quickly adds that these qualities are not peculiar to women. Quick comings and goings of passions 'we see also in some effeminate men, whose magnanimity and fiercenesse ends almost as Children do in weeping, when the adversary doth strongly oppose himselfe against them' (1658, 274). 'I do fear thy nature', Lady Macbeth says to the absent writer of the letter she has just received; 'It is too full o' th' milk of human kindness' (1.5.15–16).

Only at the end of Lemnius's anatomy of the female body do genital markers of sexual difference come into play, when he points the still curious to a possible further explanation for the quick changes in body chemistry to be observed in women:

> If any man would more neerely have the cause of this thing explain'd, and desires a more exact reason; I can find no neerer cause that can be imagined, than the venim and collection of humours, that she every month heaps together, and purgeth forth by the course of the Moon; For when she chanceth to be an[g]ry, as she will presently be, all that sink of humours being stirred fumeth, and runs through the body, so that the Heart and Brain are affected with the smoky vapours of it, and the Spirits both vitall and animal, that serve those parts are inflamed, and thence it is that women stirred up, especially the younger women, (for the elder that are past childing, are more quiet and calme, because their terms are ended) will bark, and brawle like mad doggs, and clap their hands and behave themselves very unseemly in their actions and speeches, and reason being but weak in them, and their judgement feeble, and their mind not well order'd, they are sharply enraged, and cannot rule their passions. (1658, 274)

Lady Macbeth's desire to 'stop up th'access and passage of remorse' (1.5.43) acknowledges that her body, like all women's, is leaky in comparison to the closedness and continence of men's bodies (Paster 1993, 23–63).

To equate gender with biological sex, as Aristotle and Lemnius do, is to *essentialize* gender, to give it an essence that indisputably exists. In the case of gender, the site of that essence is the sexed human body. The stability of these material differences is complicated, however, by the proposition in Galenic physiology that women's sexual organs are the inverse of men's. The vagina was thought to function as an internal penis, the ovaries as internal testicles. All human beings, according to this line of thinking, start out as females. It is the greater heat of men's bodies that causes the sexual organs to extrude. The French physician Ambroise Paré records in his treatise *On Monsters and Marvels* the case of a peasant girl named Marie who, at the age of 15, leaped over a ditch while 'rather robustly' chasing some pigs, and at that very moment 'the genitalia and male rod came to be developed' (quoted in Greenblatt 1988, 81). She changed her name to Germain. On his way to Italy, Montaigne made a detour to see her for himself. By the time of Montaigne's visit, Germain had served in the king's retinue and, though unmarried, sported 'a big, very thick beard' (quoted in Greenblatt 1988, 81). Thomas Laqueur, who has traced the history of the so-called 'one-sex model' down to the nineteenth century, argues that the effect of such thinking is to make a decisive separation of biological sex, which is the same for all human beings, from gender roles, which are culturally scripted:

> In the world of one sex, it was precisely when talk seemed to be most directly about the biology of two sexes that it was most imbedded in the politics of gender, in culture. To be a man or a woman was to hold a social rank, a place in society, to assume a cultural role, not to *be* organically one or the other of two incommensurable sexes. Sex before the seventeenth century, in other words, was still a sociological and not an ontological category. (1990, 8)

Not everyone in early modern Europe, however, accepted the one-sex model. Helkiah Crooke in his medical encyclopedia *Microcosmographia* weighs stories like Marie Germain's against the evidence of recent anatomical studies and concludes, 'Notwithstanding all this, against this opinion there are two mighty arguments. One is taken from the [Greek for 'self-evidence'] in dissection, another from reason, which two are the philosopher's bloodhounds, by which they track the causes of things' (1631, 249).

Like Crooke, who acted as personal physician to King James, the Doctor of Physic who attends Lady Macbeth in the sleep-walking scene (5.1) trusts empirical observation, reason – and the clarity of things that have been written down. Lady Macbeth's 'slumbery agitation' (5.1.11), neither sleep nor wakefulness, throws the Doctor off balance. Accompanied in his observations by Lady Macbeth's lady in waiting, the Doctor declares, 'I will set down what comes from her to satisfy my remembrance the more strongly' (5.1.31–32). Lady Macbeth, for her part, is also concerned with marks, with spots. In her case they are imagined spots of blood. She who commanded 'make thick my blood' now wonders that King Duncan should have had so much blood in him. Her speeches turn to Macduff's widow, then back to her own blood-stained hands, then to the smell of blood. Her 'O, O, O!' (5.1.50) is read by the Doctor as a symptom, as a sign of passion: 'What a sigh is there! Her heart is sorely charged' (5.1.51). Hearing her literally *incriminating* exclamations, the Doctor decides it is best to make a separation between the woman's body and the act of murder she has confessed: 'This disease is beyond my practice... More needs she the divine than the physician' (5.1.56, 71). Aristotle and his disciples would not be surprised, of course, by this outcome. Lady Macbeth's shift from murderous resolve to guilty hysteria could be predicted from the nature of her soft, moist flesh.

Mind

If Aristotle starts with sex, Plato starts with gender, with 'kind, sort, class'. Long before now, Socrates is reported as saying in the *Symposium*,

> there were three kinds of human beings... not two, as there are now, male and female. In addition to these, there was a third, a combination of those two; its name survives, though the kind itself has vanished. At that time, you see, the word 'androgynous' really meant something: a form made up of male and female elements, though now there's nothing but the word, and that's used as an insult. (189.e)[7]

'Kind', 'word', 'form', 'elements': Plato's whole scheme is a mental construction. Socrates goes on to describe what sorts of bodies the three forms possessed, but his account is clearly an etiological fable, a means of getting his fundamental idea about gender across to his listeners by making up a story that runs counter to the supposed biological facts:

> the shape of each human being was completely round, with back and sides in a circle; they had four hands each, as many legs as hands, and two faces, exactly alike, on a rounded neck. Between the two faces, which were on opposite sides, was one head with four ears. There were two sets of sexual organs, and everything else was the way you'd imagine from what I've told you. (189.e–190.a)

The separation of these round beings into halves becomes an explanation for sexual attraction that, like the original forms, comes in threes, not twos. Each half of an original male/male whole seeks another male; each half of a female/female whole, another female; each half of an androgynous whole, its *andros* or its *gyne*. Where biology leads Aristotle to a deterministic politics, gender leads Plato to a politics that allows for varying degrees of likeness among men and women. In Book 5 of the *Republic* Socrates discusses gender in terms of 'forms of difference and sameness' (454.c). The key word here is 'forms' (454.a), the ideas in terms of which discriminations are made. Biological sex is not, for Socrates, the idea that trumps all others. Men may be stronger than women, but aptitudes are distributed without respect to biological sex. When it comes to guardianship of the republic, women are the equals of men:

> Therefore, if the male sex is seen to be different from the female with regard to a particular craft or way of life, we'll say that the relevant one must be assigned to it. But if it's apparent that they differ only in this respect, that the females bear children while the males beget them, we'll say that there has been no kind of proof that women are different from men with respect to what we're talking about, and we'll continue to believe that our guardians and their wives must have the same way of life. (454.d)

Thus women should be taught music and poetry along with male citizens of the republic and receive physical training (452.a). People who would counter-argue that women are by nature less apt for these pursuits than men 'are unable to examine what has been said by dividing it up according to forms. Hence, they pursue mere verbal contradictions of what has been said and have a quarrel rather than a conversation' (454.a). What Plato does, in effect, is deconstruct biological sex as an essence. He exposes the 'verbal contradictions' in arguments that would make biological sex the guarantor of gender difference. If you start with matter and not with forms, Socrates warns, you will end up in semantic confusion.

Presentist critics, with their collapsible perspective on time, will not be surprised that Plato here anticipates Jacques Lacan – if not the other way around. In his essay, 'The Instance of the Letter in the Unconscious', Lacan tells the story of two children, a brother and a sister, who are riding in a train as it pulls into a station. 'Look', says the brother, 'we're at Ladies!'; 'Imbecile!' replies his sister, 'don't you see we're at Gentlemen?' (2005, 417). Earlier in the essay Lacan has inserted a line drawing of two visually identical doors. Introduce language and the picture changes completely. A horizontal line above the doors separates the doors below from two words above: 'Ladies' over the left door and 'Gentlemen' over the right. Two identical doors; two different significations. Two identical signifieds (s); two different signifiers (S). The conclusion: S ≠ s. Logical enough. But language seduces its speakers into assuming that S = s, and the results are played out in lived experience: 'to these children, Ladies and Gentlemen will be henceforth two homelands towards which each of their souls will take flight on divergent wings, and regarding it will be all the more impossible for them to reach an agreement since, being in fact the same homeland, neither can give ground regarding the one's unsurpassed excellence without detracting from the other's glory' (2005, 417). One door, two names, millions of consequences. Lacan's image of the two doors demonstrates graphically how gender is a construction of language. 'Ladies' need 'Gentlemen' in order to be ladies, 'Gentlemen' need 'Ladies' in order to be gentlemen. In and of themselves, the words 'Ladies' and 'Gentlemen' are empty. Without the other, against which to be different, any one of these words means nothing. And one of them must be the standard against which the other is judged to be different. 1 | 0: in the case of gender, 'Gentlemen' is that standard-defining one and 'Ladies' is the cipher.

We can see that in the prejudicial way Shakespeare and his contemporaries used the word *sex*. Here is a perfect example of the semantic confusion that Plato predicts when forms get mixed up with matter. Behavior may be a function of biology, but Lemnius is altogether typical of early modern writers in assuming that women are more susceptible to the vagaries of biology than men. 'That gentle sex', 'this weaker sex', 'the woman sex', 'the softer sex', 'the better sex', 'the fairer sex': the combinatory usages recorded in the *OED* from 1583 to 1700 demonstrate that males may constitute the standard by which difference is judged, but when it comes to 'sex', women were said to possess it to a greater degree than men. Indeed, from 1589 onward, women are *'the* sex' (*OED* 'sex', *n.* 1.e.). All 19 iterations of the word 'sex' in Shakespeare's plays and poems refer to women. Most of them, in fact, are spoken *by* women. Joan of Arc in *1 Henry 6* challenges the Dauphin: 'My courage try by combat, if thou dar'st, / Thou shalt find that I exceed my sex' (1.3.68–69). Sexual solidarity among women is important to Helena in *A Midsummer Night's Dream*. 'Your wrongs do set a scandal on my sex', she charges the importuning Demetrius (2.1.240). When Hermia seems to join the men in mocking her, Helena has these sharp words for her childhood companion: 'It is not friendly, 'tis not maidenly. / Our sex as well as I may chide you for it' (3.2.218–19). The male solidarity that Rosalind in *As You Like It* feigns when she disguises herself as Ganymede depends on distancing herself from women. Women become 'they', not 'I'. In her first interview with Orlando in the forest, she invents 'an old religious uncle' whose opinion about women she pretends to share: 'I thank God I am not a woman, to be touched with so many giddy offences as he hath generally taxed their whole sex withal' (3.2.333–34, 337–40). By maligning women, Celia complains, Rosalind has 'misused our sex' (4.1.191). Portia in *Julius Caesar* anticipates the strong women of the later plays in displaying the mettle of her father and her husband – 'think you I am no stronger than my sex, / Being so fathered and so husbanded?' (2.1.295–96) – and proves her claim by wounding herself in the thigh. Cleopatra may pretend to humble herself before victorious Caesar and own 'like frailties which before / Have often shamed our sex' (5.2.119–20), but she defies him and dies in the high Roman fashion. Innogen is so struck by the gentle behavior of Belarius, Guiderius, and Arviragus that she exclaims in soliloquy, 'Pardon me, gods, / I'd change my sex to be companion with them' (3.5.84–85). The implication is clear enough: men possess sex as white people possess race. It is the Other who is imagined to carry the physical marks of the conceptual category. The cipher (0) stands for everything that is not 'white', everything that is not 'male'.

It is curious, to say the least, that vaginas and penises are absent from Lemnius's body-based explanation of gender but figure so prominently in Lacan's language-based explanation of gender. Anatomy becomes semiology under Lacan's Law of the Father. The linguistic distinction between 'Ladies' and 'Gentlemen' needs, in Lacan's psychoanalytical theory, an enforcer who will make sure that the boy in the train never enters 'Ladies' and that the girl never enters 'Gentlemen'. That enforcer materializes in the person of 'the father', who figures first as a physical intruder in the bodily connection between child and mother and then as a linguistic intruder who inculcates the child into the symbolic order of language. The biological sex of this intruder-figure is less important than its linguistic role in turning the child into a social subject. Lacan takes the *logos* in psychology altogether literally. He retains enough of Freud, however, to find the phallus a convenient synecdoche for the brute force with which words shape the human body. For Lacan, it is not biological equipment but language that marks the social subject as male or female and determines that social subject's objects of desire. The phallus becomes 'the privileged signifier of this mark in which the role of Logos is wedded to the advent of desire' (2005, 581).

Lady Macbeth is enforcing the Law of the Father when she chides her absent husband in the sleep-walking scene, 'Fie, my lord, a soldier and afeard?' (5.1.34–35). Only a woman, she implies, would be afraid. Shakespeare's scripts are full of this sort of linguistic positioning in which gendered maleness or femaleness depends on there being an 'opposite' sex. In his first soliloquy, Richard 3, for example, articulates a dangerous unformedness *vis-à-vis* female figures: first women imagined as sexual partners ('Grim-visaged war ... now ... capers nimbly in a lady's chamber' [1.1.9, 10, 12]), then his mother (he sees himself as 'deformed, unfinished, sent before my time / Into this breathing world scarce half made up' [1.1.20–21]). It is the lack of these defining female reference points that determine Richard 'to prove a villain' (1.1.30) (Miner 1980, 35–55; Rackin 2002, 71–85). Or so it seems to him in his womanless isolation. In the course of the play he plays off a series of female antagonists, one of whom, Queen Elizabeth, commands the third largest share of lines in the script after Richard and Buckingham.[8] In *Measure for Measure,* the Duke foists the same logic on Isabella while he is pretending to ridicule the public case she brings against Angelo. Are you married, the Duke asks Isabella. No. A maid? No. A widow? No. 'Why, you are nothing then; neither maid, widow, nor wife!' (5.1.176–77). Well, she could be a whore, Lucio volunteers. The plight of Lucrece after her rape by Tarquin is precisely this. No longer the chaste wife, she can imagine no viable role for herself *vis-à-vis* her husband and her father. She may declare, 'For me, I am the mistress of my fate' (*Lucrece,* 1069), but ultimately Lucrece is what she is only in relationship to three men: her husband, her rapist, and her father.

What, in Plato's terms, are the 'forms' that determine gender in Shakespeare's works? *Différance* in Shakespeare's scripts turns on three sorts of signifiers: not just words but props and clothing. Reading the printed texts of Shakespeare's plays, we may forget how salient props and clothing were in dramatic performance as markers of gender. Famously Hercules abandoned his masculinity by taking up his mistress Omphale's distaff or spindle for winding thread. 'Do you not shrink', Deianira asks Hercules in epistle 9 of Ovid's *Heroides,* 'from laying to the polished wool-basket the hand that triumphed over a thousand toils; do you draw off with stalwart thumb the coarsely spun strands, and give back to the hand of a pretty mistress the just portion she weighed out?' (9.75–78, 113–15). Thus Goneril ridicules her husband Albany's reluctance to engage in battle by telling Edmund, 'I must change names at home, and give the distaff / Into my husband's hands' (*The Tragedy of King Lear* 4.2.16–17). The laundry basket that turns Falstaff into the butt of female tricksters in *The Merry Wives of Windsor,* Act 3, scene 3, functions in a similar way. So perhaps does Venus's traditional icon, a mirror, in *Richard 2,* Act 5, scene 1. So certainly does the knife wielded by Lady Macbeth. 'Come unsex me *here*', she commands. Where is 'here'? Does she mean in this place and time? At this moment in the fiction? On this very spot on the Globe's stage in 1606? Or does she point to the breasts that in a few seconds will come to signify her femaleness? In the course of Lady Macbeth's speech, there is a suggestive pairing of two possessive phrases, 'My woman's breasts' and 'my keen knife', each consisting of three elements: (1) the first-person possessive pronoun 'my', (2) an adjective ('woman's', 'keen'), and (3) the name of the object being possessed ('breasts', 'knife'). In the dramatic context, the knife functions as a prop, as a stage accessory (*OED* 'property' n. 3) but also as an external object 'proper' to the holder (*OED* 5) and thus as an extension of the actor's body (Harris and Korda 2002, 1–34). But a property is also an 'alienable' possession, as law terminology would it have it: the knife wielded by the actor playing Lady Macbeth took its small place among the material property owned by the King's Men (*OED* 2.a). And so, the speech implies, do 'my woman's breasts'. Earlier in the scene it is Macbeth who is imagined to possess milk-giving breasts.

Cross-dressing in Shakespeare's comedies has been extensively studied. Laura Levine in *Men in Women's Clothing* traces back to Philip Stubbes and other anti-theatrical polemicists the deep-seated fear that lack of correspondence between the signifier (female clothing) and the body being signified (a male-sexed actor) can undo the very basis of masculine self-identity among spectators of a play. Untie that knot, and behold what discord follows.[9] Critics of a more deconstructionist bent have seized on such doubts and pushed them to their ontological extreme. What has often gone unquestioned in this deconstructive free-fall is the way the very term 'cross-dressing' preserves a binary distinction between ♀ and ♂. *Cross*-dressing? Across *what*? The term entails not only a divide that has to be crossed over but an opposition between the entities on either side. To early modern eyes, cross-dressing also entailed a syntax. The satiric tract *Hic Mulier: Or, the Man-Woman* (1620) begins by pointing out the absurdity of applying the Latin male demonstrative *hic* ('this') to the Latin feminine noun *mulier* ('woman'): 'But two words, and they false Latin?' (reprinted in Shakespeare 2001, 267). If articles of clothing, 'male' and 'female', figure as qualifiers, it is the sexed human body, male and female, that figures as the substantive that those articles of clothing qualify. Moments like Orsino's address to 'Cesario'/Viola at the end of *Twelfth Night* may seem to point toward an aporia that lacks any guarantors of meaning. 'Cesario, come'. Orsino insists on calling the boy actor who has spent most of the play dressed as a boy but has now been revealed, within the fiction, to be a girl – 'For so you shall be while you are a man; / But when in other habits you are seen, / Orsino's mistress, and his fancy's queen' (5.1.381–83). However delightful it may be to count up the ironies, we are in fact stuck in the same binary conundrum as Lacan's brother and sister. To substitute 'Cesario' (♂) for 'Viola' (♀) in 1.2 and 'Viola' (♀) for 'Cesario' (♂) in 5.1 is simply to reverse the binary: 1 | 0 becomes 0 | 1. To begin with 0 is, however, more dangerous than it looks. To begin with the cipher is to set up a potentially infinite series – 0, 1, 2, 3, 4, and so on – and to end in the verbal confusion that Plato talks about in the *Symposium*. Or in the directional meaning that Lyotard finds in history.

Imagination

From a presentist point of view, it is tempting to write off Lady Macbeth's 'unsex me here' speech as an instance of 'false consciousness'. That is the label Marxist theory gives to ideology that mystifies what is *really* going on and hence diverts subordinate classes from acting in their own best interest (Holland and Wihl). Lady Macbeth, that is to say, buys into patriarchal ideology – particularly the proposition that gender differences are biological differences – and in so doing she submits to patriarchal power even in the act of trying to defy it. *False* consciousness? False to whom? False by what criterion? What we witness in this speech *is* Lady Macbeth's consciousness of her gender – or rather Shakespeare's verbal approximation of what the female body might feel like to someone possessed of a mind that belongs to a differently sexed body, a male body. Consciousness is, literally, '*with*-knowledge'. For all the talismanic power it acquired in twentieth-century academic discourse, *consciousness* entered the English language in the 1620s in quite concrete circumstances. Philip Massinger's character Camiola catches this self-reflexive quality in the word in the earliest citation recorded in the *OED*. In *The Maid of Honour*, a tragicomedy probably acted at the Red Bull Theatre in the 1620s, Camiola refuses to act on her admiration for her suitor and social superior Bertoldo. Why not, he asks her. 'The Consciousnesse of mine owne wants', she replies (Massinger sig. C4). In this statement she acknowledges differences in social class, gender, and power. These are the *with*-factors in her knowledge of the world. In the case of Lady Macbeth, the *with* includes breasts, muscles, sinews, and coursing fluids. What Lady Macbeth describes in her 'unsex me here' speech is not gender but what it *feels like* to possess gender, and she does so in terms specific to early modern culture. The sexed body is fundamental to how, in this particular time and place, gender *feels*. Lady Macbeth's organs, muscles, sinews, and body fluids both are and are not ours. Early modern discourse may have invited Lady Macbeth and her listeners to verbalize what was going on inside their bodies in terms that both are and are not ours, but words, after all, are not everything.

In the course of her speech, Lady Macbeth details just how her transformation from female to male is to be brought about. The 'spirits / That attend on mortal thoughts' are not – or at least are not *only* – the external beings, the hell-fiends that witch-lore would prompt us to envisage here, but aerated fluid that Lady Macbeth imagines to be coursing through her body. When it came to internal communication among organs, brain, and limbs, even Descartes could not imagine an alternative to the *spiritus* that Aristotle, Galen, and other authorities ancient and modern saw circulating through the body, with nerve tissues acting as conduits. Crooke in *Microcosmographia* describes *spiritus* as 'a subtile and thinne body alwayes moouable, engendred of blood and vapour, and the vehicle or carriage of the Faculties of the soule' (1631, 173–74). Lady Macbeth thus thinks of her unsexing as an act of mind over matter. It is 'spirits' that will enact the commands of her 'mortal thought', thickening her blood, stopping up her orifices, turning her milk into gall, emboldening her to take 'my keen knife' (1.5.51) in hand. The 'ministers' that will transform hostess into murderer are imagined by Lady Macbeth to be biological: they are 'sightless substances' (1.5.48), and they are not specific to sex. The passions that resulted from biochemical changes like those Lady Macbeth describes were, in fact, the early modern actor's stock in trade. Sandys recognizes as much when he describes the women's parts he saw acted at Messina as 'too naturally passionated'. In the course of a dramatic performance, so actors and listeners/spectators told themselves, an actor physiologically induced the passion he was talking about, and he communicated that passion physically to listeners/spectators through the air waves that carried his voice from his mouth to their ears and through beams sent out from his eyes that touched their bodies. A good actor had the power to turn listeners/spectators into the very sort of person he was pretending to be (Roach 1985, 23–57). In the case of the boy actor playing Lady Macbeth, that meant turning the listeners/spectators into female bodies throbbing with male ambition. In a word, the boy actor playing Lady Macbeth turned the listeners/spectators into hermaphrodites.

'Of bodies chang'd to other shapes I sing': the opening line of Ovid's *Metamorphoses* presents a third possibility for conceptualizing gender, a possibility that refuses both the binary categories of biology and the *différance* of semiology (1.1, Ovid 1970).[10] Particularly suggestive is the story of Hermaphroditus in Book 4. The son of Mercury (Hermes) and Venus (Aphrodite), Hermaphroditus combines in his person the good looks of each. Hermaphroditus's travels take him to Caria, where the water-nymph Salmacis spies his beauty and burns with desire. The other nymphs of Caria are devotees of Diana, but Salmacis refuses their manly pursuits and instead spends her time grooming her body in the stream that carries her name. When her attempts to seduce Hermaphroditus are unsuccessful, Salmacis retreats to a hiding place and watches while Hermaphroditus takes off his clothes and plunges into the stream, into *her* stream. She plunges in after him and wraps her body around his. In that posture she prays to the gods that the two of them may never be divided. Her prayers are answered when they become one body – a body that combines the external signs of male and female. In his characteristic way, Ovid tells his readers not just what the transformation looked like from the outside but what it felt like from within.

Here is the moment in the 1621 translation by George Sandys, he who had seen women 'too naturally passionated' in the theater at Messina a few years earlier:

> Even in that space
> Their cleaving bodies mix: both have one face.
> As when wee two divided scions joyne,
> And see them grow together in one rine:
> So they, by such a strict imbracement glew'd,
> Are now but one, with double forme indew'd.
> No longer he a Boy, nor she a maid;
> But neither, and yet either, might be said.

The point of view in Sandys's translation remains male. Hermaphroditus first feels estrangement from his former body:

> *Hermaphroditus* at himselfe admires:
> Who halfe female from the spring retires,
> His manly lims now softened....

Then he feels estrangement from his former voice:

> and thus prayes,
> With a voice as neither sex betrayes:
> Swift *Hermes, Aphrodite!* him ô heare

> Who was your sonne! who both your names doth beare!
> May every man, that in this water swims,
> Returne halfe-woman, with infeebled lims.
> (Ovid 1970, 182)

In Ovid's original Latin, there is a subtle and progressive shift in gender from line to line. It is a *vir* or man who has plunged into the water, but the limbs that grow soft are no longer masculine (just *mollita ... membra*), the voice in which Hermaphroditus speaks is no longer a man's voice (*iam non voce virili*), and the prayer that Hermes and Aphrodite answer is that of their 'biform (re)born' (*nati ... biforma*) (4.381–82, 387, Ovid 1929, 204).

In his extended commentary on this passage, Sandys cites both Plato and Aristotle. Plato's story of the divided self Sandys reads as 'an obscure notion ... of *Eva's* being taken out of the side of Adam' (Ovid 1970, 208). From Aristotle, Sandys takes the deterministic, biological reading we might expect: '*Aristotle* writes that that they have the right brest of a man; and the left of a woman, wherewith they nourish their children' (208). But where Plato admits of fusion Aristotle (according to Sandys) insists on separation: 'they were to choose what sex they would use, and punished with death if they changed at any time' (208). And so must androgynes in the seventeenth century. Sandys goes on to cite contemporary examples of hermaphrodites who refused to conform to one gender role or the other and the gruesome punishments that their indecision wrecked upon them:

> One not long since burned for the same at *Burges:* who elected the female, and secretly exercised the male; under the disguize committing many villanies. *Caliphanes* reports, how among the *Nasamones* there were a whole nation of these; who used both with like liberty. There are many at this day in *Aegypt*, but most frequent in *Florida*; who are so hated by the rest of the *Indians*, that they use them as beasts to carry their burthens; to suck their wonds, and attend on the diseased. But at *Rome* they threw them as soone as borne into the river; the Virgins singing in procession, and offering sacrifice unto *Juno*. (208–09)

What Sandys misses – or tries to cover up – is the very thing that made Ovid so attractive to early modern readers in the first place: his ability to dissolve binaries and to invite his readers to experience that dissolution from the inside.

Early modern ideas about imagination help us understand why Ovid was the period's favorite author. For Shakespeare and his contemporaries, the Aristotelian axiom, 'there is nothing in the intellect that was not first in the senses', gave sense experience an epistemological importance that modern science, with its protocols of objective proof, has attempted to compensate for, if not deny (Park 1988). The five external senses (sight, hearing, smell, taste, touch) were imagined to have their counterparts in five internal senses (common sense, imagination, fantasy, estimation, memory) that processed sense experiences and turned them into thoughts. Particularly interesting are the functions of imagination and fantasy. It was not just visual images, sounds, odors, tastes, and textures that imagination held in store but kinaesthetic images/sounds/odors/tastes/textures that had been fused by the faculty of common sense. These kinaesthetic *species* (to use the technical term) were then worked over by the perceiver's fantasy before being presented to estimation for a determination of how the perceiver should react. The resulting thought/action was then stored in memory. Just where estimation took place was a subject of controversy. 'Tell me where is fancy bred', asks the song in *The Merchant of Venice*, 'Or in the heart or in the head?' (3.2.63–64). Thomas Wright, in *The Passions of the Mind in General*, opts for the heart. *Phantasmata* sent from the brain via the spirits cause the heart either to dilate in pleasure or contract in abhorrence, changing the body's temperament in the process and producing the passions that determine behavior. Passion, in this model, is inescapably part of perception.

Even Descartes in *Passions de l'Ame* (English translation as *Passions of the Soule*) accepts passions as 'thoughts'. *Pensées* come in two sorts, Descartes explains, those deriving from actions of the soul and those deriving from passions. The difference seems to turn on the purposive quality of the soul's thoughts versus the passive-voice quality of passions as something that the soul 'suffers'. (The word *passion* derives from the Latin deponent verb *patior*, to undergo, to endure.) Yet even the soul's acts of will are *experienced* as passions: 'For it is certain that we cannot will anything without thereby perceiving that we are willing it. And although willing something is an action with respect to our soul, the perception of such willing may be said to be a passion in the soul' (1985, 1.335–36, 1967, 2.343). It was left to Hobbes, Locke, and Hume to limit 'thought' to syllogisms and hence pave the high road toward 'the linguistic turn' that has sent academic criticism off in a new direction since the 1970s. But that was not the direction in 1606. Even so august a writer as Edward Reynolds, John Donne's successor as preacher at

Lincoln's Inn and later Bishop of Norwich, grants imagination and fancy a scope that seems astonishing from *this* side of the Enlightenment. In *A Treatise of the Passions and Faculties of the Soul of Man*, Reynolds explains that fancy has a 'double prerogative': in the form of *phantasmata* it captures the 'quicknesse and volubilitie' of thoughts, even as it fixes objects for meditation by the understanding. And by 'thoughts' Reynolds means, not just rational propositions, but 'those springings and glances of the heart, grounded on the sudden representation of sundry different objects' (sig. D3v). Reynolds's model of perception, like Wright's, accommodates the heart as well as the brain, passions as well as reason. Hence Ovid's hold on early modern imagination. The fables in *Metamorphoses* may begin with bodies and shapes, things that can be seen and differentiated, but the focus is on change – and on what those changes feel like from the inside. Ovid invites his readers to *understand* gender not as something that is present *in* the body, as the biological model would have it, nor as something inscribed *on* the body, as the semiological model would have it, but as something experienced *through* the body, as it is in Lady Macbeth's speech.

In her speech announcing her intent to murder, we can witness Lady Macbeth's estrangement from her woman's body, but that woman's body gives Lady Macbeth the terms for *feeling* her murderous intent – and for making the audience/spectators feel it no less viscerally, no less corporeally, no less personally. When Lady Macbeth speaks, do male listeners see the breasts on someone else's body, on a female-sexed body? Perhaps that is as far as many male listeners go. Do other male listeners suddenly feel the shape of their own chests? Do they feel a slight tingling in their lips? The I-----O continuum works, not just between the 'we' who listen and watch, on the one hand, and the actors who represent the action, on the other, but among the listening and watching 'we' as it fractures into each free-standing 'I'.

'Nature' figures twice in Lady Macbeth's speech: first in her resolve that 'no compunctious visitings of nature / Shake my fell purpose' (1.5.44–45) and then in her summoning the 'murd'ring ministers that wait on nature's mischief' (1.5.49). What is 'nature' here? In the first instance, it might be heard as an attribute of milk-giving female bodies (women 'naturally' feel compunction), but in the second it has become a capacity for violence that is no more limited to maleness than, earlier, the milk of human kindness was to femaleness. The example of Aristotle prompts us to distrust the force of 'nature' as a signifier. 'The male is by nature superior, and the female inferior', Aristotle declares in the *Politics*. For Plato 'nature' is suspect as a category. It gives rise to 'verbal contradictions' that may have nothing to do with the capabilities and behavior of individual men and women. Hence, in the *Republic*, Plato's recommendation that women be trained for whatever offices they are suited. 'Nature' in Lady Macbeth's speech is less fixed than in either of these received formulations. As in Ovid's story of Hermaphroditus, Lady Macbeth's 'nature' embraces a transsexual imaginary in which male-sexed bodies can behave in 'female' ways and female-sexed bodies in 'male' ways. I take back those scare quotes. According to Galenic medicine and early modern acting theory, behavior and body do not stand in binary opposition. Lady Macbeth's unsexing is in fact a resexing. Through an act of imagination – in Descartes's terms a 'thought' willed by the soul – she attempts to transform her female-sexed body into a male-sexed body. The metamorphosis happens through body chemistry, through transmuting milk into gall and gall into milk – and through the listener's willingness to give free reign to imagination in putting together what she hears with what he sees in unexpected and perhaps socially dangerous ways. If a listener/spectator *thinks* it happens, it happens.

A presentist Ovid? Who reads Ovid? Truth be told, not many people since the peak of his popularity and influence *circa* 1600. That does not mean, however, that Ovid has nothing to say to the present. In Ovid, presentist critics can find a smart and sympathetic spokesperson for one of their own obsessions: knowing through the body. The link between body and mind that has gone missing since 1650 is not the pineal gland or neuropeptides – those, after all, have more to do with the body than with the mind – but imagination. Early modern ideas about imagination provide a way of explaining the connection between gender and sex that the material and the mind models, by themselves, do not. Imagination is not just about words: it is about visual images ('my woman's breasts'), sounds ('*m*ilk'/'*m*urd'ring'), odors (implicit in 'dunnest smoke'), tastes ('take my milk for gall'), textures ('make thick my blood', 'Come, thick night'). In a word, imagination is about *embodied* cognition. It refuses the binary markings of gender, offering instead a continuum of possible combinations of sex and gender that begins with I and ends with ∞. As such, the imagination model provides a meeting ground for past and present, and for the world's diversity of cultures. At the 1995 United Nations Fourth World Conference on Women in Beijing, a resolution was floated that would have replaced the binary markers of male/female and heterosexual/homosexual with a multi-dimensional array of possible combinations of biological sex, gender identities, social differences, and sexual behaviors.[11] In the event, the resolution failed to be ratified, but it remains an ideal for readers who want to open up possibilities for interpretation across time and across cultures, not foreclose them. Alan Sinfield has provided the outline for such a cross-cultural model, as well as an impassioned rationale for its adoption (2002, 120–38). As a model for addressing the connections between gender and sexuality, imagination's continuum offers the opportunity for a dialectic in which the movement is not one-directional, from I to O, but reversible. If I will just stop talking, O can tell I (me) a thing or two.

What this means, for our present purposes, is that sex and gender may not be the separable categories we have wanted them to be since the 1960s. The separation of sex from gender in late twentieth-century criticism has been politically useful and personally liberating for many people, myself included, but the case of Lady Macbeth suggests that if we really want to attend to our *connection* with Shakespeare's script, we must find a way of putting sex and gender back together, not just on our terms, not just on their terms, but in a mutually enabling combination of the two. Conflation of sex and gender, I would argue, is not an act of false consciousness, repeated over and over from ancient times to the 1960s, but a constantly changing phenomenon, in which sexed body and socialized behavior are brought together in culture- and time-specific ways. In the case of early modern England, penis/male/power and vagina/female/submission do not line up with anything like the precision that deconstructionist critiques have assumed. Desiring to act the man and feeling it in your breasts is not the same thing as desiring to act the man and feeling it in your penis. It is imagination, not the logic of 1 | 0, that makes the difference.

Notes

1. William Shakespeare, *Macbeth* (1.5.39–40), in Shakespeare (1998a). The dating of the script to 1606–07 is accepted by most editors. Further quotations from Shakespeare's works are taken from the revised Oxford edition and are cited in the text of the essay by act, scene, and line numbers in the case of plays, sonnet and line numbers in the case of sonnets, and line numbers in the case of narrative poems.
2. This essay began as a series of invited lectures at Rhodes College, Memphis, Tennessee; the annual meeting of the Sociedad Iberiana de Estudios Renacentistas Ingleses, Lisbon, Portugal; Manchester University, U.K.; and Otago University, New Zealand. I am grateful to the hosts who invited me to speak on these occasions and to the auditors who responded with questions and disagreements. In the transformation from lecture to essay the advice of Carol Thomas Neely has been crucial and deeply appreciated.

3. Michel Foucault's formulation in *The History of Sexuality,* Vol. 1: *An Introduction* has been taken as axiomatic for the past 25 years: 'sexuality must not be thought of as a kind of natural given which power tries to hold in check, or as an obscure domain which knowledge tries gradually to uncover. It is the name that can be given to a historical construct' (1976, 1978, 105). 'Woman' and 'female' have likewise been transformed from natural givens to historical constructs, even in works like Juliet Dusinberre's *Shakespeare and the Nature of Women* that celebrate resistance and individuality: 'Shakespeare and his contemporaries create women ready to forget the fact of womanhood in a society determined to remember it. The dramatists saw that society molds women in its own image and informs the rebels that they are not women, but men' (1975, 2003, 225). The social construction of women is the starting point for Linda Woodbridge. In her account of 'Feminist Criticism in Motion', Carol Thomas Neely (1985) notes that social strictures have had to be negotiated in all three phrases of feminist criticism of Shakespeare: a rejection of social norms in the 'compensatory' phase, an acknowledgment of the power of social norms in the 'justificatory' phase, and a negotiation of possibilities for individual difference within social norms in the 'transformational' phase (69–90).
4. Statistics handily tabulated in Alfred Harbage's *The Complete Works* give Lady Macbeth the second largest number of lines after Macbeth's, Cleopatra 622 lines to Antony's 766, Volumnia the third largest part after Coriolanus and Menenius, Innogen the largest number of lines in *Cymbeline* (522 of 3,266), and Paulina the second largest number of lines after Leontes in *The Winter's* Tale (Shakespeare 1969, 31).
5. Further quotations from Aristotle's works are taken from Jonathan Barnes's translation and are cited in the text of the essay by standard reference numbers.
6. Further quotations of Levinus Lemnius are cited in the text of the essay. Medical self-help books by Lemnius, a Dutch physician, enjoyed a long shelf-life in English translation, beginning with Thomas Newton's version of *The Touchstone of Complexions* (1565, 1576, 1581, 1633). William Burton in *The Anatomy of Melancholy* cites Lemnius frequently. For a brief account of Lemnius and his place in medical discourse of the sixteenth and seventeenth centuries, see F. David Hoeniger (1992, 48).
7. Further quotations from Plato's works are taken from John M. Cooper's translation and are cited in the text of the essay by standard reference numbers.
8. This, according to Harbage's analysis (Shakespeare 1969, 31).
9. Laura Levine in fact uses Ulysses's 'degree' speech in *Troilus and Cressida* in Act 1, scene 3, as a point of departure (1994, 33–5).
10. Further quotations of Ovid's *Metamorphoses* are cited by page number in the text of the essay.
11. Personal communication from Mary Ann Lundy, who was an official delegate to the conference. I have not been able to locate a printed or on-line confirmation of Lundy's report. The primary on-line source is to be found at http://www.un.org/womenwatch/daw/beijing/officialother.html

2

Dated and Outdated: The Present Tense of Feminist Shakespeare Criticism

Phyllis Rackin

As recent philosophers of history have repeatedly argued, there is a very important sense in which all history is present history. Any attempt to write about the past is inevitably shaped by the professional and personal interests of the historian – interests that are themselves shaped by the pressures of the time and place in which the historian writes. These pressures are everywhere apparent in the history of feminist Shakespeare criticism, although the protocols of academic discourse, with its demand for scientific objectivity, have typically rendered them unacknowledged and unrecognized.

For feminist critics and scholars, the recognition and analysis of these factors is especially necessary, not only in the interests of a more rigorous historicism but also because feminist scholarship and criticism are inevitably implicated in the political. Accordingly, this essay will examine the political implications of exemplary texts in recent feminist Shakespeare criticism – both the impact they reveal of the political pressures that produced them, and the likely political consequences of their circulation. It will also ask what issues and methodologies might best serve the feminist project in the context of the challenges that confront women in the recent political climate of backlash and retrenchment.[1]

Although feminist Shakespeare criticism has often been marginalized as a belated and unseemly intrusion into a venerable discourse that is properly concerned with more important (more universal, more serious, more elevated) concerns than the parochial interests of women, feminist Shakespeare criticism is actually nothing new. Its own history is just as venerable as that of Shakespeare criticism itself, having appeared, in fact, in the first critical essay ever published on Shakespeare. In that essay, dated 1664, Margaret Cavendish praised Shakespeare's ability to create lifelike female characters in distinctly feminist terms. 'One would think', she declared, 'that he had been Metamorphosed from a Man to a Woman, for who could Describe *Cleopatra* Better than he hath done, and many other Females of his own Creating'. She went on to list a number of others, including Beatrice, Mistress Quickly, and both of the merry wives of Windsor (Cavendish 1664, Letter 122). From Cavendish's time to our own, many other women have also written about Shakespeare from a clearly feminist perspective. In the middle of the nineteenth century, Mary Cowden Clarke, Shakespeare's first female editor, wrote that he, of all male authors, 'has best asserted womanhood's rights' (quoted in Ziegler 1997, 17). Although the terms in which both Cavendish and Clarke express their appreciation for Shakespeare's work can only be described as feminist, the first use of the word *feminist* cited in the OED did not occur until 1894, and what is usually identified today as feminist Shakespeare criticism dates from the 1970s, when it was energized by an active feminist political movement. For academic feminists, appropriating Shakespeare's authority to argue their case seemed an obvious strategy, and his sympathetic view of women seemed equally obvious. The book that is generally regarded as the foundation of modern feminist Shakespeare criticism, *Shakespeare and the Nature of Women*, was first published in 1975. In it, Juliet Dusinberre argued that both Shakespeare and the popular stage for which he wrote were 'feminist in sympathy'. Shakespeare, she argued, 'saw men and women as equal in a world which declared them unequal'. 'Where in every other field', she concluded, 'understanding of Shakespeare's art grows, reactions to his women continually recycle, because critics are still immersed in preconceptions which Shakespeare discarded about the nature of women' (1975, 2003, 135).

The year 1975 saw a number of other firsts for women. In the Central African Republic, Elizabeth Domitien became the first woman premier. During that same year, *The New York Times* reported that Cynid Meserve, a freshman at the Pratt Institute, had become the first woman to play in a National Collegiate Association basketball game, that Carol Palley joined the all-male ranks of managing editors of daily newspapers in New Jersey, that the toll-takers on the New Jersey turnpike now included four women, that a growing number of women were becoming traveling salesmen, that the International Labor Organization had called upon husbands to assume a greater share of household duties to ease the burden on wives who worked outside the home, that President Gerald

Ford had declared that he would like to have a woman in the Cabinet. The U.N. General Assembly proclaimed 1975 International Woman's Year. Canada and Australia each pledged two million dollars in support of the enterprise, and even the U.S. pledged $350,000.

All in all, the mid-1970s looked like a promising time for women. Between 1971 and 1974, the number of women serving as Foreign Service Officers in the U.S. State Department and U.S. Information Agency tripled, rising from 4.9 percent to 15 percent. In 1974, the first woman mayor of a city with a population over 500,000 (Janet Gray Hayes of San Jose, California), the first woman chief justice of a state supreme court (Susie Sharp of North Carolina) and New York's first woman lieutenant governor (Mary Anne Krupsak) were elected. Ella Grasso of Connecticut became the first woman elected governor in her own right rather than as the wife or widow of a previous governor. And a record number of 18 women were elected to the U.S. House of Representatives.

These advances were exhilarating to many women, but they also provoked significant opposition. The Equal Rights Amendment, which had seemed, only three years earlier, clearly destined for passage, was stalled four states short of ratification. Passed by Congress in 1972, the ERA received 22 of the 38 needed ratifications by individual states in one year. But as organized opposition mounted, the pace of ratification slowed and finally stopped: there were only eight ratifications in 1973, three in 1974, one in 1975, and none in 1976. In October, 1975, the National Organization for Women called for a one-day national strike by all the women in the U.S. to call attention to their roles in society. The result, however, was 'a resounding flop' ('Women in Banks' 1975, 63). As affirmative action programs began to increase women's presence in the academy, established scholars publicly worried that standards of excellence would be compromised. As President of the University of Chicago, Edward Levi had warned that 'a law against discrimination turns toward a law in favor of quotas'. In 1975, Levi became the Attorney General of the U.S. (Shiels 1975, 65).

The reception of Dusinberre's book was similarly ambivalent. *Shakespeare and the Nature of Women* had an exhilarating effect on feminist scholars who believed, as Dusinberre did, that 'the plays of Shakespeare and his contemporaries' were 'agents' for their own 'emancipation' (1975, 2003, xii); but the very power of her argument also provoked controversy. Critics were quick to emphasize the many ways in which both the women in Shakespeare's England and the female characters in his plays were disempowered, demonized, and repressed.

Dusinberre had argued that a woman ruler, such as Queen Elizabeth, 'is a spur to feminism because her position forces men to ask questions about the relation between femininity and power' (1975, 2003, 303). Other scholars pointed out that the presence of isolated 'women worthies' has little effect on the status of women in general or on attitudes toward them; and they countered the well-known evidence for Queen Elizabeth's political skills and popularity with examples of sixteenth century English expressions of resentment towards their Queen and opposition to female rule. Dusinberre had seen humanist arguments for women's education and Puritan calls for a new conception of matrimony as progressive forces for women. Other scholars emphasized the limitations of the humanist program of women's education and the decreased autonomy of wives in households shaped by Puritan ideals.

These debates reflected the ambivalence of contemporary responses to the prospect of increased power for women, but they also reflected the diversity of feminist thought, which was never so monolithic as its detractors claimed. An excellent place to see how diverse feminist thought really was is the first major book of U.S. feminist Shakespeare criticism, which also originated in the mid 1970s when Carolyn Ruth Swift Lenz organized a Special Session at the 1976 MLA convention, which she designated as 'Feminist Criticism of Shakespeare'. Lenz also began collecting essays for an anthology on the same subject, and that anthology, eventually co-edited with Gayle Greene and Carol Thomas Neely, was finally published in 1980. Entitled *The Woman's Part: Feminist Criticism of Shakespeare*, it helped to inaugurate a decade in which feminist criticism became a major – perhaps even the dominant – approach to Shakespeare's plays.

The Woman's Part reflected the multifariousness of U.S. feminist thinking during the 1970s. The essays it contained were united only by their authors' desire to pay and call attention to the importance of women's roles in Shakespeare's plays: they expressed strikingly diverse critical allegiances and equally diverse beliefs about their subject. Some contributors drew on Freudian and post-Freudian psychology to analyze both Shakespeare's characters and his own motivations, while others emphasized the specific historical context in which the plays were first produced. Some writers celebrated what they regarded as Shakespeare's challenges to patriarchal ideology, while others saw the plays as revelations of his own alignment with patriarchy and his profound fears of female sexuality.

During the 1980s and 1990s, however, this diversity gave way to a growing consensus in support of the most pessimistic views of women's lives in Shakespeare's world and of the roles of female characters in his plays. Rejecting the more optimistic feminist readings of the 1970s as unhistorical, scholars cited prescriptive texts that advocated women's subordination and demonstrated the ubiquity of patriarchal dominance. The resulting paradigm was easily – and repeatedly – summarized. Here are two of many possible examples: A textbook entitled *The Cultural Identity of Seventeenth-Century Woman* (note the author's revealing choice of the abstract term 'Woman') instructed students:

> Woman's place was within doors, her business domestic. ... Women ... themselves accepted this divorce between the private (feminine) and public (masculine) sphere and, despite the recent precedents of Mary Queen of Scots, Mary Tudor and Elizabeth, they shared the age's distaste ... for the notion of women's involvement in politics. (Keeble 1994, 186)

A well-received historical study entitled *Gender, Sex, and Subordination in England, 1500–1800* summed up its own argument in similar terms:

> It was conventional, as we have seen, to assume men and women had clearly defined gender roles indoors and out of doors .... Femininity, as we have seen, was presented as no more than a set of negatives. The requirement of chastity was, as we have seen, the overriding measure of female gender. Woman not only had to be chaste but had to be seen to be chaste: silence, humility and modesty were the signifiers that she was so. (Fletcher 1999, 120–22)

Reminders that Renaissance Englishwomen were expected to be chaste, silent, and obedient were endlessly repeated – probably more often in late twentieth century scholarly discourse than in the writings of Shakespeare's contemporaries. Readers were assured that Shakespeare's England 'was fraught with anxiety about rebellious women' (Newman 1991, 40), that 'women's reading was policed and their writing prohibited or marked as transgressive even when they were not engaged in other criminal activities' (Dolan 1996, 159) and that any manifestation of female power or authority was greeted with anxious hostility.

It is not surprising that these readings of Renaissance history were widely accepted during the last two decades of the twentieth century; the anxiety they attributed to the men of Shakespeare's England seemed entirely plausible because it resonated with the anxiety felt by academic men in a period when their own grasp on academic status – and even on tenured academic positions – became increasingly insecure. The main causes of this insecurity were a decreased population of college-age students, cutbacks in government aid to education, and the increased use of ill-paid, non-tenure-track faculty; but the growing presence of women among the already excessive supply of new PhDs and the affirmative action programs that put pressure on departments to hire and promote some of them provided a convenient focus for the anxieties and resentments of men who failed or feared they would fail to achieve the positions to which they felt entitled.[2]

Feminist Shakespeare criticism during this period often focused on plays that told stories of male misogyny and female submission. *The Taming of the Shrew* became a great favorite, and the discouraging story it told was said to express beliefs that were generally accepted by Shakespeare's first audiences. But even the plays that had seemed to present a more benevolent view of women and a more generous view of their place in society were reinterpreted to support this new orthodoxy. *As You Like It*, we learned, was designed as 'a structure for [Rosalind's] containment'. The point of the action was to secure Orlando's alliance with her father and through that alliance to restore the young man to his rightful place in the patriarchy (Montrose 1981). Some of these interpretations were quite ingenious. In *Titus Andronicus*, for instance, when Lavinia appears on stage with her hands cut off and her tongue cut out, the gruesome spectacle was said to be 'expressive of the anxieties she generates as an educated, and hence potentially unruly, woman' (Sprengnether 1996 12–13).[3] In this criticism, Shakespeare's plays were seen as complicit with a repressive gender ideology that subordinated the women in his own world. Instead of empowering subsequent women readers, his plays now appeared to validate their subjugation. The only possibility for feminist Shakespeare criticism, it now seemed, was to expose and denounce that complicity.

One way to explain these developments is to highlight the fact that women's issues had now entered the mainstream of academic discourse. As Annette Kolodny complained in 1988, 'respectability [was] eroding the revolutionary potential of feminist criticism' (1988, 52). Earlier feminist Shakespeare critics wrote from the margins of acceptable academic discourse, their work tended to be motivated by a sense of personal and political urgency, and they often found it difficult to publish. But with the growing interest in issues of sex and gender, writing about them started to look like a good career move. Conferences were organized to address those issues, and scholarly journals and academic presses were eager to publish articles and books that dealt with them. The inevitable result was that feminist studies were adopted as a conceptual tool by women and men without a serious political commitment to feminist political agendas, and scholarship designated as 'feminist' provided arguments that could just as easily be used to validate women's oppression as to oppose it. However, since academic discourse never takes place in a vacuum, it is important to remember that this backlash against earlier feminist Shakespeare studies took place during the same years when U.S. culture at large saw a widespread backlash against feminist thought and action. Many of the same themes – concerns about 'endangered masculinity', for instance – were equally prominent in studies of Shakespeare's plays and in popular culture and the mass media. It is noteworthy, for instance, that Mark Breitenberg's book, *Anxious Masculinity in Early Modern England*, probably the most sustained exposition of that subject, was written during the same years that U.S. men were flocking to weekend retreats designed to teach 'wimps' how to eradicate their feminine 'softness' and become 'real men'. Breitenberg's book, published in 1996, was written during the late 1980s and early 1990s.[4] It is more than coincidental that Robert Bly's *Iron John*, which quickly became a best-seller when it was published in 1990, was a collection of pamphlets written during the same period.[5] The leaders of the 'men's movement', like their counterparts among Shakespeare scholars, claimed that their own work was feminist in sympathy, but the animus against women's power and the sense that women had taken something that rightly belonged to men was never far from the surface. In the Grimm's fairy tale from which Bly took his title, a prince loses his golden ball when it rolls into an abandoned pond. To get it back, he must free a 'wild man' who is locked up in a cage. But to free the wild man, he must first steal the key to his cage, which the queen, his mother, keeps under her pillow.

In the feminist Shakespeare studies of this period, an obvious candidate for the role of the queen who deprived men of their rightful power was Elizabeth. One of the earliest and most influential examples of 'masculine anxiety' criticism was Louis Adrian Montrose's 1986 article, '*A Midsummer Night's Dream* and the Shaping Fantasies of Elizabethan Culture: Gender, Power, Form'. Opposing traditional interpretations that saw the play as celebrating Queen Elizabeth, Montrose argued that the story it told was shaped by masculine anxieties. These anxieties can be assuaged only by the mastery of powerful women, such as Hippolyta, the Amazonian queen, who is a surrogate for Queen Elizabeth, herself an inappropriately powerful woman who constituted a source of anxiety to her male subjects. Montrose's reading of the play became canonical because it was perfectly suited to the intellectual climate – and the gender politics – of the times. New historicist critics were fascinated by questions of royal power, especially that of King James. In the case of James's vastly more capable and successful monarchical predecessor, Queen Elizabeth, what seemed most important now was evidence that her rule was less popular than previously assumed. The story of Essex's rebellion was told again and again. By 1998, there was even an anthology entitled *Dissing Elizabeth: Negative Representations of Gloriana* (Walker 1998).

The Shakespearean canon was similarly revised, as critics mined the plays for stories in which female power was contained and punished. *The Taming of the Shrew* became a great favorite, both among the theater-going public and among Shakespeare scholars, who saw fit to write about it over twice as often as any of Shakespeare's other early comedies (Rackin 2005, 11, 51). At the same time, ubiquitous self-help books and articles in women's magazines advised women on ways to get and please husbands. As we have seen, even so obedient a daughter as Lavinia in *Titus Andronicus* was now seen as a source of anxiety, simply because she could read and write, her rape and mutilation symbolic punishments for her literacy. This interpretation seems willfully eccentric in the context of the play, where female literacy – indeed, literacy itself – seems at best a peripheral concern; but it resonated with the anxieties of late twentieth-century academic men confronted by a shortage of tenured positions and increasing competition from women whose academic credentials rivaled or surpassed their own.

The anti-feminist backlash of the last two decades of the twentieth century had serious economic consequences for women, driving many of them out of the workforce and confining them to their homes. According to reports from the U.S. Census Bureau, 13 percent more children were being raised at home by full-time mothers in 2002 than had been in 1994 (Shulevitz 2005, 12). Women's earnings in a variety of fields were also decreasing. A 2002 study prepared by the U.S. General Accounting Office showed that women in management positions now earned only 73 percent of what men made, while in 1995 they had earned 86 percent (Henry 2002, C2). It is doubtful that the remarkable (although relatively unpublicized) success of the anti-feminist backlash could have been achieved without the cooperation of women as well as men. The noisiest advocates of what became known as 'the Mommy track' were women, and even unmarried women bought into the story of male anxiety and the resulting need for female repression. Uncomfortable spiked, pointed-toed shoes and super-feminine clothing became all the rage – designed and promoted mostly by men, but enthusiastically adopted by women who did not want to lose their 'femininity'. In the 1970s, pantsuits and comfortable shoes were fashionable, but they were now rejected in favor of garments that proclaimed women's sexual availability while inhibiting their mobility.

Many academic feminists adopted these fashions, along with the fashions in thought and feeling they expressed. The best we could do, it now seemed, was to expose the faultlines in the now-dominant patriarchal narrative. An early and influential practitioner of this strategy was Coppélia Kahn, who demonstrated in her 1981 study *Man's Estate: Masculine Identity in Shakespeare* that since 'a woman's subjugation to her husband's will was the measure of his patriarchal authority and thus of his manliness', patriarchy made men 'dependent on women indirectly and covertly for the validation of their manhood'. 'Paradoxically', she concluded, 'their power over women' made men 'vulnerable to women' (1981, 15–17). Kahn's thesis provided provocative and influential new readings of a variety of Shakespearean texts, ranging from the early history plays to the late Romances, and much of the most powerful feminist Shakespeare criticism of the following decade was based on similar arguments. Witches and other demonized women became popular subjects. Catherine Belsey argued in 1985 that the scaffolds upon which women were executed for witchcraft 'paradoxically ... offered women a place from which to speak in public with a hitherto unimagined authority which was not diminished by the fact that it was demonic' (1985, 190–91). As late as 1994, Frances E. Dolan argued that 'accounts of domestic violence' were 'one set of scripts in which women could be cast as agents, albeit in problematic terms' (1994, 5).

These arguments used a kind of intellectual jujitsu to turn the now-dominant patriarchal master narrative against itself and in so doing to open a space within it for women's agency. That is the strategy I used in my early work on Shakespeare's history plays, conceding that women were cast as outsiders and opponents to the history-making project of the English protagonists but arguing that those very exclusions empowered their roles and voices (1985, 1989, 1991). The power of that interpretive strategy, like the power of the female characters it featured, was severely limited: women were able to trouble the masculine historical narrative and sometimes to subvert it, but the narrative itself remained as a given. Kathleen McLuskie's astute observation about *Measure for Measure* – that feminist critics were 'restricted to exposing [their] own exclusion from the text' – now seemed applicable to the entire Shakespearean canon (1994, 97).

By the end of the twentieth century, feminist Shakespeare criticism, like the feminist political project itself, seemed to have reached a dead end, and scholars – even women scholars – increasingly turned in other directions. Some of these, like the rediscovery and revaluation of women's own writings, enabled work that continued to advance a feminist agenda; but many constituted a genuine retreat from feminism, as women positioned themselves in the mainstream currents of contemporary academic thought. These were the same years that women's progress in the U.S. academy also reached a dead end. A 2005 study revealed that although women had constituted nearly half of the graduate and professional students at U.S. doctoral institutions for most of the previous decade, the number of women full professors at U.S. research universities had not increased at all during the past five years and that women were still over-represented at the lowest ranks and under-represented at the top (White 2005).

At this point, feminist scholarship no longer looks like the cutting edge in Shakespeare studies. Graduate professors advise their students that feminist approaches are 'outdated'; and, in the conservative political climate of George W. Bush's U.S., the production of feminist criticism and scholarship no longer looks to ambitious young scholars like a shrewd professional move. A quick survey of the online edition of the *World Shakespeare Bibliography* reveals that in 1994 there were 82 English-language entries for the topic women, but only 61 in 2004. Under the keyword 'feminist' there are 24 entries for 1994 but only 17 in 2004. A survey of the most selective journals, I believe, would reveal an even greater discrepancy.

This does not mean, of course, that all the questions raised by previous feminist scholarship have been answered or that important work does not continue to be published. Recent feminist historical scholars, for example, have contested the patriarchal master narrative that had dominated the thinking of their predecessors, emphasizing that repressive prescriptions should not be regarded as descriptions of actual behavior, and they have also been recovering the materials for alternative narratives. Three paradigms that exercised a powerful influence on previous scholarship – the gendered division between public and private spheres, the legal doctrine of coverture, and the theory of the traffic in women – have all been challenged in recent feminist studies. Lena Cowen Orlin produced a formidable array of evidence in her pioneering 1994 book, *Private Matters and Public Culture in Post-Reformation England*, to demonstrate that the division between public and private spheres was accepted only slowly and with difficulty in precapitalist England.

Natasha Korda's *Shakespeare's Domestic Economies: Gender and Property in Early Modern England,* published in 2002, cites a variety of contemporary documents that record married women's ownership, management, and contestation of their husbands' claims to various kinds of property. She shows that women's control over household property – both *de facto* and *de jure* – was far more extensive than a too-simple understanding of the doctrine of coverture and an uncritical application of the theory of the traffic in women have seemed to suggest (7). Pamela Allen Brown and Peter Parolin have recently published an anthology entitled *Women Players in England, 1500–1660* that effectively refutes the notion that Shakespeare and his fellow dramatists wrote for an 'all-male stage'. Women, the authors demonstrate, performed in a variety of professional and amateur settings, and they were deeply involved in the business of professional theatrical production. Women also exerted their influence on those productions, both as the patrons of theatrical companies, and as paying customers in the playhouses. All of this work effectively answers the grim generalizations that dominated feminist Shakespeare criticism during the years of the backlash, when the most optimistic feminist readings were discredited as unhistorical. The only truly historical reading, it seemed then, was from the point of view of a male spectator, threatened by any manifestation of female power or autonomy. These new feminist historical scholars are now showing that Shakespeare's countrywomen were not as marginalized and repressed as we have been led to believe. They are also giving feminists the materials to contest our own marginalization as readers of Shakespeare's plays.

My insistence that feminist Shakespeare criticism shows the pressures of the larger culture in which it is conducted might seem to support the often-heard objection that feminist questions are too 'trendy' and 'tendentious' to justify serious study. However, it would be difficult to find any form of Shakespeare criticism – or academic inquiry, for that matter – that is not 'trendy' – not, that is, shaped by the political and professional pressures that influence the beliefs and preferences of the scholars who produce and consume it. The recurrent dream of a scholarship that will ascend (or escape) to the empyrean realm of timeless, transcendent truths becomes most attractive at particular historical moments. Current emphases in Shakespeare studies are a good case in point. Aesthetic questions are now enjoying a resurgence, as are old-fashioned bibliography and antiquarianism, newly remodeled as 'history of the book' and 'the study of material culture'. And more and more scholars are finding that classical texts and the intricacies of religious doctrine had a profound influence on the playscripts that William Shakespeare produced for the popular commercial stage. Of course, only a few minutes' reflection will demonstrate how very trendy all these currently popular approaches are. The last time aesthetic questions dominated the study of literature was during the McCarthyite 1950s, when applicants for positions at New York's publicly supported institutions of higher learning were required to sign loyalty oaths before they could be hired, and tenured professors were brought up before the House UnAmerican Activities Committee and asked whether they had ever been members of the Communist Party (and some of them lost their jobs for refusing to answer). Both material objects and the physical properties of books can help to reveal the political and cultural history of the worlds in which they were produced and used, but they can just as easily become the fetishized objects of elegant connoisseurship. The Renaissance revival of classical learning and the Reformation controversies over religious doctrine can provide insight into the interests and motivations that shaped the responses of Shakespeare's contemporaries; but the intensity of current fascination with them can tell us just as much about the interests and motivations that help to shape our own scholarly choices.

Notes

1. For earlier examinations of these questions, upon which the following discussion will draw, see my essay, 'Misogyny is Everywhere', and my book, *Shakespeare and Women,* especially chapter 1.
2. By 1986, women accounted for 59 percent of the PhDs in English and foreign languages. This figure, reported by the National Research Council, is quoted by Annette Kolodny (1988, 52).
3. This quotation, taken from the Introduction, comes from Sprengnether's summary of Eaton's argument.
4. Breitenberg cites three earlier publications that contained, he writes, 'earlier versions of material in this book'. The first of these was published in 1988.
5. On Bly's campaign to restore what he perceived as the endangered masculinity of men and other manifestations of the men's movement during this period in U.S., see Susan Faludi (1991, 304–11).

Part II

Making War/Making Histories

3

'Mirror[s] of all Christian kings'[1]: Hank Cinq and George Deux

Evelyn Gajowski

We are no tyrant, but a Christian king.

–King Harry, *Henry 5* (1.2.241)

Tyranny has come to America.

–Former U.S. Vice President Al Gore

'Which Plantagenet do I most remind you of?' asks a fictional political leader, U.S. President Jed Bartlet of the TV series, *The West Wing*, about a historical dynasty of monarchs. In posing the question, the character, played by actor Martin Sheen, suggests resonances among medieval British monarchs and contemporary U.S. Presidents. Indeed, a glance at the regimes of another pair of fictional and historical political figures – Shakespeare's Henry 5 and President George W. Bush – yields several provocative, striking parallels. Both are reformed prodigal sons of national leaders – sons who themselves go on to inherit the mantles of their fathers. Both conduct imperialistic invasions of sovereign foreign nations, recruiting soldiers from the working classes to do so. Both violate war etiquette and international treaties regarding the treatment of prisoners of war, prompting charges of 'war criminal' to be lodged against them.[2] Both believe in the absolute power of their respective offices – power that is, moreover, divinely inspired. Negotiating between fictional and historical records, as well as between past and present, this essay attempts to read Shakespeare's *Henry 5*, the historical Battle of Agincourt, and the 2003 U.S. invasion and consequential occupation of Iraq intertextually, with a focus on the ways in which military invasion is gendered as a masculinized venture and the vanquished country and war critics alike are gendered as feminized, emasculated, or effeminate entities. It examines the implications of these intertextualities for the construction of meaning in the contemporary imperialistic, political climate in which we find ourselves enmeshed, as well as Shakespeare's dramatic texts.

Daddies' boys

Prodigal sons Henry 5 and George W. Bush undergo reform before following in the footsteps of their fathers, Henry 4 and George Herbert Walker Bush, in assuming the positions of King of England and U.S. President, respectively. Shakespeare's *Henry 4* plays dramatize Prince Harry's abrogation of political responsibility, his participation in the satiation of the bodily appetites that Falstaff and the Carnivalesque world of the Boar's Head tavern represent, and his subsequent rejection of them. Harry predicts at the outset of *1 Henry 4* that his prodigality would eventually serve to underscore his future heroism: '[W]hen this loose behaviour I throw off', he confides to the audience, 'My reformation, glitt'ring o'er my fault, / Shall show more goodly and attract more eyes / Than that which hath no foil to set it off' (1.2.186–93). When Falstaff protests, while role-playing, 'Banish plump Jack, and banish all the world', Harry's response is sobering, and foreboding: 'I do; I will' (2.5.438–39). The exchange is a dress rehearsal, of course, for his refusal to acknowledge Falstaff at the conclusion of *2 Henry 4* – 'I know thee not, old man' (5.5.45) – and his ultimate banishment of him:

> Presume not that I am the thing I was,
> For God doth know, so shall the world perceive,
> That I have turned away my former self;
> So will I those that kept me company...
> ....
> ...I banish thee, on pain of death,
> As I have done the rest of my misleaders,
> Not to come near our person by ten mile.
> (*2 Henry 4*, 5.5.54–63)

In *Henry 5*, scenes in which the tavern characters speak feelingly of Falstaff's broken heart over Hal's rejection and his impending death enclose the scene that depicts Harry's unfeeling treatment of the traitors at Southampton. On 6 July 1986, his fortieth birthday, George W. Bush gave up alcohol. As he later explained to friends, Laura had issued an ultimatum: 'It's me or the bottle'. Because of his short temper, which he shares with his mother, the Bush family never thought he would become U.S. President, but since he quit drinking he has exercised discipline to control his temper. *New York Times* columnist Maureen Dowd notes what she sees as the Oedipal drama being played out between George W. Bush and George Herbert Walker Bush: whereas the father did not take the U.S. invasion of Iraq to Baghdad during the first Gulf War, failed to please his radical right-wing base, and did not win re-election, she notes, the son does everything in his power to achieve these objectives. In view of the diplomatic labor that George Herbert Walker and Herbert Walker had performed in years past, moreover, for George W. Bush to become the unilateralist that he has amounts to the greatest teenage rebellion in the history of the Presidency – 'like crashing the family car into a tree', as Dowd puts it.

Pretenders to the throne

A deep sense of illegitimacy pervades the regimes of both Henry 5 and George W. Bush. *Richard 2,* the first play in Shakespeare's second tetralogy, dramatizes the usurpation of Richard's throne by Harry's father. In *1 Henry 4,* Prince Harry appropriates imagery associated with Richard when he proclaims, 'Yet herein will I imitate the sun' (1.2.175). Instead of naturally being associated with the sun as rightful king, however, he can promise only to '*imitate* the sun', as Alexander Leggatt points out – to produce, as his father did, 'a good *performance* in the role of king' (1988, 89, emphasis mine). The sins of the father are visited upon the son throughout the dramatic action of *Henry 5* – Harry is possessed by an acute sense of guilt over the illegitimacy of his rule. Time and again, Shakespeare's King Harry demands confirmation that his invasion of France is justified and that he is not responsible for the horrors of war. Ever conscious of and remorseful for his father's usurpation of Richard's throne, he prays on the eve of Agincourt: 'Not today, O Lord, / O not today, think not upon the fault / My father made in compassing the crown' (4.1.274–76). After listing the acts of penance he has performed in the past to expiate his father's crime, he concludes by admitting that 'all that I can do is nothing worth, / Since that my penitence comes after ill, / Imploring pardon' (4.1.285–87). The Harry who fashions himself on Shakespeare's stage is, unlike the image of perfection completed in the past and evoked by the Chorus, a Harry in quest of both monarchical authority and a place in history, as Phyllis Rackin observes (1990, 167). So much depends on his victory in France that he feels that if he fails there he will be worthless; he will

> ... lay these bones in an unworthy urn,
> Tombless, with no remembrance over them.

Either our history shall with full mouth
Speak freely of our acts, or else our grave,
Like Turkish mute, shall have a tongueless mouth
Not worshipped with a waxen epitaph.
(1.2.228–33)

What the imperialistic venture in France is all about, indeed, is shoring up his sense of the legitimacy of his reign: 'No king of England, if not king of France' (2.2.189). And bound up in that attempt to acquire authority and legacy is an attempt to prove his manhood. Here, as elsewhere in Shakespeare's dramatic texts, masculinity, warriorship, and empire are so inextricably entangled with one another as to be difficult to tease apart for analysis.

On 12 December 2000, the U.S. Supreme Court, in a partisan vote, appointed the losing Presidential candidate to the White House. George W. Bush displays none of Henry 5's awareness of the illegitimacy of his regime. Yet Operation Iraqi Freedom, his March 2003 invasion and consequent occupation of Iraq, is haunted by the specter of illegitimacy – an attempt to acquire his authority and his place in history by breaking out of the shadow of his father, who, as mentioned, did not take the U.S. invasion of Iraq to Baghdad during Operation Desert Storm in 1991. Despite approval ratings that have plunged to all-time lows and public criticism about the Iraq War that has risen to all-time highs five years after the U.S. invasion,[3] George W. Bush remains confident that history will vindicate him. 'Be it thy course to busy giddy minds / With foreign quarrels', father advises son in *2 Henry 4*, 'that action hence borne out / May waste the memory of the former days' (4.3.340–43). Both Henry 5 and George W. Bush exploit the tried-and-true political strategy of deflating domestic criticism of one's legitimacy, as well as one's former profligate ways, by deflecting public attention onto an enemy abroad. And each attempts to insure a glorious legacy in the bargain.

Empire building

To the Boskovitch family: I wish to offer my heartfelt sympathy. I served with your son during his early enlistment period at Brook Park, Ohio. I can express no words that can return him to you but only to offer to you the consolation of what his service as a Marine means to me. As written by William Shakespeare in *Henry 5*,

From this day to the ending of the world
But we in it shall be remembered,

We few, we happy few, we band of brothers.
For he today that sheds his blood with me
Shall be my brother.

Semper Fidelis.

–Lt. Col. John P. Boland, USMCR[4]

Henry 5's invasion of France, a chapter in the Hundred Years' War, was conducted in part to improve his financial position by gaining lands that would secure him economic revenue. George W. Bush's invasion of Iraq, nominally to find weapons of mass destruction (WMD) initially and then a component of a political strategy to bring democracy to the nation, was in fact conducted at least in part to gain economic control of the second-greatest oil reserve in the world. 'I am saddened that it is politically inconvenient to acknowledge what everyone knows', Alan Greenspan admitted in print in September 2007: 'the Iraq War is largely about oil' (2007, 463). According to the former Chair of the Federal Reserve, the attention that developed nations give to the political situation in the Middle East is directly tied to oil security: 'whatever their publicized angst over Saddam Hussein's "weapons of mass destruction"', Greenspan notes, American and British authorities 'were also concerned about violence in an area that harbors a resource indispensable for the functioning of the world economy'.[5]

The question of troop strength in both imperialistic invasions has been a hotly contested one. Whether the number of U.S. troops under former Secretary of Defense Donald Rumsfeld's newly streamlined Pentagon was adequate to maintain the occupation of Iraq following the invasion was the subject of much debate from March 2003 until his resignation on 8 November 2006, the day after the U.S. midterm elections. Early on, General Eric K. Shinseki had argued that the U.S. would need hundreds of thousands of troops to keep the peace, and he was stripped of his post for doing so. Since Rumsfeld's resignation, the Bush administration's 'surge' in troop strength, an about-face in policy, has only intensified debate about its Iraq War strategy. Similarly, contemporary historians contest the myth that Henry 5's small 'band of brothers' miraculously and heroically defeated the French at Agincourt – a myth that has held sway for nearly six centuries and in which Shakespeare's dramatic text participates. According to tradition, the French outnumbered the English by a ratio of four to one (i.e., 24,000 to 6,000). Based on recent research into enrollment records in the National Archives in London and the National Library in France, however, historian Anne Curry argues that the numbers of the English have traditionally been underestimated and the numbers of the French have been overestimated – for patriotic reasons. According to her calculations, the French outnumbered the English, but by a ratio of three to two (i.e., 12,000 to 8,000).[6] She thus deflates the myth of Agincourt, theorizing that it was constructed around Henry 5 to enhance his reputation as a masculinized warrior king.

Whatever the numbers, the English defeated the French at Agincourt despite being outnumbered by them. How did they manage to do so? Again, as tradition would have it, the technological superiority of the English longbow archers was the major factor. The longbow was the machine gun of the middle ages; its arrowhead, the bodkin point, was its bullet. An arrow shot from a longbow moved at 37.9 meters per second (38 joules); because its shape had less resistance, a bodkin point arrowhead was supposedly able to penetrate armor and make a deeper wound ('Agincourt' 2005). The French used steel armor, however, a vast improvement over iron armor, and contemporary tests demonstrate that the bodkin point does not pierce steel. Both Agincourt and the Iraq War are examples of asymmetric warfare, that is, war between opponents whose relative power differs significantly. When two opponents of unequal power attempt to exploit each other's weaknesses, one may deploy a technological advantage to offset the numerical advantage of the other; the English use of the longbow at Agincourt has served as a traditional example of this strategy. A weaker force, particularly one in a defensive position, under attack, or under occupation, may deploy unconventional strategies and tactics, such as guerilla warfare, improvised explosive devices (IEDs), and hit-and-run attacks to compensate for its deficiencies and harass a stronger opponent.

Recent research suggests instead that several decidedly non-heroic factors contributed to the English defeat of the French. For one, Charles 6, King of France, was not present on the battlefield. Instead, his commander, Bouciqualt, led the French troops into battle. Too, although the French knights were protected by steel armor, their horses were not, as John Keegan notes (1983). Then there is the matter of ransom. One of the primary reasons for war in medieval Europe was money; in the heat of battle it was crucial, therefore, to be able to identify a soldier and his worth, heraldry being the method for doing so. Whereas the English forces were of mixed classes, the French were primarily noblemen. The English longbow archers disregarded the noble ranks and the heraldry of the French, however, and this breakdown in battle etiquette threw the French into disarray.

As in the English defeat of the Spanish Armada nearly two centuries later, weather played a significant role in the English defeat of the French at Agincourt. The soil was unusually muddy from rainfall, causing the French literally to fall down in their armor. Unable to get up, they suffocated to death. Contemporary tests of soil samples taken from the battlefield at Agincourt demonstrate that it neither repels water, as does clay, nor soaks up water, as does sand. For a French knight trying to pull his foot out of the mud, it would have felt like 15 one-pound bags of sand hanging on his foot. The English soldiers, on the other hand, were more lightly armored, primarily wearing cloth, and this factor may have worked in their favor by granting them greater mobility than the heavily armored French.

Perhaps the most crucial factor at Agincourt was topography. The landscape itself was Henry 5's greatest ally. The French were drawn in a southerly direction from a broad plain 773 meters wide in the north down into a funnel only 350 meters wide in the south – a 50 percent reduction in area that resulted in simply too many men crammed in too little space, causing the French, literally, to fall ('Agincourt' 2005). The effect of the funnel-shaped topography on the crowd of French soldiers was that it pushed them together toward the center. Ranks broke up; confusion and chaos reigned. This situation offered the classic makings of a crowd disaster: too many people; a rapid reduction in space; a massive increase in density; and a sudden reduction in forward movement. Even without the English longbow archers, then, the French would have suffered great losses due to topography alone. Far from the mythological heroic victory of English longbow archers over the French, Agincourt instead is a military victory snatched from chaos by a ruthless king.

Boys will be boys

> A world that truly includes the feminine is a world in which history cannot be written.
>
> –Phyllis Rackin, *Stages of History*

It is curious that *Henry 5* manages as well as it does to celebrate masculine English heroism, Robert Ornstein points out, when it makes such scathing revelations about the conquerors of France and dramatizes so clearly the human cost of the imperialistic venture (1972, 175). King

Harry's ability to imagine and dwell on the human suffering that his invasion will inflict on the French people is remarkable:

> ... many a thousand widows
> Shall this his mock mock out of their dear husbands,
> Mock mothers from their sons, mock castles down;
> Ay, some are yet ungotten and unborn
> That shall have cause to curse the Dauphin's scorn.
> (1.2.284–88)

Shakespeare repeatedly represents the French forces as effeminate. His portrait of the French is limited to the overconfidence and incompetence the effete, foppish generals who bet on the number of English they will kill and does not include any equivalents of the discipline, good cheer, decency, matter-of-factness, sturdiness, loyalty, and stoutness that characterize common English soldiers such as Williams and Bates. The dramatic text identifies the trappings and ideology of chivalry as French and genders them as feminine, as Jean Howard and Phyllis Rackin note (1997, 187). In fact, Shakespeare represents the entire French kingdom as a woman to be conquered by the masculine force of the English army (1997, 213).

The dramatic action of *Henry 5* emphasizes the conflation of military conquest with sexual violation at least twice: Harry's threat to the citizens of Harfleur in Act 3 and his 'wooing' of Catherine in Act 5. In a speech that is Shakespeare's invention (3.3.78–120), Harry threatens the citizens of Harfleur with the slaughter of their women and children and the rape of their daughters. While Holinshed mentions the threats, he does not mention sexual violation; Shakespeare's Harry, on the other hand, configures violence against the French in terms of rape three times:

> The gates of mercy shall be all shut up,
> And the fleshed soldier, rough and hard of heart,
> In liberty of bloody hand shall range
> With conscience wide as hell, mowing like grass
> Your fresh fair virgins and your flow'ring infants ...
> ....
> What is't to me, when you yourselves are cause,
> If your pure maidens fall into the hand
> Of hot and forcing violation?
> What rein can hold licentious wickedness

When down the hill he holds his fierce career?
. . . .
...in a moment look to see
The blind and bloody soldier with foul hand
Defile the locks of your shrill-shrieking daughters.
(3.3.87–91, 96–100, 110–12)

Curiously, Harry's tone is one of detachment from the sexual violence he threatens at length. Like Othello at the murder of Desdemona ('It is the cause, it is the cause, my soul' [*Othello*, 5.2.1]), impending male violence toward the female is conceived of and articulated as an impersonal force beyond the control of the male protagonist. Moreover, in a clever logical and rhetorical gambit on Harry's part, should the threatened violence, including sexual violation, come to pass, it is the citizens of Harfleur – and not he – who would be to blame. Should they refuse to surrender to his forces, he will destroy their city because they will be 'guilty in defense' of it (3.3.120). Despite the fact that Harry is wracked with guilt over his father's usurpation of Richard's throne (or perhaps because of it), he repeatedly blames others for his offenses – whether it is the citizens of Harfleur who are at fault for the slaughter he threatens or his soldiers who are to blame for their actions at Agincourt, as his argument with Williams and Bates in Act 4, scene 1, attests.

Harry's 'wooing' of Catherine in Act 5 resonates with his earlier threat to rape the maids of Harfleur in Act 3. As a political pawn, of course, she has no power. Harry views her as war booty, the supreme symbol of his imperialistic victory in France.[7] In possessing her, he possesses France, as Robert Ornstein points out (1972, 200). In representing the promise of producing an heir, moreover, she serves to consolidate his political power as king of England – as of France. In Harry's wooing of Catherine, he is always mindful of his own status as victorious imperialist and her status as his prize of war, his 'capital demand' (5.2.96). It may not be the custom for maids in France to kiss before they are married: *'Les dames and demoiselles pour etre baisees devant leurs noces, il n'est pas la coutume de France'* (5.2.240–41). However, while simultaneously making light of the matter – 'nice customs curtsy to great kings' (5.2.250) – Harry forces Catherine to endure his kiss in what Jean Howard and Phyllis Rackin rightly call a symbolic rape (1997, 214). He wants her and he will have her, according to the political negotiations worked out between him and her father, the King of France. For all the humor of his inept attempts at wooing, 'will you, nill you, I will marry you' (2.1.263),

Petruchio's matter-of-fact warning to another Katherine (that of Shakespeare's *The Taming of the Shrew*) is the subtext of the final scene of *Henry 5*. Whether Catherine desires Harry in return is, of course, of no consequence. Her role, like that of the other aristocratic female characters in the play, is to provide sexual titillation for the audience, as Howard and Rackin point out, and a bride for the masculinized soldier hero (1997, 206). Moreover, in *Henry 5*, for the first time in Shakespeare's plays, rape is a paradigm for the masculine performance of dominance (1997, 196). The personal is political, indeed.

Shockingly, the degradation, killing, and rape of civilians by U.S. troops have become commonplace in Iraq, as Chris Hedges and Laila Al-Arian report in their exhaustive investigative article, 'The Other War', based upon interviews with 50 combat veterans from around the U.S. Court cases, such as those surrounding the massacre in Haditha and the rape and murder of a 14-year-old girl in Mahmudiya, and news reports suggest just how widespread attacks on civilians are. Despite the large number of incidents, however, the vast majority are not reported, let alone tried and punished. 'You physically could not do an investigation every time a civilian was wounded or killed', a Marine Reserve Lieutenant admitted, 'because it just happens a lot and you'd spend all your time doing that' (2007, 11). The impossible mission, poor training, and inconsistent and irresponsible rules of engagement, coupled with a low level of understanding of Iraqi culture, have led many U.S. soldiers to believe and behave as though endangering civilians is simply the cost of business. Indeed, the occupation has become a classic example of an 'atrocity-producing situation', according to psychiatrist Robert Jay Lifton. The eroding moral constraint that interviewees witnessed is confirmed by a survey conducted by the U.S. Army Medical Command in May 2007: only 45 percent of soldiers and 38 percent of marines agreed that civilians should be treated with any kind of dignity and respect ('Deadly Occupation' 2007, 3). These practices on the part of U.S. troops in Iraq violate, moreover, the *Geneva Conventions*. Of the 159 Articles and three Annexes of *Convention 4: Relative to the Protection of Civilian Persons in Time of War* of 12 August 1949, of which the U.S. is a signatory, Part Three, Article 27, stipulates the minimum protections regarding humane treatment that must be afforded civilians:

> Protected persons are entitled, in all circumstances, to respect for their persons, their honour, their family rights, their religious convictions and practices, and their manners and customs. They shall at

> all times be humanely treated, and shall be protected especially against all acts of violence or threats thereof and against insults and public curiosity. Women shall be especially protected against any attack on their honour, in particular against rape, enforced prostitution, or any form of indecent assault. Without prejudice to the provisions relating to their state of health, age and sex, all protected persons shall be treated with the same consideration by the Party to the conflict in whose power they are, without any adverse distinction based, in particular, on race, religion or political opinion.

Despite the fact that George W. Bush went AWOL while performing military service in the Air National Guard during the Vietnam War (or perhaps because of it), his administration consistently deploys a rhetorical strategy that attempts to emasculate and feminize critics of its Iraq War policy, including decorated Vietnam War veterans who are prominent politicians, such as 2004 U.S. Presidential candidate Senator John Kerry (D-MA), former U.S. Senator Max Cleland (D-GA), and U.S. Congressman Jack Murtha (D-PA). In high contrast to the genuine heroism and sacrifice on the part of these former military figures, some of whom left limbs on the battlefield in Vietnam, on 1 May 2003, George W. Bush made a cartoonish (and buffoonish) jet landing on the deck of the USS *Abraham Lincoln* to proclaim to the nation that the Iraq War was a 'mission accomplished' a mere six weeks after his 20 March 2003 invasion.[8] The proclamation has turned out to be premature, of course, as the Iraq War has since proven to be the longest military conflict in which the U.S. has ever been involved – longer than World War 2, longer than the Vietnam War – and cause for ironic commentary and political satire.[9] The incident, complete with the rumor that George W. Bush stuffed several socks into the crotch of his flight suit (in an improvised twenty-first century version of a codpiece) to enhance the fantasy of virile, heroic leadership, is the result of deliberate fashioning of a macho guise and masculine bravado. Likewise, despite the fact that critics often depict Harry as a man of action, the dramatic action of *Henry 5* does not once demonstrate his physical prowess. To represent this masculine trait on screen during World War 2, in fact, Sir Laurence Olivier had to invent a scene for his cinematic text that is not in Shakespeare's dramatic text.

George W. Bush's former Deputy Chief of Staff has made explicit his role in constructing Bush's Iraq War in overtly masculine terms and its critics in overtly feminine terms. On 15 August 2007, two days after announcing his departure from the White House, Karl Rove went on the attack, labeling critics of George W. Bush 'elite, effete snobs', echoing former Vice President Spiro Agnew's attack of Vietnam War critics under the Nixon administration more than three decades earlier.[10] In constructing critics of the Bush administration in this way, he overlays gender and class binary oppositions upon that with which the U.S. public has become all too familiar: critics are traitors, while, by implication, supporters are patriots. According to this configuration, traitors are intellectual, upper-class effeminates, as well, while, by implication, patriots are robust, virile, working-class men of action – the same young males it shamelessly uses as cannon fodder.[11]

Shock and awe

> France being ours we'll bend it to our awe,
> Or break it all to pieces.
>
> –King Harry, 1.2.224–25

> Agincourt is one of the most instantly and vividly visualized of all epic passages in English history... Visually it is a pre-Raphaelite, perhaps better a Medici Gallery print battle.... It is a school outing to the Old Vic, Shakespeare is fun, *son et lumiere*, blank verse, Laurence Olivier in armour battle;... It is also a story of slaughter-yard behaviour and outright atrocity.
>
> –John Keegan, *The Face of Battle*[12]

The English forces suffered relatively low casualties at Agincourt: 25 'of name' (4.8.99), or high rank, and 100 common soldiers. For the French, however, it was a disaster: 5,000 war dead and 1,000 prisoners of war. Whereas the French prisoners of war, being of noble rank, should have been taken to England for ransom according to medieval European war etiquette, Harry ordered his English longbow men to slaughter them by the hundreds. George W. Bush, as Commander in Chief, is ultimately responsible for the torture of people at Abu Ghraib, Guantanamo, and numerous black sites throughout eastern Europe, the Middle East, and Afghanistan. Indeed, in the latter, a kind of 'reverse ransom' is in effect: the U.S. military pays Afghans $5,000 for each person turned in as an 'enemy combatant', people whom it then sends to Guantanamo. The injustice of the 'reverse ransom' practice is exacerbated by the fact that no customary battlefield hearings, a component of military justice used in Vietnam and World War 2, are being convened immediately following combat to separate enemy combatants from shepherds and other innocent bystanders who have simply gotten caught up in the crossfire. The result, according to Jack Hitt, is that only 5 percent of Afghans apprehended are enemy combatants (2007).

Both Henry 5 and George W. Bush, then, disregard international agreements regarding the treatment of prisoners of war: where one violates medieval war etiquette, the other violates the *Geneva Conventions* *The British Manual on Military Law* describes the customs of war concerning the treatment of prisoners of war over the centuries:

> Few of the customs of war have undergone greater changes than those relating to the treatment of prisoners. In ancient time captured soldiers were killed, mutilated or enslaved. In the Middle Ages they were imprisoned or held to ransom. It was only in the 17th century that they began to be regarded as prisoners of the State and not the property of individual captors. (Part 3, 45)

Of the 143 Articles and five Annexes of *Convention 3: Relative to the Treatment of Prisoners of War* of 12 August 1949 of the *Geneva Conventions*, of which the U.S. is a signatory, Part Two, Article 13, stipulates the minimum protections regarding humane treatment that must be afforded prisoners of war:

> Prisoners of war must at all times be humanely treated. Any unlawful act or omission by the Detaining Power causing death or seriously endangering the health of a prisoner of war in its custody is prohibited, and will be regarded as a serious breach of the present Convention. In particular, no prisoner of war may be subjected to physical mutilation or to medical or scientific experiments of any kind which are not justified by the medical, dental or hospital treatment of the prisoner concerned and carried out in his interest. Likewise, prisoners of war must at all times be protected, particularly against acts of violence or intimidation and against insults and public curiosity. Measures of reprisal against prisoners of war are prohibited.

Yet the George W. Bush administration has attempted to evade the *Geneva Conventions* by arguing that prisoners in its custody are 'unlawful combatants' who do not fall into the categories of prisoners of war that the *Conventions* spell out in Article 4, a strategy that has stoked international controversy.[13]

Holinshed goes into gory detail on the killing of the French prisoners by the English:

> When this dolorous decree, and pitifull proclamation was pronounced, pitie it was to see how some Frenchmen were suddenlie sticked with daggers, some were brained with pollaxes, some slaine with malls, other had their throats cut, and some their bellies panched, so that in effect, having respect to the great number, few prisoners were saved. (quoted in Bullough 1962, 397)

In contrast, Shakespeare's reference to the killing of the French prisoners occurs in perfunctory, brief commands on the part of Harry, Fluellen, and Gower, while the action itself may or may not be set on stage.[14] The slaughter of the French prisoners provides Shakespeare with an opportunity, nevertheless, to dramatize with profound ambivalence the nature of masculine, imperialistic heroism.

Shakespeare's Harry gives the order to kill the French prisoners of war twice. The first time, the rationale is fear of another attack: 'The French have reinforced their scattered men. / Then every soldier kill his prisoners, / Give the word through' (4.6.36–38). Holinshed describes the 'lamentable slaughter' as follows:

> he doubting least his enimies should gather togither again, and begin a new field; and mistrusting further that the prisoners would be an aid to his enimies, or the verie enimies to their takers in deed if they were suffered to live, contrarie to his accustomed gentlenes, commanded by sound of trumpet, that everie man (upon paine of death) should incontinentlie slaie his prisoner. (quoted in Bullough 1962, 397)[15]

Harry may be capable of threatening to kill infants at Harfleur, yet the one time he loses his temper in France is when he learns of the French murder of the English boys guarding the luggage. It serves as his rationale, in fact, for giving the order a second time to kill the French prisoners: 'Kill the poys and the luggage! 'Tis expressly against the law of arms', Fluellen proclaims, ''Tis as arrant a piece of knavery, mark you now, as can be offert. In your conscience now, is it not?' (4.7.1–3). In Holinshed, the French,

> hearing that the English tents & pavilions were a good waie distant from the armie, without anie sufficient gard to defend the same,

> either upon a covetous meaning to gaine by the spoile, or upon a desire to be revenged, entered the kings campe, and there spoiled the hails, robbed the tents, brake up chests, and caried awaie caskets, and slue such servants as they found to make anie resistance. (quoted in Bullough 1962, 397)

In response, Shakespeare's Harry 'most worthily hath caused every soldier to cut his prisoner's throat. O 'tis a gallant king' (4.7.7–8), as Gower reports. Harry himself proclaims, 'we'll cut the throats of those we have, / And not a man of them that we shall take / Shall taste our mercy' (4.7.55–57). His response is self-admittedly one of rage: 'I was not angry since I came to France / Until this instant' (4.7.47–48). His anger had long ago been described by his father as a force to be reckoned with: 'being incensed, he is flint, / As humorous as winter, and as sudden / As flaws congealed in the spring of day' (*2 Henry 4*, 4.3.33–35). Fluellen's educated comparison of Harry and Alexander emphasizes the point: one warrior is like the other 'in his rages and his furies and his wraths and his cholers and his moods and his displeasures and his indignations' (4.7.28–30).

Both Henry 5 and George W. Bush evade moral responsibility for their soldiers' actions, including their mistreatment – whether execution or torture – of prisoners of war. Because their behavior is divinely ordained, the problem of ethical choice exists for others, not for them. The psychological and moral conflict that occurs on the eve of Agincourt takes up more space in Shakespeare's dramatic text than the battle itself. The climactic confrontation of the dramatic text pits Harry not against the French, as Robert Ornstein notes, but his own English soldiers, who debate with him his responsibility for the impending slaughter (1972, 176). Although Harry, in disguise, acknowledges his commonality with Bates – 'the King is but a man' (4.1.99) – he simultaneously perpetuates the myth of masculine monarchical heroism for the sake of military morale: 'Yet, in reason, no man should possess him with any appearance of fear, lest he, by showing it, should dishearten his army' (4.1.106–08). At issue in his debate with Williams and Bates is the extent of a king's moral responsibility for his soldiers' actions and fates:

> Bates: If his cause be wrong, our obedience to the King wipes the crime of it out of us.
>
> Williams: But if the cause not be good, the King himself hath a heavy reckoning to make, when all those legs and arms and heads chopped off in a battle shall join together at the latter day ... Now, if these men

> do not die well, it will be a black matter for the King that led them to it – who to disobey were against all proportion of subjection. (4.1.125–38)

When they refuse to endorse Harry's claims about the rightness of his cause, he responds by denying his responsibility for his soldiers' lives:

> The King is not bound to answer the particular endings of his soldiers ... Then if they die unprovided, no more is the King guilty of their damnation than he was before guilty of those impieties for the which they are now visited. Every subject's duty is the King's, but every subject's soul is his own'. (4.1.146–65)

Yet even as the dramatic text concentrates ideological power in Henry's character, as Jonathan Dollimore and Alan Sinfield point out, so too does it concentrate responsibility in his character, as well (1985a, 222).

The issue of moral responsibility for war-time atrocities has contemporary resonances, of course, whether in the war crime trials in Nuremburg following World War 2 or in the present U.S. occupation of Iraq. George W. Bush responded to the publicity of the torture of prisoners at Abu Ghraib, for example, by advancing the theory of 'a few bad apples' that places blame on the rank and file. Low-ranking soldiers such as Lindsay England take the fall, while those higher up in the chain of command, including the Secretary of Defense, the Vice President, and the Commander in Chief himself – although reviled throughout the rest of the world – escape legal incrimination within the U.S. And Alberto Gonzales, author of the White House 'torture memo' that was used to rationalize and justify practices forbidden by the Geneva Conventions, went on to be promoted from White House legal counsel to U.S. Attorney General – a position in which he served until his resignation on 17 September 2007 amid controversy over his role in the dismissals of nine U.S. Attorneys for political reasons and accusations of perjury before Congress on the National Security Agency's surveillance programs.

Henry 5 and George W. Bush also perform surveillance of their military troops and their citizenry, respectively. While the disguised Harry spies on his troops on the eve of Agincourt, George W. Bush conducts warrantless wiretaps and issues a signing statement proclaiming his right to read the mail of U.S. citizens, invoking post-9/11 national security concerns as justification for doing so.[16] Rather than the praise of the king by his troops that is conventional in situations such as this, Harry is put in a position of having to defend himself against the stout opposition of Williams and Bates. Bush administration policies are shrouded in secrecy, on the other hand, disallowing the U.S. public from the benefit of any kind of debate about the legitimacy of the Iraq War, let alone responsibility for war-time atrocities. The breadth of illegal, domestic spying continues to be covered up, thanks to Bush's self-serving interpretation of U.S. law and the U.S. Constitution. 'The public did not know what power the President took unto himself', remarks Anthony Romero, ACLU Executive Director, on the Bush administration's arrogance and secrecy in violating U.S. citizens' first-amendment rights in a bid to consolidate power. The disappearance of privacy rights in dribs and drabs prevents the public from becoming aware of and protesting their loss. The public therefore gradually grows accustomed to the erosion of privacy – first wiretapping, then email, and finally the U.S. Postal Service – until the guarantees insured by the fourth amendment to the U.S. Constitution no longer exist. Indeed, the primary concern of Vice President Cheney and his fellow neo-conservative architects of the Iraq War is not finding WMD, spreading democracy, or fighting terrorism. It is, rather, consolidating the power of an imperial presidency – one without any checks, without any balances.

Divine right

> But this lies all within the will of God.
>
> –King Harry, *Henry 5* (1.2.289)

> Now it is our turn to take up the cause. Our struggle is not with a monarch, named George, who inherited the crown – although it often seems that way. Our struggle is with the politics of fear and favoritism in our own time, in our own country. Our struggle – like so many others before – is with those who put their narrow interests ahead of the public interest. ... For centuries, kings ruled by what they claimed was divine right – they could not be questioned, they could not be challenged. The people's fate was not their own.
>
> –U.S. Senator Edward Kennedy (D-MA)

Henry 5 is a powerful Elizabethan fantasy simply because it represents a single source of power in the state: 'Nothing is allowed to compete with the authority of the King', as Jonathan Dollimore and Alan Sinfield note (1985a, 220). According to the politically absolutist doctrine, the divine right of kings, the rule of a monarch derives its authority from the will of God rather than the will of subjects or any other political entity. In the early modern period, James 1 of England and the French bishop Bossuet expanded the doctrine, using it as a mechanism to increase the power of monarchs relative to the aristocracy and subjects. Yet the concept of divine right shaped European organization since the eighth century, tracing its origin to the writings of Augustine of Hippo and Paul of Tarsus.

The dialogue between the Archbishop of Canterbury and the Bishop of Ely with which the dramatic action of *Henry 5* opens emphasizes the extent of the conversion of the former pseudo-libertine. Now 'the King is full of grace and fair regard' (1.1.23), Canterbury remarks, to which Ely chimes in, 'And a true lover of the holy Church' (1.1.24). In the conflict between the Church and Parliament of which they speak, King Harry is 'rather swaying more upon our part / Than cherishing th'exhibiters against us' (1.1.74–75). Indeed, their support of his rationale for the impending invasion of France is a *quid pro quo* for his support of their efforts to prevent the Church from losing half its assets in taxes. As early as *1 Henry 4*, Harry repeatedly invokes God's will to justify his intended political and military accomplishments:

> And I will call him [Percy] to so strict account
> That he shall render every glory up,
> Yea, even the slightest worship of his time,
> Or I will tear the reckoning from his heart.
> This, in the name of God, I promise here.
> (3.2.149–53)

When he brags to the French Herald before Agincourt, he perpetuates his habit of referring to his impending military actions as divinely ordained:

> But by the mass, our hearts are in the trim.
> And my poor soldiers tell me, yet ere night
> They'll be in fresher robes, as they will pluck
> The gay new coats o'er your French soldiers' heads,
> And turn them out of service. If they do this –
> As if God please, they shall – my ransom then
> Will soon be levied.
> (4.3.115–21)

Yet all the English soldiers believe in Harry's invasion of France; they all believe that God and history are on their side. 'All share the imperial impulse', Robert Ornstein observes; 'all are inspired by memories of a glorious past and hopes of crowns and coronets to come' (1972, 180). In France, they intend not only to improve the material conditions of their existence but also to prove their manhood. Both King Harry and George W. Bush look for vindication for decisions they have already made; both 'cherry-pick' evidence, finding rationales to put into practice that which they have planned all along and finding scapegoats to shoulder the burden of moral responsibility. And both do so in an attempt to legitimize their regimes. Harry's pious insistence that God won the Battle of Agincourt is an attempt to imbue himself with 'the mystifying force of divine right', as Barbara Hodgdon puts it, that was Richard 2's special province (1991, 188).

Would it be overstating the case to claim that George W. Bush, like Henry 5, believes that his regime is divinely ordained? The Bush administration deliberately invokes the political absolutism inherent in the doctrine of divine right to advance the concept of the 'unitary executive' and to cultivate the notion that George W. Bush is infallible. One of his own infamous statements, 'If this were a dictatorship, it would be a heck of a lot easier – just so long as I'm the dictator',[17] blatantly configures a desire for absolute power in contemporary terms. Indeed, George W. Bush's particular manifestation of absolute power has been dubbed 'executive tyranny' by *Harper's* magazine editor Lewis Lapham.

In June 2003, according to Nabil Shaath, a Palestinian negotiator, Bush said to all present at a meeting during Israeli/Palestinian negotiations: 'I'm driven with a mission from God. God would tell me, "George, go and fight those terrorists in Afghanistan". And I did, and then God would tell me, "George, go and end the tyranny in Iraq". And I did'. (Kamen 2005). In July 2004, George W. Bush stopped to campaign with some Amish folks at Lapp Electric Service in Smoketown, Pennsylvania. Just as the meeting ended, Bush told the group, 'I trust God speaks through me. Without that I couldn't do my job', according to Jack Brubaker, columnist for the *Mennonite Weekly Review* (Kamen 2005). In invoking God, in speaking to 'a higher father', and so on, George W. Bush is imbued with the belief that he can do no wrong, as Harvard law professor Lawrence Tribe observes. Both King Harry and George W. Bush believe that in every war one side is right and the other is wrong; they are sure, moreover, that right is on their side. Commenting on the certitude, or the sense of messianic zeal, that possesses some people when they become people of faith, political pundit/comedian Bill Maher states of George W. Bush: 'Because he believes he was called by God to bring freedom to the world, this guy is so sure he's doing the right thing that he could be 2 percent in the approval ratings, and he wouldn't care'. The rule of the divinely-ordained political leader is owing to the will of God rather than the will of subjects, or citizens.

What are the odds that a U.S. President preparing to invade Iraq would not consult a former President who had done so? The most infamous moment in *Plan of Attack*, Bob Woodward's first in a series of three books on the Iraq War, records his exchange with George W. Bush on whether he sought advice from his father, George Herbert Walker Bush, who as President had conducted the first Iraq War. 'Here is the one living human being who's held this office who had to make a decision to go to war', Woodward observes. 'And it would not be credible if you did not at some point ask him, What are the ingredients of doing this right? Or what's your thought, this is what I'm facing' (2004, 420). 'Look, I talk to him, of course', George W. Bush replies, concluding, 'You know, he is the wrong father to appeal to in terms of strength. There is a higher father that I appeal to' (2004, 421). Indeed, the Bush administration's foreign policy is driven by a fundamentalist, apocalyptic view not only of Iraq, but the entire Middle East.

Woodward was further surprised to learn that George W. Bush did not consult relevant cabinet members in making the decision to go to war: he asked neither his Secretary of Defense, Donald Rumsfeld, nor his Secretary of State, Colin Powell, for a recommendation. When George W. Bush acts as an authoritarian political leader who does not believe in asking for the opinions of advisors, he is enacting the model of not only divine right, but also the authoritarian father of a patriarchal family who does not believe in asking for the opinions of other family members. This model has its origins in the conservative religious ideology of the radical religious right in the U.S., particularly that of James Dobson, as George Lakoff observes (2004, 6–8).[18] According to this logic, consulting with an entity such as the U.N. regarding the invasion of Iraq would be unthinkable: because the U.N. is constituted of nations inferior to the superpower that is the U.S., George W. Bush would no sooner consult it than would an authoritarian father of a patriarchal family consult his children before making a decision.

Ron Suskind characterizes the methodology that George W. Bush employs for making policy decisions as 'faith based', as opposed to 'reality based' (2004b). Time and again, religious faith trumps science in the present White House. Regardless of whether the issue is global warming, evolution, or stem cell research, scientific evidence is eschewed, while gut reactions are manifold, and preferred. In a political environment such as this, it is entirely plausible that CIA intelligence regarding the absence of WMD in Iraq was ignored in favor of a decision to make a pre-emptive strike – a decision that was made prior to George W. Bush's assumption of the Presidency, as Suskind and others have pointed out (2004a, 70–76).[19] The result is that 'the delusional is no longer marginal' in U.S. politics; as Bill Moyers put it in a 2004 speech: 'it has come in from the fringe to sit in the seat of power in the Oval Office and in Congress' (quoted in Rothschild 2005). For the first time in U.S. history, from 2001 to 2006 under the regime of George W. Bush and a Republican-controlled Congress, theology and ideology held a monopoly of power in Washington.

A couple of broader, deeper questions emerge from my consideration of the politics/war/religion nexus of Hank Cinq and George Deux. Is the problem that King Harry and George W. Bush fashion themselves in the image of a virtuous political leader ordained by a Christian God, while in fact their policies and practices are remarkably un-Christian? Even anti-Christian? Vile, in fact? Or is the problem, rather, that Harry *is* 'the mirror of all Christian kings'? And that, at the present moment – in view of an unjust war, the slaughter of 400,000 Iraqis, more than 4,000 U.S. war dead, the practice of torture, warrantless wiretapping of U.S. citizens, and the dismantling of habeas corpus – the same is true of George W. Bush?

Notes

I am appreciative of the opportunity to present my ideas on the Hank Cinq/George Deux connection at several professional venues, including the annual Shakespeare Symposium, 'Shakespeare's Couples, Shakespeare's Couplings', sponsored by UCLA's Center for Medieval and Renaissance Studies in May 2007, and a couple of recent annual meetings of the Shakespeare Association of America. Audience members at UCLA were notable for their constructive, engaged responses to the ideas I tried out on them. At SAA, I would like to single out Kathryn Schwarz for the thoughtfulness of her response to my work.

1. 2.Chorus.6. All quotations of Shakespeare's texts are from *The Norton Shakespeare*. In employing the 'mirror' trope to convey Harry's virtue, Shakespeare follows his predecessors and contemporaries. In his primary source, the third volume of *The Chronicles of England, Scotland, and Ireland*, Raphael Holinshed concludes by commenting on the development of Prince Harry's character as follows: 'a majestie was he that both lived and died a paterne in princehood, a lode-starre in honour, and *mirrour of magnificence*' (quoted in Bullough 1962, 408, emphasis mine). In book four of *The Civile*

Wars between the Two Houses of Lancaster and Yorke, Samuel Daniel follows Hall and Holinshed, describing Harry as a '*Mirror of vertue*, miracle of worth' (stanza 15, quoted in Bullough 1962, 424, my italics).

2. See John Sutherland's and Cedric Watts's *Henry 5, War Criminal? and Other Shakespeare Puzzles*. Independently of the development of my own ideas, some of these parallels were set forth in the popular media on the eve of the Iraq War and following public disclosure of the violations of the Geneva Conventions at Abu Ghraib. See, for example, Judith Shulevitz's article in *The New York Times* in January 2003 and Bob Thompson's article in *The Washington Post* in May 2004, the latter of which reviewed a mock debate among political pundits at The Shakespeare Theatre in Washington, DC, on 17 May 2004.
3. U.S. public support of the Iraq War has dramatically eroded since the U.S. invasion of Iraq in March 2003. Three years after the U.S. invasion of Iraq, a CBS-TV News poll found that by a ratio of two to one the U.S. public believed that U.S. efforts to bring stability to Iraq were going badly – the worst assessment of progress in Iraq to that date (February 2006). According to the same poll, George W. Bush's and Dick Cheney's approval ratings fell to all-time lows of 34 percent and 18 percent, respectively. Since the Congressional midterm election on 8 November 2006, itself a repudiation of the Iraq War, polls find that the U.S. public overwhelmingly favors the ability of Democrats over Republicans to extricate the U.S. from Iraq and that, furthermore, it suffers Bush fatigue, wanting his Presidency to be over and done with. At the fifth anniversary of the U.S. invasion of Iraq, George W. Bush's approval rating had dropped to 19 percent, lower than that of any U.S. President in history, even Harry Truman during the Korean War and Richard M. Nixon at the point of his resignation under the pressure of impeachment because of the Watergate scandal.
4. When the Pentagon instituted its campaign of distributing military books, including Shakespeare's *Henry 5*, to U.S. soldiers in Iraq in December 2003, as Ellen Caldwell points out, it co-opted Shakespeare to support a masculine 'warrior culture' and promote identification with earlier, successful armies of invasion (2006, 15). Perhaps Marine Lieutenant Colonel Boland's familiarity with *Henry 5* and his ability to quote it on the occasion of the death of his military 'brother', fellow Marine Corporal Jeffrey A. Boskovitch, is evidence of the Pentagon's successful appropriation of Shakespeare for this purpose.
5. According to the U.S. Department of Energy, Iraq's export of crude oil to the U.S. before the Iraq War averaged 800,000 barrels a day – 8.6 percent of total U.S. crude oil imports – making it the sixth-largest supplier to the U.S. after Saudi Arabia, Mexico, Canada, Venezuela, and Nigeria.
6. On the other hand, historian Juliet Barker reinscribes the myth of a heroic English victory at Agincourt, arguing, based on a French heraldic source, that the ratio of French to English was six to one (36,000 to 6,000). I should note that some of the information in the following paragraphs is drawn from 'Agincourt' (2005).
7. In this regard, the victorious Harry is not unlike Octavius Caesar, who would drag Cleopatra caged back to Rome to display her as the supreme symbol of his imperialistic victory in Egypt (*Antony and Cleopatra*, 5.2.194–217). See my *The Art of Loving*, 114.

8. Everything about the public relations stunt proved to be controversial: the 'mission accomplished' banner prominently displayed behind George W. Bush, his jump suit, his mode of transport. The fact that Bush made a dramatic arrival on the aircraft carrier via jet rather than helicopter, the customary mode of transport for distances of 30 miles or less, was the subject of heated commentary in the news media at the time.
9. Since 1 May 2003, Keith Olbermann has concluded nightly broadcasts of his MSNBC news show, *Countdown with Keith Olbermann*, by stating the number of days that have passed since 'the declaration of "mission accomplished" in Iraq'.
10. On 22 May 1970, Agnew labeled the college student anti-Vietnam War protesters of the 1960s 'an effete corps of impudent snobs who characterize themselves as "intellectuals"', driving a wedge between those wealthy enough to afford a college education and the working classes who were drafted for military service. The parallels between the 2007 U.S. Constitutional crisis and that of Watergate under the Nixon administration, while too numerous to analyze within the purview of this essay, are nevertheless striking and significant.
11. Note that both Karl Rove and Spiro Agnew exploit the prevalent anti-intellectual attitudes of the U.S. public. Cultivation of anti-intellectualism, exploitation of a cult of masculinity, overt expressions of Christianity, and the selective, emphatic use of the Texas drawl are all components in the arsenal from which George W. Bush's public persona is deliberately fashioned, according to political commentator, Molly Ivins (2004).
12. Barbara Hodgdon takes up the contradictions and ambivalence characterizing the historical and fictional representations of Henry 5 and Agincourt that John Keegan articulates as follows:

    > critical narratives as well as theatrical representations have fractured *Henry 5*, the most generically flexible of Shakespeare's histories, more or less along its fault lines to view its king either as the chroniclers' 'blazing comet' King of Desire or as the prisoner-killing warmonger, and so have read the play as a nationalistic pageant-drama or, especially at times of national or world crisis, as an ironic critique of successful military endeavor. (1983, 185)

    Earlier critics such as Norman Rabkin were concerned, instead, to argue for the 'complementarity' of these contradictions in both Shakespeare's dramatic text and his representation of the monarch (1981).
13. The disregard of war etiquette and international treaties concerning the humane treatment of prisoners of war on the part of both Henry and George W. Bush stands in high contrast to the policy of another George W. – General George Washington at the battle at Drake's Farm during the Revolutionary War. After seven Revolutionary soldiers, including a colonel, had surrendered to the British, as David Hackett Fischer relates, the British ran them through with bayonets and crushed their skulls with muskets. When the Revolutionary troops recovered the bodies, they were shocked at the mutilations. The atrocities, together with the British commander's denial of responsibility for them, inspired Revolutionary troops to follow a higher code of military conduct. Rather than reprisal, Washington ordered his troops to preserve the honor and dignity of all combatants by providing

comfort and healing to prisoners of war in their possession, even offering them the option of farm labor. Washington's policy was so successful that more than 25 percent of the British captives, including Hessian mercenaries, decided to remain in the U.S. rather than return to their homeland (2006). I am indebted to Willis Barnstone for bringing this information to my attention.

14. *The Norton Shakespeare*, based on the Oxford edition, prepared by Gary Taylor and Stanley Wells, makes this note at the stage direction, '*[The soldiers kill their prisoners]*' (4.6.37). Setting the killing of the prisoners off stage has been the editorial consensus over the past four centuries. In his Introduction to his Oxford edition of *Henry 5*, however, Taylor makes the argument that the killing of the prisoners should occur on stage:

    This squeamishness has been echoed in all but the most recent productions of Shakespeare's play, and I believe that I am the first editor to specify that the prisoners should be killed on stage, though the text unequivocally implies this, having brought the prisoners on for no other discernible purpose. The unwillingness of playwrights, producers, and editors to show Henry's order being carried out belies the scholarly defence of it as an obvious military necessity no Elizabethan would have condemned…legal arguments and prose descriptions of far-away wars are one thing; *seeing* such an order carried out in front of your eyes is another…Shakespeare…. could hardly have failed to realize how strongly audiences would respond to the cold-blooded atrocity he calls them to witness. (1982, 32)

15. In Holinshed, as in Shakespeare, the two rationales for the killing of the prisoners are conflated with one another. In Holinshed, it is only 'when the outcrie of the lackies and boies, which ran awaie for feare of the Frenchmen thus spoiling the campe, came to the kings eares' (quoted in Bullough 1962, 397) that Henry expresses concern about the regathering of the French forces. In Shakespeare, Harry responds to the news of the boys' deaths – 'I was not angry since I came to France / Until this instant' (4.7.47–48) – with the threat that he will cut the throats of any French who refuse to either fight or 'void the field' (4.7.50–51).
16. The disclosure in December 2007 that the Bush administration's violation of U.S. citizens' right to privacy under the Fourth Amendment preceded 9/11 exposes its post-9/11 national security concerns as a ruse.
17. George W. Bush uttered this statement, a kind of wish-fulfillment fantasy that ultimately came to pass, on 18 December 2000, while waiting for the recount of the vote in the state of Florida during the U.S. Presidential election.
18. James Dobson heads up a 100–200 million dollar-a-year operation. So many people are ordering his books and pamphlets on the authoritarian-father or strict-father family model that the USPS has assigned him his own zip code.
19. Ron Suskind gives an account of George W. Bush's initial meeting with the principals of his National Security Council on 30 January 2005, ten days after his inauguration: 'Ten days in, and it was about Iraq', he concludes. 'Getting Hussein was now the administration's focus, that much was already

clear', Paul O'Neill, Secretary of Treasury at the time, recalls about the meeting, which had seemed scripted:

> Was this multipronged assault on Saddam Hussein really a priority in early 2001? The dialogue today had been mostly about *hows* – how to weaken or end Saddam's regime. With the administration at the start of its second week, O'Neill wondered, when, exactly, the *whys* – why Saddam, why now, and why this was central to U.S. interests – were to be discussed. (2004a, 75–6)

4

Ventriloquized Sentimentality, or, the Theory and Practice of Women in War

Kathryn Schwarz

It is easy to see, and easy to say, that sports enable a kind of inconsequential homosocial sentimentality. Fantasy teams, voyeurism, fetish gear, the passionate rhetoric of love and hate: the clash of rivalry and desire, which is, as Eve Sedgwick has shown, no clash at all, yokes 'my guys' to 'your guys' in an illusion of battle played out in safe space.[1] Unless it is a very bad day in sports, no one dies.

On a good day in war, many people may die, as long as they are, as after Agincourt, 'ten thousand French' and, in that peculiarly chilling small phrase, 'none else of name' (*Henry 5*, 4.8.80; 105).[2] War is necessarily consequential, its stakes not only life and death, but implication in the outcome of that grim either/or. Yet an analogy as irresistible as that which links writing to childbirth binds sports to war. Thrills of victory, agonies of defeat, acts of heroism and the grace of God are game-day clichés, appropriated so effortlessly and naturalized so seamlessly that their origins disappear. Only when the referent comes too close does the simulacrum waver and become vulnerable to demystification: so, in the weeks following 9/11, *Sports Illustrated* suspended the feature 'This Week's Sign of the Apocalypse'. It was now – *then*, for those few weeks – a sign of poor taste.

War, too, is a homosocial fantasy. It may concern women – as strategists, victims, monarchs and soldiers – but it is not particularly concerned *with* women, at least not in a way that accommodates heterosociality. As Carol Burke writes, 'Official segregation may be on the wane, but a more insidious system of gender subordination takes place as the military aggressively practices the unofficial rites handed down from man to man through the generations' (2004, xiv). From

Elizabeth's 'heart and stomach of a king' to the 'suck my dick' apotheosis of G. I. Jane, war enacts a masculinist appropriation, an effective translation of speaking parts. It does this not only to protect homosocial exclusivity, but simultaneously to incite and to sanitize violence: the feminine is not that with or against which one fights, but that for which one fights. War requires a mediation that sports do not; it needs a high ground for its argument, something apparently, if not actually, more sophisticated than 'our hats are blue'. In Burke's terms,

> Moral justification, palliative comparison, euphemistic labeling, displacement of responsibility, and diffusion of responsibility offer ways in which repugnant conduct is transformed into sanctioned behavior. The soldier executes violence not as the aggressor but simply as the justified moral agent. (2004, 48)

In this project of displacement, mediation, and endorsement the rhetoricians of war turn, repeatedly, to a chiastic iconicity that both suppresses and fetishizes female bodies: dislocated into historical mythology or chauvinist personification, 'women' become precedent signs of military valor and immanent articulations of nationalist agendas, appropriated, in both cases, to a valorizing genealogy of masculine martial subjects. Embedded in generative legend, femininity provides a chastised sentimental discourse that men deploy in the service of violence, even as they shield themselves from intimations of hysteria, madness, appetite, corruption, and histrionic display. Wars can thus be ideologically repopulated, fought not by vicious and greedy opportunists but by the heirs of exemplae in the names of mother countries and mother tongues. It is perhaps worth noting that, while many soldiers claim a mother country, few athletes have a mother team.

Yet that rhetorical move is neither entirely persuasive nor fully prophylactic. In practice, it proves oddly difficult to invoke an idealized instrumental femininity without incurring the risk that actual women may show up. We might think briefly of one figure for whom the analogic distance between war and sports collapsed: Pat Tillman, the NFL safety who, in the aftermath of 9/11, left the Arizona Cardinals, trained as an Army Ranger, and was killed in Afghanistan by friendly fire. If there seems to be some harmonic irony in those two abused terms – 'safety' and 'friendly fire' – there is something still more symptomatic in the frame *Sports Illustrated* constructs for Tillman's story. In a story titled 'Remember His Name', Gary Smith compresses three reference points onto a single page (2006).

The first:

> [Russ] wasn't ready. As the grim news crackled, he grabbed a mate's *Maxim* magazine, fixed his eyes on a naked woman, nudged his neighbor and said, 'Hey, look at this chick'... Pat reached over, took hold of Russ's hands and said softly, 'Can you please put that away? Some of our guys are getting hurt right now. We need to focus on them'.

The second:

> That's how they found themselves atop a bunker south of Baghdad late one night in March 2003, on the eve of the rescue of Army Pfc. Jessica Lynch, knowing a bloodbath might await them the following night, when they would encircle the hospital in Nasiriyah where she lay wounded.

The third:

> Russ didn't know yet that Pat had written to his mom.

Recruited into the project of 'remember[ing] his name', which of these trails are we to follow? And what would it mean to follow any one of them: the picture of the naked chick, the rescue of the female soldier, the letter to his mom? A textual turn around feminine clichés – away from the pornographic, toward the maternal – brackets a woman, at once comrade and casualty, already inscribed into layers of myth. Sex as distraction, victim as motive, mother as home: the tropes proliferate and collide, not only *as* tropes, but in their competing claims on something that might, in both a Lacanian and a colloquial sense, be termed the Real. For all its immediacy – both its historical presentness and its rhetorical confounding of mediation – this is, I would argue, a markedly early modern problem.

In 1559, in *An Harborowe for Faithfull and Trewe Subjectes,* John Aylmer deploys a familiar trope, rendering nationalism in a mother's voice.

> Do you not heare how lamentably your natural mother your countrey of England, calleth upon you for obediences saying. Oh, remember remember my dear children in what case you stande, your enemies be round about you, lyke unsaciable ravenours to pluck me from

> you, to cast you out of my lap where I have this.110 yeres lyke a faithful mother nourished you.... Lette me rather satisfie my thirste with their effeminate bloud, then they should pluck from you my motherly breastes: Sticke to youre mother, as she sticketh to you. (1559, sig. R1^{v}–R2)[3]

Neatly ventriloquized, the mother country makes all the right moves, recalling nurture, anticipating violation, consolidating alliance by modeling fidelity. Yet can these in fact be the right moves, voiced as they are? Lynn Enterline describes the risks of what she terms 'cross-voicing' in Ovidian narratives: 'As soon as Ovid's poems provoke the Barthesian question – "whose voice is this?" – one can no longer say, with any certainty, whose "experience" of violence or desire the text is representing, or for whom its stories may be said to "speak"' (2000, 11). The questions of propriety and control certainly speak to Aylmer's text: cast as inspiration, it begins with a demand for obedience and ends with a fantasy of cannibalistic emasculation. Whose agency operates here, and on what instrument?

Early modern rhetorical theory anticipates that Barthesian question, returning again and again to the tension within 'figure' – figure as body, figure as trope – that informs the practices of signifying femininity. The rhetoric that seeks and claims to master its subjects attempts to confirm its genealogy by way of women; men write themselves into authority through the feminization and sexualization of language, a strategy which, predictably, returns upon itself. Language appears as a subject in the sense that it defines an area of inquiry, but also in the sense that it has qualities attributed to personhood: idealized and debased; compliant and resistant; faithful and treacherous; committed to a communal cultural purpose and inclined to obscure, disrupt, or stray from that goal. Theories of discourse present their subject not only as unpredictably counterfactual but as potentially counter-intentional, suggesting that it may work against or away from the purpose that makes use of it. The appearance of a generative femininity in these characterizations collapses the social and sexual project of securing meaning through women with the rhetorical project of securing meaning through language, and reflects a suspicion that both women and language are inadequate or inappropriate media, opaque where they should be transparent, wayward where they should be circumscribed, entirely too apt to assume a significance other than that assigned to them. Masculine speaking subjects unravel the fabric of articulate singularity as they indistinguishably remember, invent and invoke a will to language other than their own; through the analogies and genealogies that link it to femininity, language itself appears willful, an agent that means equivocally even when it means well.

The problem of a partial and contested agency in language only reiterates the problem of being a subject in language at all. In *Excitable Speech*, Judith Butler writes, 'The one who acts (who is not the same as the sovereign subject) acts precisely to the extent that he or she is constituted as an actor and, hence, operating within a linguistic field of enabling constraints from the outset' (1997, 16). Agency begins in and through the experience of constraint – 'one reason that "agency" is not the same as "mastery"' (1997, 26) – and always reflects back on that experience, constituting identity through dependence and instituting a process of memory which, as it yokes need to damage, circulates in the present tense. As Butler argues,

> There is no way to protect against that primary vulnerability and susceptibility to the call of recognition that solicits existence, to that primary dependency on a language we never made in order to acquire a tentative ontological status. Thus we sometimes cling to the terms that pain us because, at a minimum, they offer us some form of social and discursive existence. The address that inaugurates the possibility of agency, in a single stroke, forecloses the possibility of radical autonomy. (1997, 26)

It is in this sense impossible to speak as and for one's self, to forget or ignore the interpellation that confers an agency dependent on its limits and haunted by its relational contingency. If early modern theorists of language cannot leave women alone, their failure or refusal to do so recalls the failures and refusals of language itself, which will not leave the masculine speaking subject alone, but instead resolutely denies him the space of autonomous mastery:

> The ritual dimension of convention implies that the moment of utterance is informed by the prior and, indeed, future moments that are occluded by the moment itself. Who speaks when convention speaks? In what time does convention speak? In some sense, it is an inherited set of voices, an echo of others who speak as the 'I'. (Butler 1997, 25)

Preoccupied with linguistic conventions, rhetorical theorists and practitioners are at the same time pre-scripted by their implication in social conventions, by those recognitions of vulnerability and susceptibility that erupt into their texts when, in speaking of women and language, they re-imagine the subjects who have previously spoken them.

These processes constellate around the symptomatic and oddly somatic travels of the phrase 'mother tongue'. Deployed as a synonym for 'vernacular' or 'vulgar' or 'native', the term repeatedly exceeds its figurative use, recurring to and materializing the feminine subjectivity from which it derives. William Austin, in *Haec Homo*, argues that men depend on women for the use of language: 'For from *their voyce* men learne to frame *their owne*, to be understood of others. For in our infancy, we learne our language from them. Which men (therein not ingrate-full) have justly termed our *Mother tongue*' (1637, 133). Matthew Sutcliffe elevates this developmental debt to the status of a monarchical gift, crediting Queen Elizabeth for 'the Scriptures and publicke prayers in our mother tongue' (1629, 2). And in what might, for English audiences, represent a kind of super-ambivalence about both generation and faith, William Annand argues in *Fides Catholica* for the unity of the Roman churches: '[B]ut yet there is one Roman speech that is used by all these together, and is the Dialect of them all in common. Well we may cal it their mother tongue, since we know she who suckled them, taught them also to speak' (1661, 64). In 'Sins of the Tongue', Carla Mazzio writes,

> The spectacle of the independent organ of speech, mobile even while dislodged from its bodily surround, in many ways perfectly embodies anxieties about reference itself, not only about the movement of speech *away* from the individual body but also about the movement of signs away from any singularly discernable, naturalized context. (1997, 54)

The rhetorical turn to 'mother tongue' occurs at this intersection of the material and the symbolic, and as the sign moves away from its speaker and from the naturalized contexts of nationalism, religion, sovereignty and privileged articulation, it reveals that other, perhaps more obviously natural, link to women.

Women who teach the mother tongue also speak it, with effects not easily accommodated to the disciplinary projects of homosocial masculinity. The line from *Westward Hoe* – 'Why mistris, railing is your mother tongue as well as lying' (Scaena Prima) – resonates with assumptions about the proper, and in another equally compelling sense, improper, speech of women. The repeated associations of a maternalized vernacular with witchcraft escalate this impropriety; in *The admirable historie of the possession and conversion of a penitent woman. Seduced by a magician that made her to become a witch*, the preface assures the reader that 'those that are possessed ordinarily spake their mother tongue' (Michaelis 1613).[4] And George Abbot's account of vernacular preaching records a different kind of possession, which leads to the production of a counter-narrative:

> When *Hus* began first to preach, the people which used handy craftes, did with great desire heare his sermons, and did reade the Scriptures, being turned by him into their mother tongue; so that they could dispute with the Priests: which the very women were able to do; yea and one woman did make a booke. (1604, 37–38)

The women who employ and inhabit the mother tongue may be variously nurturers, railers, teachers, witches, authors, sovereigns, or whores, but they consistently disrupt the normative relations presumed and produced by appropriative speech. Carla Freccero describes the way in which 'queer' functions as a force in language:

> [Q]*ueer* can also be a grammatical perversion, a misplaced pronoun, the wrong proper name; it is what is strange, odd, funny, not quite right, improper. Queer is what is and is not there, what disaggregates the coherence of the norm from the very beginning and is ignored in the force to make sense out of the unintelligibilities of grammar and syntax. (2006, 18)

'Mother tongue', metonymically bound to feminine subjects who both are and are not there, is a queer locution, an acknowledgment, both perverse and misplaced, of the vulnerability of heterosocial hierarchy to its own improper terms.

In plays in which women take part in war, Shakespeare dramatizes this tendency of a feminized rhetoric to find its own, unexpected and unaccommodated situation of utterance. We might think of Volumnia's assertion to Coriolanus – 'Thy valiantness was mine, thou suck'st it from me' (3.2.129) – and remember that the play balances Coriolanus's failure or refusal to use his legacy of speech against his mother's all too effective language. We might remember, too, who emerges in triumph as the savior of Rome. Margaret Ferguson writes, 'In figuring the vernacular itself or the vernacular text as feminine, the male author repeatedly risks losing his own stereotypical gender bearings in his linguistic matrix' (2003, 124).[5] Like any fantasy of a return to origins, the maternal vernacular stands as an anterior truth about legitimacy, unity, and identity misshapen and deferred by its projection backward from an altered state. Again and again, invocations of the mother tongue evoke the impossibility of speaking as a man without in some sense speaking among women, as if the triumphs of appropriation, of recuperation, and of conquest must be muted and challenged by the stubborn memory of native inhabitants.[6] In the context of these confused and contested subjective questions – where am I speaking from? what am I speaking as? – it is not surprising that use of that too-expressive mother tongue carries the burden not only of privilege but of risk.

This problem, of a linguistic inheritance turned askew or perhaps set adrift by the medium through which it passes, preoccupies the early history plays. I have argued elsewhere that Margaret, in *3 Henry 6*, and Constance, in *King John*, disrupt patriarchal logic precisely by acting as its informed and willful advocates.[7] Here I want to take a different approach to that disruptive effect, locating it at the intersection of maternal rhetoric and violent acts. I suggest that these characters, who act not only as but like mothers in their bellicose interventions, provide a site of origin for chauvinist articulations that dislocates those articulations from their masculine homosocial project. I am pursuing the possibilities generated by an alternative referential relation: a vocabulary of war structured by an abstract and largely tacit filial piety turns, through the material presence of feminine speaking subjects, to become an explicit maternal demand. Such speaking subjects are decidedly anachronistic in the context of a project that wants only to use their names – to encounter a mother in the motherland is to experience a crisis of re-appropriated referentiality – and that anachronism intervenes in the theoretical arguments and quotidian practices of socialized violence.

In *Engendering a Nation*, Jean Howard and Phyllis Rackin write of the history play that 'its masculinity was identified with its function as an ideological apparatus for the construction of an emergent national consciousness' (1997, 47). The masculine homosocial processes that construct such a consciousness work, through war, by destroying the other in the name of the same; at the same time, more insidiously, they work to demonstrate that the other *is* the same, indiscriminately assimilable through obliteration and recognition, through conquest and alliance. 'Nothing, perhaps, could be more banal than the role of violence in awakening desire', René Girard writes. 'Two desires converging on the same object are bound to clash. Thus, mimesis coupled with desire leads automatically to conflict' (1977, 144, 146). Understood as a mimetic relation, war may kill individual men, but it does not threaten the masculine homosociality secured by triangulation through an absent feminine presence. Jonathan Dollimore's comment on sexuality applies as well to other, more explicitly violent modes of identification: 'Within masculine sexuality the most significant other is the male – but it is a significance which presupposes, and is rehearsed in relation to, the female' (1991, 302). But what if the medium that should guarantee a clear line of sight instead effects an interruption? What if the female is rehearsing too?

To imagine an answer, we might turn to the extraordinary scene in *King John* in which Constance breaks the truce. That truce, formed through the marriage of John's niece Blanche to the French Dauphin, efficiently turns the material female body to the project of masculine alliance: 'My uncle's will in this respect is mine. / If he see aught in you that makes him like, / That any thing he sees, which moves his liking, / I can with ease translate it to my will' (2.1.510–13). But Constance's response – 'Gone to be married? Gone to swear a peace? / False blood to false blood join'd!' (3.1.1–2) – suggests that feminine will is a far more volatile and volitional agent than such a formula can describe. This war, for Constance, is fought in the name of her son, a name that cannot be restored by a contract among other men. But perhaps more accurately and certainly more urgently, it is fought in the name of her *relation* to her son; so, in response to Arthur's 'I do beseech you, madam, be content', she replies,

> If thou that bid'st me be content wert grim,
> Ugly, and sland'rous to thy mother's womb,
> Full of unpleasing blots and sightless stains,
> Lame, foolish, crooked, swart, prodigious,
> Patch'd with foul moles and eye-offending marks,
> I would not care, I then would be content,
> For then I should not love thee; no, nor thou
> Become thy great birth nor deserve a crown.
> But thou art fair, and at thy birth, dear boy,
> Nature and Fortune join'd to make thee great.
>
> (3.1.42–52)

Marking the truce as a betrayal of her own maternal claim, Constance subjects its agents to that claim:

> Let kings assemble; for my grief's so great
> That no supporter but the huge firm earth
> Can hold it up. Here I and sorrows sit;
> Here is my throne; bid kings come bow to it.
> (3.1.71–4)

What seems a fantasy or at best a figure becomes, instead, a speech act, as the ratification of peace devolves into an increasingly ineffectual attempt to resist this maternal imperative. Constance's reproach to the French King defines masculine sovereignty as false show, a disingenuous and devalued signifier detached from its validating cause.

> You have beguil'd me with a counterfeit
> Resembling majesty, which, being touch'd and tried,
> Proves valueless. You are forsworn, forsworn!
> You came in arms to spill mine enemies' blood,
> But now in arms you strengthen it with yours.
> The grappling vigor and rough frown of war
> Is cold in amity and painted peace,
> And our oppression hath made up this league.
> Arm, arm, you heavens, against these perjur'd kings!
> A widow cries; be husband to me, heavens!
> Let not the hours of this ungodly day
> Wear out the day in peace; but ere sunset,
> Set armed discord 'twixt these perjur'd kings!
> Hear me, O, hear me!
> (3.1.99–112)

Removed from its foundation in sentimentalized maternity – disconnected from Constance, so often critiqued for her excess of maternal sentiment – the bond among men is 'painted peace', as the men themselves are counterfeit, valueless, perjured, forsworn.[8] 'Lady Constance, peace!' pleads Austria, to which Constance replies, 'War, war, no peace! Peace is to me a war' (3.1.112–13). That act of translation usurps the masculine privilege of authorized language, returning a ventriloquized rhetoric to the feminine subject who insists on the propriety of her own speech.

Constance wins, if we can allow for a highly vexed and compromised notion of winning. The introduction of a maternalism that privileges one man disarticulates the homosocial consolidation embodied in Blanche:

> Which is the side that I must go withal?
> I am with both, each army hath a hand,
> And in their rage, I having hold of both,
> They whirl asunder and dismember me.
> (3.1.327–30)

Instrumental femininity gives way to volitional femininity; as a heterosocial intervention in the name of patrilineality opposes homosocial alliance, feminine abstractions become not motives for masculine efficacy, but disciplinary instruments deployed against masculine inadequacy. Phyllis Rackin writes, 'Patriarchal history is designed to construct a verbal substitute for the visible physical connection between a mother and her children, to authenticate the relationships between fathers and sons and to suppress and supplant the role of the mother' (1985, 337).[9] Radically unsuppressed, the role of mother in *King John* is particular in its attachment and indiscriminate in its devastation, introducing the specter of an alternative contractual model that cannot be approximated to the autonomous and self-perpetuating logic of the state. As Constance argues,

> when law can do no right,
> Let it be lawful that law bar no wrong;
> Law cannot give my child his kingdom here,
> For he that holds his kingdom holds the law;
> Therefore since law itself is perfect wrong,
> How can the law forbid my tongue to curse?
> (3.1.185–90)

The agency of ventriloquism shifts: Constance's curse substitutes for sovereign law, and when Pandulph, the Pope's legate, attempts a return to the masculine appropriation of maternal rhetoric, he reiterates and furthers this specific mother's cause.

> All form is formless, order orderless,
> Save what is opposite to England's love.
> Therefore to arms! be champion of our Church,

Or let the Church, our mother, breathe her curse,
A mother's curse, on her revolting son.
(3.1.253–57)

The agent that imposes form and constitutes order is war, a war conceived by a mother against the sovereign masculine subjects of the mother country herself.

As she provides an all too local, all too vocal habitation for maternal authority, Constance undoes the homogenous masculinity that produces nationalism as at once natural and obvious. There *is* no obvious nationalism in *King John*: is the battle over Arthur's rights a foreign invasion, or a civil insurrection? Constance's maternal will conflates the threat of domestic division with that of external conquest, making the integrity and even the nature of the state both fragile and opaque. That will becomes not the ventriloquized form for chauvinist sentimentality, but a feminine sentimentality turned against the legibility of chauvinist self-justification. A maternal rhetoric occupied and deployed by its presumptively abstract referent has a life of its own, an embodied volition which exposes masculine autonomy as both fantastic and contingent, at once insufficient for and destructive to its own ends. The Bastard's reproach to his countrymen makes this crisis vividly clear:

And you degenerate, you ingrate revolts,
You bloody Neroes, ripping up the womb
Of your dear mother England, blush for shame;
For your own ladies and pale-visag'd maids
Like Amazons come tripping after drums,
Their thimbles into armed gauntlets change,
Their needl's to lances, and their gentle hearts
To fierce and bloody inclination.
(5.2.151–58)

Only wives and daughters can defend the mother country against her degenerate and revolting sons; an exclusively masculine martiality gives way to a closed circle of women. Edward's reproach to Margaret in *3 Henry 6* – 'No, wrangling woman, we'll no longer stay, / These words will cost ten thousand lives this day' (2.2.176–77) – echoes here, with its eerie return to the opening scene of Part 1:

Posterity, await for wretched years,

When at their mothers' moist'ned eyes babes shall suck,
Our isle be made a nourish of salt tears,
And none but women left to wail the dead.

(1.1.48–51)

The mother land threatens, through the invocation of mothers, to become a space only of mothers, a collapse of sign into body from which there seems no escape. Even the Bastard's final words in *King John* promise only a subjunctive return, explicitly both partial and contingent:

This England never did, nor never shall,
Lie at the proud foot of a conqueror,
But when it first did help to wound itself.
Now these her princes are come home again,
Come the three corners of the world in arms,
And we shall shock them. Nought shall make us rue,
If England to itself do rest but true.

(5.7.112–18)

What restoration inheres in those dangerous deictics of 'when' and 'now', that ominous subjunctive 'if', those uneasy pronominal shifts between 'it' and 'her'?

Pursuing an alternative historiography, seeking 'an approach to history – and to justice – that would neither "forget the dead" nor "successfully" mourn them', Freccero writes, 'The past is in the present in the form of a haunting. This is what, among other things, doing a queer kind of history means, since it involves an openness to the possibility of being haunted, even inhabited, by ghosts' (2006, 78, 80). We might say, in this sense, that *King John* does a queer kind of history, deliberately summoning its ghosts: of Arthur's matrilineal right; of an England violated by English men and defended by English women; of sovereign subjects – Arthur, the Bastard, King John himself – through whom the collective fantasies of nationalism and homosociality disintegrate into individual masculine identities determined by maternal will. And we might say, to glance again at the present, that this is promise as well as threat. To be haunted in this way by the bodies and effects of women is to be open to an alternative future, revisionary and destabilizing in potentially productive ways. As Louise Fradenburg and Carla Freccero write in the introduction to *Premodern Sexualities*,

> [P]ositing the power of the past to disrupt and remake the present is not necessarily to adopt a naÏve continuism ... The past may not *be* the present, but it is sometimes *in* the present, haunting, even if only through our uncertain knowledges of it, our hopes of surviving and living well. (1996, xix; xxi)

If, as I have argued, the tendency of ventriloquized maternal rhetoric to produce immanent maternal agents disrupts a seamless masculine homosociality, it does so in the name of difference. For *King John*, it is the difference between a war that consolidates nationalist meanings and a war that interrogates and unsettles those meanings. The question of utility, of what that war gave or proved or did or made, refuses any comforting or comfortable answer, and we might take that refusal, with its hints toward something different, as our own enabling ghost.

Notes

1. Sedgwick writes of René Girard's mimetic model, 'The bonds of "rivalry" and "love", differently as they are experienced, are equally powerful and in many senses equivalent' (1985, 21).
2. All quotations from Shakespeare's texts are from The Riverside Shakespeare (1974).
3. In citing early modern texts, I have retained their spellings; however, I have modernized typography in several ways. Consonantal *u* and *i* have been revised to *v* and *j*, and vocalic *v* has been revised to *u*; long *s* has been revised to *s*; ligatures of æ and œ have been expanded; & and *y*e have been altered to *and* and *the*; where a macron over a vowel indicates the suspension of *m* or *n*, I have supplied the letter.
4. See also Heywood (1624, 406), Scot (1651, 308), and de Torquemada (1600, 81).
5. For discussion of the gender ambiguity of the tongue, and of language itself, see Mazzio (1997, especially 60);and Stallybrass (1991b, especially 215).
6. Parker, tracing 'the complex concerns about virility at work in the period's repeated diatribes against the "female" tongue', describes the quest for a more masculine style as 'haunted by both the female and the effeminate', by 'anxieties both about the ambiguous gender of men of words and about the activity of writing itself' (1996, 201, 206, 216). See also Wall, who, in her reading of the relationship between nationalism and domesticity, writes, 'Like the household in which early education and language acquisition took place, the native tongue was both a national ideal and a sign of the abject' (1998, 15).
7. See Schwarz (2003).

8. For accounts of the challenge posed by feminine speech to patriarchal authority in *King John*, see Howard and Rackin (1997, 119–33), Vaughan (1989, 62–75), Levin (1987, 219–34), and Dusinberre (1990, 37–52).
9. See Rackin's reading of the disintegrating effect of women in *King John* (1985, 338–43); she writes, 'In the world of *King John*, women no longer serve their traditional functions as creators of male bonds and validators of male identity' (1985, 338).

5

A Presentist Analysis of Joan, la Pucelle: 'What's past and what's to come she can descry'

Kay Stanton

> There is a history in all men's lives,
> Figuring the nature of the times deceased,
> The which observed, a man may prophesy,
> With a near aim, of the main chance of things
> As yet not come to life, which in their seeds
> And weak beginnings lie intreasurèd.
>
> –*2 Henry 4*, 3.1.80–5[1]

> Glory is like a circle in the water,
> Which never ceases to enlarge itself
> Till by broad spreading it disperse to naught.
> With Henry's death the English circle ends;
> Dispersèd are the glories it included.
>
> –*1 Henry 6*, 1.2.133–36

On the basis of a flimsy, convoluted, and unprovable claim, an English-speaking country has, with the endorsement of those of its religious leaders with vested interest, declared war upon, invaded, and attempted both to efface the culture and to exploit the natural resources of a foreign country. Such is the story of Shakespeare's *Henry 5* – yet, but for 'a little variations' (*Henry 5*, 4.7.18), it is also contemporary U.S. story, history in progress. The present, as it is perceived by many of us in the U.S., can be seen as eerily 'present' in many quotations from Shakespeare's English history plays, with a few examples from *2 Henry 4* serving to make the point. The presidency of George Bush, in his first term, was 'an honor snatched with boisterous hand' (*2 Henry 4*, 4.5.191) away from the legitimate winner of the election, Al Gore; perhaps 'God knows' everything about 'By what bypaths and indirect crooked ways' (*2 Henry 4*, 4.5.184) Bush obtained the presidency in 2000, and 'won' it in 2004; we mortals of the opposition just have our suspicions and some fact-finding done by a few – too few – brave reporters[2] who risk, and usually suffer, retribution from the White House, or slander and/or effacement by its minions, for communicating truths. As for the remainder of the contemporary U.S. news media,[3] they, for the most part, are of the 'household' of Rumor, whose 'pipe / Blown by surmises, jealousies, conjectures' is 'of so easy and so plain a stop / That the blunt monster with uncounted heads, / The still-discordant wavering multitude' – in our case, particularly bloggers and talk-radio callers – 'Can play upon it', and, as for We The People, 'which of [us] can stop / The vent of hearing when loud Rumor speaks?' (*2 Henry 4*, Induction 22, 15–20, 1–2). Rumor certainly spoke loudly, and long, in the 2004 Presidential campaign, through the 'continual slanders' (*2 Henry 4*, Induction 6) issued by the 'Swift Boat Veterans' and others. But there are also egregious instances of propaganda in current play, issuing directly from the White House: the planting of paid mouthpieces of the administration in the guise of military experts and 'objective' reporters, whose job it is to 'bring smooth comforts false, worse than true wrongs' (*2 Henry 4*, Induction 40), for example, in regard to the situation in Iraq and social and economic issues. Most horrifying and most difficult to combat, however, are administration tactics that 'speak of [freedom] while covert enmity / Under the smile of safety wounds the world' (*2 Henry 4*, Induction 9–10). Except that it is eloquently stated, therefore beyond Bush-capacity, the advice that father Henry 4 gives to son Henry 5 is identical to the strategy of both father George Bush and son George Bush: 'Be it thy course to busy giddy minds / With foreign quarrels, that action, hence borne out, / May waste the memory of former days' (*2 Henry 4*, 4.5.213–14). Furthermore, we are presently witnessing history being written, right before our eyes, as lies. We are told, as if undisputable truth, that *everyone* in the U.S. believed, prior to our invasion of the country, that Iraq had weapons of mass destruction and that Saddam Hussein was in league with Osama Bin Laden to attack us on 11 September 2001 – which is definitely *not* the case, nor is it the case that *everyone* supported the invasion. Millions of us opposed it and thousands of us protested it – with these voices of opposition and protest given minimal media coverage, treated as un-American and/or traitorous, and, needless to say, unheeded, because unlistened to, by the Bush–Cheney–Rove administration. What, then, is the situation in the present time of those of us who oppose and protest our government's war-mongering, as well as its projects of dismantling environmental conservation and protection, social and educational programs, and rights of women and homosexuals? One way to express it is to say that it is precisely the situation of the women of Shakespeare's history plays.

The female voices of Shakespeare's history plays were mostly 'unheard' in criticism, even in feminist analyses, until about 20 years ago. One of their earliest and best listeners, Phyllis Rackin, states that these women 'are typically defined as opponents and subverters of the historical and historiographic enterprise – in short, as anti-historians'; their voices challenge 'the logocentric, masculine historical record', threaten 'to invalidate the great, inherited historical myths that Shakespeare found in historiographic sources and imply that before the masculine voice of history can be accepted as valid, it must come to terms with women and the subversive forces they represent'. Yet when Shakespeare 'attempts to incorporate those feminine forces', she continues, 'historiography itself becomes problematic, no longer speaking with the clear, univocal voice of unquestioned tradition but re-presented as a dubious construct, always provisional, always subject to erasure and reconstruction, and never adequate to recover the past in full presence' ('Anti-historians' 1985, 329–30).[4] Not simply a spokeswoman but a *champion* of the 'anti-historical voice' emerges in *1 Henry 6*: Joan of Arc, 'la Pucelle', whom Coppélia Kahn aptly describes as 'a composite portrait of the ways women are dangerous to men' (1981, 55).

In *1 Henry 6*, Joan is, of course, one of three powerful French female characters (the others being the Countess of Auvergne and Margaret), each of whom positions herself against the English narrative of history, with each voice's impact reinforced by their combined choral effect, making this play among the English histories speak the female oppositional voice most strongly. Leah Marcus notes that 'Taken in the rough order of their composition and performance, Shakespeare's history plays from *Henry 6* to *Henry 5* progressively marginalize the dominant woman' (1988, 94), yet 'We who read the plays in the order of their composition and staging can supply the ironic coda that the cycle is poised to begin all over again: after Henry triumphs at Agincourt, he dies, and with his death we are thrown back into the woman-dominated world of *Henry 6*' (1988, 95). Shakespeare's two tetralogies self-consciously highlight this cyclical movement not only by their order of composition and staging, but also by his having the Chorus of *Henry 5*, who has, throughout that play, served as the King's 'press agent' and 'spin doctor', turn on him in the epilogue and reveal not simply the transitory nature of the glory that the King achieved through conquering France, but also the fact that that triumph's aftermath 'made... England bleed' in Civil War, 'Which oft our stage hath shown' (*Henry 5*, Epilogue 12, 13), in the *Henry 6* plays. As Rackin determines, *Henry 5* is 'Not only the last play in the two tetralogies, it is also their center; for the plot of Shakespeare's historical reconstruction bends the teleological, chronological line of his historiographic sources into a circle, beginning and ending with the death of Henry 5'; this circle 'is joined at the point that represents the moment of loss, and, like the 'wooden O' of Shakespeare's theater, it circumscribes an absence – the heroic past and royal authority that the name of Henry 5 denotes'. Thereby it 'replaces the purposeful, linear progress of history with the endless work of historiography and the endless repetition of theatrical performance, obsessively moving about a lost center they can never recover' (*Stages* 1990, 84). Additionally, Rackin suggests, that 'image of the circle itself circles back' to Joan's 'circle' speech, also 'associated with Henry's death and the erasure of English heroic history', in *1 Henry 6* (1990, 85): 'Glory is like a circle in the water, / Which never ceaseth to enlarge itself, / Till broad spreading it disperse to naught;' for 'With Henry's death the English circle ends, / Dispersèd are the glories it included' (1.2.133–37). Furthermore, as Gabriele Bernhard Jackson states, 'Joan's image of the circle in the water is not only the most poetically resonant statement in the play, it is also specifically borne out by the action' (1988, 21). Arguably, then, over the course of the two tetralogies, Shakespeare ultimately aligns himself with and endorses the position articulated by the Chorus's epilogue to *Henry 5*[5] and to the oppositional voice of Joan in *1 Henry 6* – although he does also allow Rumor to play its pipe so loudly in accompaniment to Joan's voice that it almost drowns it out.

Throughout *1 Henry 6*, English male characters, in rather pathetic attempts to deal with the power, military skill, superb rhetorical ability, and stunning charisma of virgin warrior Joan, resort to labeling her as a witch and joking tirelessly in speculation about her sexual experience – and, in turns that have surprised or shocked many readers and viewers, Shakespeare seems to prove those slanders true, by her own admission. In 5.3, Joan calls upon her familiars, identified in the stage direction as 'Fiends', and refers both to the assistance that they have previously provided her and to her witchcraft-defined means of having obtained it, and in 5.4, after she denies to his face that her shepherd father sired her, claiming instead 'noble birth' (5.4.22), she asserts, 'I am with child' (5.4.62), naming first Alençon and then Reignier as its father. Peter Saccio comments as follows: 'revealed as a sorceress, a whore, and a vixen of monstrous pretensions and ingratitude', the 'real Joan of Arc was of course none of these, but Shakespeare is dramatizing a common English view of her' (1977, 110). Yes, but it was not the *only* 'English view of her', and it was a view also held, at times, among some of the French.[6] Jackson discusses Joan in regard to Elizabethan commentary on positive and negative female exempla ('chosen from history, the Bible, and legend' 1988, 24), noting her representation in the play as 'a tangle of contradictory allusions: she is among other identifications a Sibyl, an Amazon, Deborah, Helen the mother of Constantine, and Astraea's daughter to the French, but Hecate and Circe to the English' (1988, 25). Besides, the exempla genre 'itself was tolerant of, not to say dependent upon, divergent evaluations of the same phenomenon', with some figures assigned either to the positive or negative category, dependent upon the author's evaluation: 'one man's Sibyl is another man's Hecate' (1988, 25). Jackson determines that 'Joan is evaluated by French choice of exempla at the beginning and by the English choice at the end' (1988, 25). Although Jackson's analysis is helpful, we are still left with some nagging questions. Why does Shakespeare's Joan herself give credibility to the English male characters' view of her? And into which category would we, in the present, place the historical Joan of Arc? Beyond question, she was an exemplum of female accomplishment, particularly in light of the fact that she was an illiterate peasant who managed to convince various nobles and the French heir to the throne that she could do wonders, she did indeed accomplish great feats before dying at the extremely young age of 19. But she also insisted that she saw visions of and heard instructions from saints sent from God, and these assertions remain problematic for evaluation of her in the present.

If Shakespeare may be said to turn on Joan, as noted above, he also turned on Henry 5. Besides, when one examines the actual content of these extremely controversial scenes of 5.3 and 5.4, it may be noted that Shakespeare does not slander her as much as readers and audiences lead themselves to believe. As is often discussed in the criticism on this play, Shakespeare deliberately contrasts French peasant-girl Joan against English nobleman Talbot, and he also self-consciously alters several facts of the 22-year period covered in *1 Henry 6* to suit his artistic design. However, these deliberate alterations are doled out to favor English and French fairly evenly, and some elements that initially seem to favor the English, upon closer examination, actually ameliorate Joan's stance. Furthermore, although Shakespeare changes some historical facts, there are others that he correctly includes and/or indirectly references that were unavailable to him in Hall and Holinshed, and some of these facts help to clarify the presentations of Joan in 5.3 and 5.4.

To most critics, Joan's denial of her father seems crude and heartless and thereby contrasts sharply with what is read as the touching and noble relationship between Talbot and his son, but historical facts omitted from the play complicate both parent–child interactions, and even within the play, Joan may be understood as taking the wiser position. Talbot and his son spend the entirety of 4.5, 55 lines, arguing about which, if either of them, should try to flee from the battle, in order to stay alive to revenge the anticipated death of the other. Neither wants to look ignoble by fleeing; *both* could have escaped within that space of time. The scene ends with Talbot saying, 'Come, side by side together live and die, / And soul with soul from France to heaven fly' (4.5.54–5). In the opening lines of 4.6, Talbot complains that 'The Regent hath with Talbot broke his word / And left us to the rage of France his sword' (4.6.2–3): thus the very leader on whose behalf father and son Talbot fight has betrayed and abandoned them; the chivalric ideal, though sustained by father and son, cannot be trusted to be maintained throughout the chain of command. However, their continued presence on the field has allowed son Talbot the opportunity to prove himself in battle and father Talbot the opportunity to avenge his son's wounding in that battle. After praising themselves effusively over these incidents, they then resume the flight-argument for another 30 lines, with the scene ending in Talbot's statement, 'If thou wilt fight, fight by thy father's side; / And, commendable proved, let's die in pride' (4.6.56–7). In the next scene, they both do indeed die, but *for* pride as much as in pride, and Joan summarily triumphs over such pride's pretensions: 'Him that thou magnifi'st with all these titles / Stinking and fly-bown lies here at our feet' (4.7.75–6).[7] The Talbots' noble pride has been both evanescent and suicidal; both die of it, and such substance as it had immediately afterwards not only decays and rots but also stinks.

Joan's scene with her father does indeed provide a contrast. Like Talbot, Joan's father laments the idea of seeing his child die, and he too vows, 'I'll die with thee' (5.4.6), but a major difference is that, unlike Talbot when he had stated that intention, Joan, being already a captive of the enemy, has no opportunity to fly – but her father *has*. By denying that he sired her, she saves her father's life. Busy with their glee over Joan's 'Wicked and vile' (5.4.16) denial of her father, the English make no effort to interfere with his departure. She had not hidden or lied about her parentage when presenting herself to Charles: 'Dauphin, I am by birth a shepherd's daughter' (1.2.72). She lies about her parentage only to her English captors: 'You have suborned this man / Of purpose to obscure my noble birth' (1.2.21–2). Her claim to noble birth[8] not only distracts them from harming her father, but it is probably also the first of her desperate attempts in this scene to save her own life. She has to this point witnessed much evidence, particularly in regard to Talbot, that the English put great store in noble birth. Could she convince them that she were born noble, that might save her, perhaps by ransom, a means usually honored by both English and French nobility. A historical incident involving Suffolk, described by Joan of Arc biographer Marina Warner, provides further evidence of the English snobbism: when Suffolk 'was captured at the siege of Jageau in June 1429 by one of the French soldiers with Joan of Arc, he asked his captor if he was noble. When the latter said no, Suffolk told him to kneel and dubbed him, then and there, a knight. Only then did he yield himself up', because 'For an earl to have been taken by a commoner would have been degrading; consequently, for a commoner, winning such a prize in battle meant a sudden rise in the world' (1981, 160). Furthermore, Suffolk's noble lineage itself did not reach back very far, as noted by Saccio: 'Despite his claim in Shakespeare to Lancastrian blood, Suffolk was not a Plantagenet but the descendant of a Yorkshire wool merchant': his 'grandfather Michael had been raised to the peerage by Richard 2'; Suffolk himself 'inherited the earldom at the age of 19, after his father and elder brother perished in Henry 5's Agincourt campaign' (1977, 120). Although Shakespeare omits these details, he does depict Suffolk, in the scene directly after the one in which Joan claims nobility, counseling Henry 6 to break his oath to an 'earl's daughter' (5.5.34) for more a high-status marriage to Margaret, whose 'father is a king' (5.5.39), even though, as Gloucester notes, Margaret's 'father is no better than an earl, / Although in glorious titles he excel' (5.5.37–8). If Joan's attempt to raise herself to nobility is a desperate lie to save her life, Suffolk's aggrandizement of Margaret's nobility is an insidious attempt to enhance his life and increase his power, as well as to satisfy his sexual lust for her. He ends the scene, and with it the play, with his vow to 'rule both her, the King, and realm' (5.5.108). Between Joan and Suffolk, whose assertion of nobility is more deceitful and treacherous?

The historical Joan of Arc, however, never denied her parentage, and she turned down the opportunity for ennoblement for herself, though a coat of arms had actually been bestowed by Charles on her brothers.[9] Joan's 'nobility' scene in *1 Henry 6*, 5.4, includes another historical inaccuracy as well. In it, Joan's father answers her assertion of 'noble birth' by affirming, ''Tis true, I gave a noble to the priest / The morn that I was wedded to her mother' (5.4.22–24), implying Joan to be not merely lowborn, but furthermore illegitimate. Not only was the historical Joan *not* born illegitimately, as court records show her mother to have testified under oath, but neither did her father sire any illegitimate child – in contrast to Talbot. As Shakespeare knew from Hall, in addition to young John, Talbot had another son, Henry, who also died on the same day, but Henry was illegitimate and is not mentioned in *1 Henry 6*. Critics who, from reading Hall, know about Talbot's illegitimate son, say that Shakespeare suppressed this fact, but close reading of the father–son Talbot scenes reveals that it is Talbot himself who is suppressing the matter. He never directly says that John is his only child; instead he is careful to specify that young John is his *wife's* only child: 'Shall all thy mother's hopes lie in one tomb?' (4.5.34) and 'In thee thy mother dies, our household's name' (4.6.38). Interestingly, however, son John brings up the issue of illegitimacy: 'O if you love my mother, / Dishonor not her honorable name / To make a bastard and a slave of me!' (4.5.13–15). This could have been a perfect opportunity for Talbot to mention young John's half-brother, but he refrains. If Shakespeare's Joan denies being the illegitimate child of her father, Shakespeare's Talbot denies claiming his illegitimate son. Rather than confess to such siring, he allows John to believe that if there were to be any illicit sexual activity in the Talbot household, it would have been done by his mother rather than his 'noble' father. Yet young John has been wounded by bastardy, described by Talbot in a bizarrely sexualized way: the wound was rendered by 'The ireful bastard Orleans, that drew blood / From thee, my boy, and had the maidenhood / Of thy first fight' (4.6.16–18) – as if the virgin boy were raped, and thereby bled, by Bastardy. Father Talbot then 'quickly shed / Some of his bastard blood' (4.6.19–20); he met up with young John again while 'purposing the Bastard to destroy' (4.6.25). If we may read the Bastard of Orleans as a symbolic stand-in here for Talbot's bastard son Henry, we can see that Talbot's 'nobility' destroys both of his offspring killed that day. A further clue is provided that links the Talbot and Joan father–child scenes. Talbot's repeated attempt to convince John to fly from the battle provokes John's comment that 'The sword of Orleans hath not made me smart; / These words of yours draw lifeblood from my heart' (4.6.42–3); the words of Joan's father will be an echo: 'Ah, Joan, this kills thy father's heart outright!' (5.4.2). These historical inaccuracies, interpreted from this perspective, show that what seems to be an ahistorical denigration of Joan's character reveals that, for the English, she, simply by being

French, female, and of non-noble lineage, is a convenient scapegoat for their own ignoble behavior.

The scene, however, also manages, by its historical inaccuracies, additionally to register some historical truths about Joan in artistically transformed ways. Her lie about her parentage perhaps symbolically represents the historical fact that she refused to swear to tell the truth and nothing but in her trial, and her revision of attribution of identity of her supposed impregnator perhaps stands for the historical fact that, following her trial, while imprisoned and under duress (and almost certainly misled as to the document's content), she had signed a 'confession' of heresy and afterwards refuted it. But the deck was stacked against the historical Joan, and she became well aware of that, as does Shakespeare's Joan. It is far from being the case that if Joan *had* sworn to tell the truth and had indeed told only the truth that her English captors and the Church's inquisitors would have spared her. It was merely a show trial, which even some of its contemporary witnesses recognized and documented.

There are also, interestingly, ways by which the historical Joan in a sense did indeed 'deny' her father, by circumventing and then escaping from his authority over her. As Mary Gordon states, 'The first dream of Joan of Arc was dreamed by her father. He saw his daughter traveling with an army: a camp follower'. Upon waking, 'he told her brothers that if this ever happened, he would ask them to drown her, and if they refused, he would do it himself' (2000, 1). Perhaps this incident can be seen as behind the raging remarks made by the shepherd to Shakespeare's Joan: 'Dost thou deny thy father, cursèd drab? / O, burn her, burn her! Hanging is too good!' (5.4.32–3). Furthermore, it seems that, not long before she had set off on her mission, the historical Joan's father had arranged a marriage for her that she refused to accept; a breech of contract suit followed. Thus, as Marina Warner describes it, 'Joan was, in fact, a run-away' (1981, 154). She had told no one about her visions, which she had apparently been having for about five years before her departure, and when she was permitted to leave home, it was for her to help a relative through the birth of her child. Instead of going directly to her pregnant relative, en route she convinced Duand Laxart, her relative's husband, to take her instead to Robert de Baudricourt, Provost of the royal fortress of Vaucouleurs, whom she ultimately persuaded to take her to the Dauphin.

The historical Joan may further be interpreted as 'denying her father', Jacques Darc, because she never used his name. Biographers often comment on the irony that she herself never identified herself by the name that we use for her, Joan of Arc. Instead, she called herself, as does Shakespeare's Joan, 'la Pucelle'. Marina Warner notes that *Pucelle* means 'virgin', but in a special way, 'with distinct shades connoting youth, innocence and, paradoxically, nubility'; it is 'the equivalent of the Hebrew *'almah*, used of both the Virgin Mary and the dancing girls in Solomon's harem in the Bible', and it 'denotes a time of passage, not a permanent condition', as a word 'that looks forward to a change in state' (1981, 22). The word *pucelle* was also 'used in gallant contexts'; it 'implied no rank, and it was current at every level in society', which 'made it an inspired choice in Joan's case', as it 'cancelled out her background, without denying it' (1981, 23). Joan thereby 'picked a word for virginity that captured with doubled strength the magic of her state in her culture', expressing 'not only the incorruption of her body', but also 'the dangerous border into maturity or full womanhood that she had not crossed and would not cross', thusly, Warner adds, 'In this sense she was a tease' (1981, 23).

Besides being enabled to laugh at Joan's pretensions to nobility, her English captors in 5.4 are also treated to Joan's 'confession' both of pregnancy,[10] and, supposedly, promiscuity, which especially delights them, as throughout their encounters with her, they have wanted to believe her to be what they habitually call her, a whore.[11] This 'confession' is also non-historical, but it is perhaps part of Shakespeare's version of what Warner calls the historical Joan's being 'a tease'. Both English and French male characters habitually assume implied seductiveness in any word Joan speaks that can be twisted into a sexual pun, but there has been no evidence that she is other than a virgin. She had even turned down the offered chance to become the Dauphin's paramour: 'I must not yield to any rites of love, / For my profession's sacred from above' (1.2.113–14). Most critics assume with the English, wrongly, that Shakespeare's Joan is actually confessing to promiscuity, finally 'revealing' herself as the whore she is, without even considering the *prospect* of what is the *likelihood*: that her only 'sins' here are in grasping at *anything* that might save her life – 'Will nothing turn your unrelenting hearts?' (5.4.59) – and in believing that the English do indeed, as they profess to do, respect and protect as yet unborn and thus innocent life: 'Murder not then the fruit within my womb, / Although ye hale me to a violent death' (5.4.63–4). Needless to say, they do not: 'We'll have no bastards live' (5.4.70), 'It dies an if it had a thousand lives' (5.4.75), 'Strumpet, thy words condemn thy brat and thee. / Use no entreaty, for it is in vain' (5.4.84–5). That is the behavior of a Herod, not of those who truly are, as they represent themselves to be, civilized, humane, chivalric, supposedly Christian members of the English 'nobility'. In fact, by their mocking exclamations of 'The holy maid with child? / The greatest miracle that e'er ye wrought' (5.4.65–6) and 'It's a sign she hath been liberal and free. / And yet, forsooth, she is a virgin pure!' (5.4.83–4), York and Warwick reveal that, had they the pregnant Virgin Mary herself before them in Joan's position of vulnerability, they would have executed both her and the 'illegitimate' fetus, her Son, their God. And if they do not credit Joan's claim to pregnancy, then neither have they any right to credit the idea of her supposed promiscuity or even absence of virginity. Once again, in a scene in which Shakespeare seems ahistorically to denigrate the character of Joan, the English come off as being much worse than she.

According to many critics, in this scene Joan confesses to having had sex with nearly the entire French camp, but she does not; it is York, not Joan, who assumes that 'she knows not well [who the father of her professed child may be], / There were so many, whom she may accuse' (5.4.80–1). Only a total of three names is proposed, and the first of these is Charles, named by York. Joan, denying that it was he, names Alençon, historically her closest friend among the French nobles, one who is also high-born enough, she probably at that point believes, to impress the English. When they instead (anachronistically) label him a 'Machiavel' (5.4.74), whose child they would certainly kill, she moves up the social register to one, and only one, additional name, which happens to be that of the same man that Suffolk himself will soon use to work influence on the king, 'Reignier, King of Naples' (5.4.78), but her captors focus, disapprovingly, only on his status as a married man. Shakespeare's handling of the issue is, I believe, intentionally ambiguous; in one sense Joan's claim of pregnancy allows the English to support their claim for her promiscuity, which, however, also grants her the power of sexual 'trangressiveness' that will be continued in *2 Henry 6* by Margaret (Howard and Rackin 1997, 62–3). In a symbolic sense, she is also 'pregnant', as the 'mother' of other female Shakespeare characters to be born in the future: not only Lady Macbeth and the witches, but also the comedies' cross-dressing heroines.

The historical Joan almost certainly died a virgin. There were, however, both English and French suspicions to the contrary, and she had several times had to endure being examined, usually by noblewomen, to verify her claim of virginity; each time she passed the test. Sometimes she herself had suggested such testing. Her virginity was supremely important to her, for many reasons, not the least of which because it allowed her independence from male control. Within

5.4, the 'promiscuity' and 'pregnancy' scene, Shakespeare also gives his Joan words that are in keeping with the attitude of the historical Joan: calling herself 'A virgin from her tender infancy, / Chaste and immaculate in very thought', she contrasts herself with her English captors, 'you, that are polluted with your lusts, / Stained with the guiltless blood of innocents, / Corrupt and tainted with a thousand vices' (5.4.50–1; 5.4.43–5), who in their hypocrisy presume to pass judgment on her.

Within that same speech in 5.4, however, Joan also maintains that, being 'Virtuous and holy', she was 'chosen from above / By inspiration of celestial grace / To work exceeding miracles on earth' and that she 'never had to do with wicked spirits' (5.4.39–42), even though she had just been seen in 5.3 attempting to commune with her 'fiends'. As Dominique Goy-Blanquet rightly notes, *1 Henry 6* maintains throughout a 'double system of interpretation': the 'characters explain successes and reversals by supernatural causes, in which they believe if we do not', although 'the interference of superior powers in human affairs, always to be reckoned with as a likely possibility, does not exclude the more prosaic reality of facts' (2003c, 54). But the presentation of Joan with her familiars *does* assert a kind of perceived reality for the supernatural, and even here, I believe, Shakespeare is being fair to the historical Joan. To her, her voices and visions had both a reality and an authority that trumped all patriarchal authority – not merely of her father, but also the Church and even her king.

During her trial, under unrelenting pressure to provide details to her inquisitors of her supernatural encounters, the historical Joan, after long resistance, ultimately identified Saints Catherine, Margaret, and Michael as those who had visited her and informed her of her destiny and mission. Marina Warner and Karen Sullivan both suggest, however, that Joan's actual experiences may not have been so particularized. Sullivan notes that these names are not specified in any documentation prior to that of Joan's trial (1999, 24); Warner opines that Joan, lacking the sophistication of language by which Teresa of Avila eloquently described her similar experiences, nonetheless 'gave an answer that is a model of mystical description: "The light comes in the name of the voice"' (1981, 122–23). What seems clear is that Joan had visual and auditory experiences that she entirely believed were divine in origin, and, although both Warner and Sullivan find an appropriateness in her choice of saints to whom to attach the experiences (as their stories were well-known, and there may have been statutes of them, in Joan's home locale), the fixing of their specific identities was more of an obsession to her interrogators than to her, and hallucinators may incorporate their individual frames of reference into what they believe they have experienced. Rather than naming those specific saints, Shakespeare has his Joan tell the Dauphin that 'God's mother deignèd to appear' to her, 'in a vision full of majesty' (1.2.78–9). Just as the historical Joan initially had spoken in the singular about the divine 'voice' coming from God, but when under pressure and in mortal danger had changed to the plural and differentiated saints' 'voices' (Sullivan 1999, 26), so Shakespeare's Joan initially centers her vision on the singular, 'God's mother', then, when the battle goes badly and she realizes her danger, the supernatural is pluralized as 'spirits', moving lower (as do saints) in the hierarchy as 'speedy helpers, that are substitutes / Under the lordly monarch of the north' (5.3.5–6). For both the historical Joan and Shakespeare's Joan, the divine takes both male and female form, as does she through being the maid in male garb.

Unlike those who have simply dismissed the historical Joan as a charlatan or a sufferer of mental illness, then, Shakespeare takes her seriously by granting Joan, and only Joan among those who in the play bandy about the idea of supernatural influence, a tangible relationship with other-worldly beings. He does, though, choose the English attribution of these forces to witchcraft (as did the Burgundian French and, for many years, the Catholic Church) in 5.3, but, interestingly, witchcraft has re-emerged in the present as an explanation of the historical Joan's 'visitations', though now through positive, rather than negative interpretation of what 'witchcraft' constitutes: a survival of pagan goddess-associated religions.

In 1921, anthropologist and Egyptologist Margaret Murray published her study *The Witch-Cult in Western Europe*, in which she argued that evidence suggests that Joan participated in pagan rites, among which were ingestion of psychoactive plants that produced hallucinogenic experiences including visions, voices, and prophetic ability. Her book provoked controversy upon its publication, with many trying to discredit it. Although some elements of the case that Murray makes for Joan being 'The Maiden' of her local Dianic cult are not entirely convincing, the book was very instrumental in overcoming some of the Christian propaganda associating the pagan 'old religion' with demonic evil. What seems likely is that Joan had been exposed to some pagan practices and rituals, and had learned some herbal and medicinal treatments, without recognizing that the church condemned them and without interpreting them as being contradictory to her deep commitment to Christianity.

In the 'witchcraft' segment of 5.3, Joan calls for help from 'charming spells and periapts' (5.3.2), 'choice spirits' that 'give [her] signs of future accidents', and the 'substitutes / Under the lordly monarch of the north' (5.3.56), with most commentators assuming the latter designation to refer to Satan, as depicted through Christian religion, thus aligning Joan with his evil. In witchcraft/Wicca, however, it has no such connotation. Within the witchcraft circle, four points are marked, to 'orient the circle to the four cardinal points' of east, south, west, and north (Buckland 2002, 92), and these four points represent the four elements of air, fire, water, and earth, respectively. The earth, thus the north, 'is connected with the Goddess, the Mother' (Buckland 2002, 145), as well as with gnomes, or 'knowing ones', as its 'elementals', or means to accomplish magic (Buckland 2002, 147). Among the associations of the north are the female principle, practicality, and the materialization of cosmic powers (2002, 148), all very much needed helpers for Joan as she sees that 'The Regent conquers, and the Frenchmen fly' (5.3.1). But the 'familiar spirits, that are culled / Out of the powerful regions under earth' (5.3.10–11), rather than assisting Shakespeare's Joan in this instance, instead 'forsake' her (5.3.24), mutely, just as the historical Joan had said that her 'voices' abandoned her, without explanation, near the end of her life. Once the forces assisting each Joan left her 'circle', she was subject to the earthly powers that captured, imprisoned, and ultimately executed her.

In the present, explanations of Joan's 'other-worldly' experiences remain ambiguous, as they are in *1 Henry 6*, but in the worldly frame of reference, her impact was most strong, and thus most troubling to her enemies, because it encompassed not only spiritual, but gender/sexual, military, and political 'cardinal' points of power. The 'circle', then, of this uneducated peasant girl ultimately proved more powerful than the 'circle' of ever-widening glory of Henry 5, which did in fact, as Shakespeare's Joan had predicted, 'disperse to naught', whereas the historical Joan, in the present, has more fame and relevance than he, the result that Shakespeare himself definitely foresaw.

Within Shakespeare's tetralogies, Joan's claim that she was 'issued from the progeny of kings' (5.4.38) *is* in a sense true: she is the symbolic offspring of the mating of Henry 5 with Katherine of France. When 'wooing' French princess Katherine, Henry asserts both that she is 'like an angel' and that she has 'witchcraft in [her] lips' (*Henry 5*, 5.2.110, 267). He believes that because he loves her 'cruelly' and gets her with 'scrambling' (*Henry 5*, 5.2.197), she must therefore 'prove a good soldier-breeder' (*Henry 5*, 5.2.200), and 'between Saint Denis and Saint George', they will 'compound a boy' (*Henry 5*, 5.2.201) that will extend his military triumphs. But it is scrambling angel-witch, saint-soldier, male-attired Joan, more than biological son Henry 6, who compounds these qualities, and, as symbolic daughter to the sexually and politically exploited Katherine, Joan, wielding the sword of Saint Katherine, rights the silenced French princess Katherine's wrongs and inspires France to reverse Henry 5's triumphs and free itself from English subjugation.

The English habit throughout *Henry 5* of regarding France as a female to be conquered is epitomized in the play's last scene in Henry's description of his 'love-blindness', by which he 'cannot see many a fair French city for one fair French maid that stands in [his] way' (*Henry 5*, 5.2.304–06). Yet, as the King of France reminds him, 'you see them perspectively, the cities turned into a maid; for they are all girdled with maiden walls that war hath never entered' (*Henry 5*, 5.2.307–09). Through a perspective trick, the as yet unconquered French cities telescope into the French maiden; by entering her 'breach', he also enters theirs. But in order to enter them, he needs to 'conjure up the spirit of love in [Katherine]' (*Henry 5*, 5.2.279–80). Burgundy advises him that 'If you would conjure in her, you must make a circle; if conjure up love in her in his true likeness, he must appear' as a 'naked blind boy in her naked seeing self' (*Henry 5*, 5.2.282–84). Her 'naked seeing self' is of course her vagina, and the 'naked blind boy' is both Henry's erect phallus and the son that he hopes to conceive through it by means of the circle that he will make by rupturing Katherine's maidenhead. This act will be the climax of his glory, the conquest by England of France, yet in *1 Henry 6*, Joan pronounces that 'With Henry's death the English circle ends; / Dispersèd are the glories it included' (1.2.133–37). Henry's 'death' of course is literal, but by pun it is also his sexual climax in the circle, the ultimate ejaculation of his glory, and it is also the symbolic conception of Joan. Had Henry not exploited the female, first in his outlandish claim through descent by his female French ancestor, and then by his sexualized invasion of and seizure of France as his 'wife', Joan would not have been 'born' to become the militant la Pucelle, champion and savior of France. Joan, the visionary, is the center of the conjuring circle, the 'naked seeing self' of the female 'anti-historical' perspective that can disperse the spirit of Henry 5 and deny his patriarchal authority.

In convincing Charles to meet with Joan in *1 Henry 6*, the Bastard of Orleans states that 'What's past and what's to come she can descry' (1.2.57). The historical Joan heeded a prophecy from the ancient past, said to date from Merlin, and repeated by others across time, that France would be lost by a woman and regained by a virgin, and, speaking the will of voices and visions that only she could hear and see, she saw herself, and made others see her as, that virgin, and she did go on correctly to voice prophecies of the future – and Shakespeare himself also correctly prophesizes *her* future: 'Joan la Pucelle shall be France's saint' (1.6.29). The process of Joan's canonization did not begin until 1869, and she was not formally declared a saint until 1920. We of the present may not lay claim to mystical prophetic abilities as did the 'glorious prophetess' of France (1.6.8), but, by reading Shakespeare's history plays, we can better equip ourselves to observe 'the nature of the times deceased' and learn by them to 'prophesy, / With a near aim, of the main chance of things / As yet not come to life, which in their seeds / And weak beginnings lie intreasurèd' and will 'become the hatch and brood of time' (*2 Henry 4*, 3.1.80–6). In the twentieth century, the U.S. made a big splash on the world's stage, and its glories spread in ever-widening circles of influence. In the twenty-first century, U.S. glories, already quickly dispersing in world opinion, are at high risk of turning to naught.

Through Joan, Shakespeare shows that, in trying to predict what will be the 'hatch and brood of time', the oppositional 'female' 'anti-historical' voice *must* be listened to carefully. By means of the ambiguities of Shakespeare's presentation of Joan, we may read her as the 'enemy', one whom the English-speaking power-elite may demonize as an 'evil-doer', but also one whose own culture could valorize as a martyr, and one whose voice, when allowed to be heard by any in the world above the din of slandering Rumor, can articulate the hypocrisies, hollow pretensions, and self-destructiveness of her oppressors' ruling ideology. Joan, however, had not only to combat the English, but also those of her own country who had turned their backs on their true national identity, and we in the U.S. who believe that the Bush administration and its supporters have turned their backs on *our* true national identity can read her as both a positive exemplum and a champion, one whose voice and influence, 'anti-historical' in her own time, has proven to have more historical import over the centuries than that of Talbot or even Henry 5.

As Shakespeare shows us through another female voice in *1 Henry 6*, that of the Countess of Auvergne, a figure like Talbot is merely 'a silly dwarf', a 'weak and writhled shrimp' (2.3.2–23), until his power is magnified by the anonymous soldiers who follow him and thereby constitute his 'substance, sinews, arms, and strength' (2.3.64) that wreak destruction on her country. This idea re-emerges in the Prologue to *Henry 5*: 'a crooked figure [zero] may / Attest in little place a million': it is those who stand behind the figure that increase his or her influence, worth, magnitude, and historical stature, as 'ciphers to this great account' (*Henry 5*, Prologue.15–17) of history, past and present. Those who refuse contribute to dispersing that figure's influence to 'naught'. We are these circles, the ciphers, for it is we who empower the historical figures that we stand behind. Rather than having our circles entirely dispersed, we can line up our 'ciphers' in the oppositional voice's account and hope that a champion of our perspective can be conjured up to lead our column away from naught. Such champions might be seen in Cindy Sheehan and Code Pink and other women's groups in their activist efforts against the Iraq War; others may be found in editor of *The Nation* Katrina vanden Heuvel and progressive radio talk show hosts Randi Rhodes and Rachel Maddow. Though propagandists slander and abuse them, such female champions are emerging and gaining ground. In solidarity with them, Joan, and other Shakespearean female 'anti-historians', I hereby leave my mark: O.

Notes

1. All quotations from Shakespeare's plays are from Bevington's edition. Authorship and date of composition issues had preoccupied many twentieth century scholars who commented on *1 Henry 6*. See Geoffrey Bullough's Introduction to the play in Vol. 4 of his *Narrative and Dramatic Sources of Shakespeare* and Kenneth Muir's *The Sources of Shakespeare's Plays* for summaries of the cases for various collaborators. Bullough acknowledges that 'We cannot be sure that Shakespeare did not write all of *1 Henry 6*' (34), and I not only concur but furthermore regard the cases for various collaborators to be flimsy and based on rather preposterous grounds. Most absurd to me regarding these issues is the basis for positing that Parts *2* and *3* were composed prior to Part *1* being that Talbot is not mentioned in *2* or *3*. One of the main arguments of *1 Henry 6*, in my interpretation, is that the glory of Talbot, like the glory of Henry 5, is fleeting, with the long-range consequences of these imperialistic leaders' ideologies more harmful than beneficial. These points are evident in the epilogue of *Henry 5*, which, in its reference to the *Henry 6* plays, also constitutes a strong argument for Shakespeare's sole or at least main authorship of the first as well as the second tetralogies, all plays of which were included by Shakespeare's actors in the First Folio.
2. See Mark Crispin Miller's book and article (2005, 2006) and the article by Robert F. Kennedy, Jr. (2004).
3. For documentation of the mainstream (i.e., corporate) media's uncritical coverage of the Bush administration from the beginning of the first term until recently, see Eric Boehlert's book; for ongoing monitoring of the problem, see David Brock's website.
4. Phyllis Rackin's book, *Stages of History,* continues the project begun in this article, as does the book she co-authored with Jean Howard, *Engendering a Nation.*

5. Not all readers and critics, of course, share this position; many prefer to believe that Shakespeare glorifies Henry 5 throughout. See Norman Rabkin's insightful analysis of the way in which Shakespeare has constructed the character of Henry 5 as a gestalt figure, the duck-rabbit, which enables interpretation of this king in two entirely contradictory ways. To me it seems that Shakespeare also wrote his character of Joan in this way.
6. Françoise Michaud-Fréjaville notes that 'Various sensitive issues stood in the way of early modern writers' in France in regard to Joan:

   How, for instance, were they to account for the verdict and execution of Joan without exposing the Church as either merciless or misled, and the King as too timid to rescue her from prison, or worse still, envious of the fame won by a mere peasant girl? To give the Pucelle a large share in the eviction of the English armies was to minimize the achievements of Charles the Victorious (as the once retiring Dauphin would henceforth be called) and of his successors, or the validity of a war effort costly enough in men and money not to be wasted on propaganda for a divine mission one could hardly hope to repeat. It would have been inopportune, at any time after 1525, in a country deeply upset by the Reformation, to anathematize a group of clerks for having deluded an innocent girl or themselves. Nor was it advisable to recall the tales of witchcraft used against Joan while the witch hunt against women allegedly possessed by the devil was at its peak, and the least suspicion of occult practices could lead to a trial. (2003, 40)
7. Nina S. Levine comments that 'Radically altering the chronology of his sources, Shakespeare cuts Talbot's life short by nearly a quarter century in order to allow Joan to triumph over his death. That Shakespeare might just as well have allowed Talbot to triumph over Joan at her death, with far less offense to the historical record, raises questions about the political and cultural forces at work in this highly charged scene' (1998, 39).
8. Dominique Goy-Blanquet states that 'Strangely enough, this scene parallels a rumor of no less obscure origin, making Joan an adulterous child of Queen Isabel and her brother-in-law Louis, the Duke of Orleans', thus the Dauphin's half-sister (2003b, 13). She continues that 'Despite any solid evidence and many efforts [by professional historians] to deny it, the bastardy theory, as it is called, still has a few supporters' (2003b, 13). (One may currently find websites supporting the idea.) Intrigued as to the source of the rumor, Goy-Blanquet traced it to Pierre Caze, a 'minor government official in Bergerac' in 1805; thus it was 'a nineteenth-century hoax' that was 'adopted wholesale by a set of gullible amateur historians' (2003b, 13). She believes that Caze took the idea from this scene in Shakespeare's *1 Henry 6* (2003b, 14).
9. Being granted a coat of arms did not induce 'noble' behavior in Joan's brothers. Following her death, they 'participated in a scheme to pass off an imposter as the real Joan, a kind of sideshow. They did it for the money' (Gordon 2000, 2).
10. The historically inaccurate rumor that Joan had claimed to be pregnant was mentioned in *The Brut* and in Holinshed and was employed as an explanation for delaying her execution until gestation time would have expired, as Goy-Blanquet points out (2003b, 12). Although there is no truth behind either idea, Shakespeare uses that of the pregnancy rumor, but not the supposed

leniency granted in the execution's delay, in ways that, I argue, are more favorable to Joan than to the English. Among the charges originally brought against Joan, however, was an accusation of impurity compounded by blasphemy, based on the story that she had boasted to Robert de Baudricourt that 'after her mission was accomplished, she would have three sons, of whom the first should be pope, the second emperor, the third king'. Robert was said to have answered that 'he should like to father one of them himself, but Joan rebuked him, saying her children would be the work of the Holy Spirit'. Not only did Joan deny the charge, but it 'had not been even raised during her interrogation', though the source was cited to be Robert himself (Warner 1981, 108). Perhaps Shakespeare had heard of this story and his treatment of the pregnancy claim is his version of it.

11. As I have elsewhere noted, the 'whore' label, in Shakespeare's works and currently, carries slippery connotations, meaning any of the following:

> professional prostitute, promiscuous woman, woman who has had sexual relations with more than one man; woman who has had or seems to want sexual relations with a man other than the one laying claim to her; woman who has had, or is believed to have had, sexual relations with men, or even only one man, without marriage; woman who, consciously or unconsciously, provokes sexual desire in men; woman who has, or attempts to take or maintain, control over her own sexuality, integrity, or life; and woman who has gone, or has expressed a desire to go, into territories, geographical and/or professional, claimed exclusively for men. But each of these very different meanings slides into the overall connotation of professional prostitute. (Stanton 2000, 81)

Part III

'A kiss is just a kiss'/ Performativities

6

'You'll be the man!': Homophobia and the Present in Performances of *Twelfth Night* and *Romeo and Juliet*

Adrian Kiernander

In this article I examine evidence, taken from the performance history of Shakespeare's *Twelfth Night* and *Romeo and Juliet*, of changes in Western society to the acceptance of public performances of homosexual desire between men. Part of my interest is to see how theater practice can reflect and encourage the evolution of social attitudes toward issues of sexual morality and behavior. I am interested in the intersection of three significant concerns for modern society and scholarship: the role of Shakespeare's plays in performance as a feature of our society around the turn of the twenty-first century; the rapidly changing attitudes towards non-heterosexual and non-monogamous relationships; and the emerging critical move called presentism that has been developed and explored in the work of Terence Hawkes, Hugh Grady, Ewan Fernie and others. One specific aspect of my interest in presentism in this context is to see how the underlying presentist approach is manifested, both similarly and differently, in theater scholarship and theater practice.

It is indisputable that issues of gender and sexuality, current practices in performance and criticism of Shakespeare's plays, and a serious scrutiny of the rapidly changing present moment in which we are living have all become intertwined. Many of the plays themselves repeatedly deal in interesting ways with the diversity and uncontrollability of gender and sexuality. Orsino's line to Viola at the end of *Twelfth Night*, where he says 'while you are a man' rather than the more accurate 'while you are in men's clothes', suggests an awareness of the mutability of sex. This in itself often feels, or can be made to feel in production, both modern and daring; I have argued elsewhere (Kiernander 1998) that one image in *As You Like It* is currently so dangerous as to be all but unperformable in the way that we assume it to have been presented in Shakespeare's own theater. In Act 4, scene 1, what takes place on the stage is a mock wedding between an adult male and a pre-pubescent boy, this theatricalized sacrament conducted by another boy dressed as a woman. It is true that the young actor acting the boy bride is, within the fiction, playing a woman disguised as a boy, but what the audience actually sees is a boy marrying a man; this goes beyond the current controversies about gay marriage between adults, and would be likely to provoke outrage if performed in even the most open-minded parts of the Western world today. If a company performing this image on a stage today were threatened with official censure and legal sanction, part of their defense might be that they were performing a play by Shakespeare under original conditions; however, such an image in a play by a less revered playwright, such as John Lyly, whose *Gallathea* presents other examples of risky sexual playfulness, would not have such an excuse. Contemporary plays dealing in similar ways with these issues could provoke major scandal. Comparable anxieties, less extreme perhaps, might be provoked by boy actors playing roles in scenes from Shakespeare's plays that involve the prospect of explicit sexual activity with an adult male, such as Juliet in Act 3, scene 5, Marina in Act 4, scene 6, of *Pericles* or Innogen in the final scene of *Cymbeline*. This risky portrayal of sexuality, combined with the mainstream popularity and public nature of Shakespeare performance, suggests that the plays of Shakespeare can be a particularly privileged and powerful location for the exploration of dangerous or innovative ideas about sexuality in our time. In this article, I shall be looking at some images that would have been offensive to many people in the recent past but have now become acceptable.

While you are a man, or what you will

My starting point is a photograph of two men kissing.[1] The kiss is passionate, mouth to mouth, bodies charged with energy, though perhaps one of the men seems less engaged than the other; certainly, with one arm awkwardly outstretched, he looks as if his attitude is ambivalent, neither wanting to engage fully, nor to break away. The photo, dating from the early 1980s, is of Ariane Mnouchkine's production at the Théâtre du Soleil of *Twelfth Night* (translated into French as *La Nuit de rois*). It shows Antonio and Sebastian, and I want to use it to illustrate two points regarding theater in the present.

First, the photographed kiss was taking place publicly in the present tense. While there is an element of fiction to the embrace that sets the act in a theatrical locus, Illyria, which is not-here and not-now, there is also the friction of physical contact, the corporeal touch of lip against lip and hand pressed against chest, which is happening on a stage in front of an audience even as they watch. While Fabian might condemn *Twelfth Night* as an improbable fiction, the audience watching two men, Maurice Durozier and Jean-Pierre Marry, had to acknowledge this moment (whether with condemnation or approval) as an undeniable fact. This much is a commonplace understanding of live theater, though an action like an onstage kiss highlights the issue vividly.

But there is a second aspect to this presentness that has more at stake. We know that the occurrence of this kiss meant something in the first half of the 1980s that would mean something different at other times. The physical contact is not only a fact but a complex series of meanings that are located in the period in which the act took place. There is potentially a lot at stake in the theater at moments like this, and the consequences could have been extreme. For example, in New Zealand, where I lived until 1984, and in Queensland, where I moved a few years later, homosexual acts were illegal at the time this production was staged, and kissing in public was forbidden for men. In theory, at least, the two actors could have been arrested and prosecuted in many parts of the world, not for indecently representing an unlawful action (like the mock sodomy in *The Romans in Britain*) but for actually committing one.[2]

A further danger in this act (involving the possible exchange of real bodily fluids) was the question of the transmission of AIDS, which at the time was only coming to be known, and where the possibility of contagion through the saliva had not been ruled out. In the atmosphere of hysteria and uncertainty, the kiss was a particularly dangerous one.

My point here is that this moment in Ariane Mnouchkine's *La Nuit des rois* was, in important ways, new and took place, significantly, in the present. It was certainly not the first time that Antonio's love for Sebastian had been treated as overtly homosexual desire; Laurie E. Osborne (1996, 123) writes that the BBC video that preceded this production by about a year was 'remarkably receptive to the homoeroticism of Antonio's love' (though the expression of sexual desire by Maurice Roëves as Antonio is very understated) and there must have been many live productions around the world at the time where an overtly gay approach was taken, though most of these are unrecorded and unrecoverable; ephemerality and the risk of oblivion are of course one consequence of the presentness of theater.[3] Nevertheless, it seems fairly clear that there is something new happening in this onstage kiss, not least in the suggestion that Antonio's sexual desire for Sebastian has been reciprocated and consummated. In this case, accepting for a moment the traditional association of homosexuality with effeminacy and gender inversion, Sebastian's claim at the end of the play to be both 'maid and man' could take on quite the opposite meaning from what he presumably intends it to signify.[4]

After all, even the question of Antonio's sexuality as represented in the text is unresolved. On the page, it seems almost certain that we have a portrayal of sexual desire, that this is what Shakespeare 'must have meant', and that the play on the stage must have presented the obvious possibility of this reading throughout history. However, perceptions differ; for example, the Royal Shakespeare Company director John Caird argues that Antonio's love for Sebastian cannot possibly be sexual. He concedes (or complains) that the sexualization of Antonio's desire has become commonplace in theater, dating the start of this approach to about 1980, the date of both the BBC video and Mnouchkine's production (Billington 1990, 95–6).

The earlier stage history of the play tells us next to nothing about the way the sexual orientation of Antonio might have been perceived in the past. The first performances of the play about which we have much information seem to have diminished the importance of the characters of Antonio and Sebastian, with the effect that their relationship is not much of an issue (Greif 1982; Osborne 1996). Later performance editions, throughout the nineteenth century and beyond, seem to have deliberately cut some of Antonio's more unambiguously passionate declarations of love so as to avoid any suggestion that the character could be read as homosexual (Osborne 1996, 84). This stage history raises many questions but provides few answers about how the play might have been received in the early years of the seventeenth century; it would be equally easy to argue that Shakespeare and his audience must have read Antonio as sexually engaged with Sebastian, and that they could not possibly have imagined this. Certainly this feature of the play did not raise John Massingham's eyebrows when he recorded his impressions of a performance on 2 February 1601, so if the text he saw was anything like that which survives in the Folio, he found Antonio's desire either sufficiently commonplace as not to require noting, so outrageous as not to be mentioned, so understated that he didn't register it, or simply unthinkable.

If it is the case that Antonio's desire has been a non-issue until recently, that it has been not sexual but rather an intense form of comradeship, this suggests that in our current present day the play means something quite radically different from what it has meant throughout the rest of the 400 years of its life. This may sound like an extreme statement, but the now-almost-unthinkable possibility that actors could at various points of history and geography have been imprisoned or worse for playing the roles in this way suggests that it is not out of the question. If the relationship between the world and the play has changed so much, what are the implications for performance today?

Before looking at questions of staging today, I want to spend a little more time thinking about the changes to how we read sexuality and gender. Terence Hawkes in *Shakespeare in the Present* convincingly argues that one of the issues that preoccupied Shakespeare and those he wrote for was the question of the nation of Great Britain. Hawkes makes a case that the English history plays, especially *Henry 4* and *Henry 5*, are an intervention in the then-current debate about the concepts of England versus Britain, and the awkward place of the Welsh, Scots and Irish within the new nation that was at a significant stage in its development at that time. He points out that now is an appropriate time to explore that debate and Shakespeare's part in it because we can for the first time see it from the outside. He argues that in the late twentieth century the political agenda shifted from national integration to devolution, and that the Great Britain project is now at an end, enabling commentators to view and describe its entire trajectory. While it would be a great exaggeration to announce the death of gender in the same way, it is arguable that the changes in how we perceive issues of sexuality and masculinity are similarly important. Randolph Trumbach's vision of the present day (which he dates back to *c.* 1960) supports the notion that we are living within a different epistemological framework, in terms of gender and sexuality, from that in which the performance traditions for this play were established:

> No-fault divorce, widespread pre-marital sexual relations between men and women who were not engaged to marry, widespread birth control, the expectation that women should have equal pay and equal access to work and that men should share in the duties of childrearing, the decline in prostitution, the control of venereal disease, and the appearance for the first time in most Western societies of a gay and lesbian movement – all these occurred together in a single generation, and in the very same countries that first experienced

around 1700 the modern sexual system that these new forms of behavior have to some extent displaced. (1998, 22)

My own research, with Jonathan Bollen and Bruce Parr, into the changes in theatrical enactments of masculinity in Australian theater since the 1950s shows a parallel 'seismic shift' in the portrayal of gender. Of the items on Trumbach's list, only extra-marital sex is an issue that was performed in front of Australian audiences in the 1950s, or even recognized as a topic for discussion. Mnouchkine's kiss between Antonio and Sebastian is unthinkable in these theaters. I need to note, however, that Trumbach locates the beginning of the previous 'sexual system' at about 1700, a century after *Twelfth Night*. In particular, Trumbach identifies the beginning of the eighteenth century as the origin of the radical split of men's sexualities into homosexual and heterosexual for the first time in history. This might imply that Antonio's desire, and even Sebastian's compliance, might have been seen as less consequential in 1601 than it would have seemed a century later.[5] The play can therefore potentially have had many different shifts of sexual meaning over time.

In this light, I would like to concentrate briefly on questions of masculinity in the script. If Shakespeare was operating in a world different from our own in this regard, and from that of the intervening period, it is interesting to focus on how the play explores the gender possibilities for the male characters. This is a question that is usually, and justifiably, pushed into the background by a focus on the female characters and the lesbian 'dangers' that arise when Olivia falls in love with Cesario. However, when the gender of the characters is examined, the surprise in the script is that, according at least to traditional understandings, there is not a single male character whose masculinity is unproblematic. Orsino is (in most productions) too poetical, unstable and narcissistic, and he fails according to his own criteria for the ideal man's resilience in love. Sir Toby is too dependent on Olivia and Maria, Sir Andrew too much of a loser, and Feste too much an underling and an outsider. Malvolio, starting from a position of domestic servitude and professional asexuality, spectacularly attempts to perform a more overt masculinity, and even more spectacularly fails. Fabian is too inconsequential to register, as are Curio and Valentine. Sebastian and Cesario, on the basis of being attractive to Olivia, are candidates, but they are too close to being boys (if Malvolio's description of Cesario is accurate) to be fully acceptable, and in any case Olivia, like the play itself, is interested in something other than conventional masculinity in men since she falls in love with someone who presents 'himself' as a eunuch, one whose state is signaled even in 'his' name. The one visible difference between the twins in the play is that Sebastian knows how to use a sword and is not terrified when it comes to a fight; otherwise, the script insists that the two are indistinguishable. The play's history is full of references to actresses who were praised for not abandoning their womanliness when playing Cesario, and a few who were criticized for appearing too convincingly like men, so it is hard to see someone who looks, sounds and acts like Viola in drag as masculine.[6] That leaves only Antonio, who would be conventionally masculine were it not that he is devotedly in love with Sebastian. That fact itself would have been enough to disqualify him from manliness until the 1960s, but it is interesting that in every other way he is the epitome of ideal masculinity: he is strong, courageous, outspoken, faithful, generous, and a good fighter. Stephen Orgel perceptively describes him as the only 'real' man in the play (1996, 81). The image of the muscular, macho, and physically active gay man has become recognizable in recent times, but one important question that (regrettably) no amount of historicizing can answer is how this combination of qualities might have been understood by members of Shakespeare's audience in the moment of performance; but, whether his desire was seen by them as sexual or companionate, whether he himself was seen as too masculine, not masculine enough, or just right, there is no permanent place in Shakespeare's Illyria for someone like Antonio. All this, combined with Olivia's foregrounded double bereavement with the deaths of both father and brother, and the problematic femininity of the three female characters, suggests that the play could work in performance today as a dramatic experiment in imagining and representing a society where gender differentiation is attenuated to the point of near non-existence; the image of a beautifully lachrymose, luxurious, and indolent Georges Bigot as Orsino (See Figure 6.1) indicates that this may have been part of Mnouchkine's thinking when she directed the play.[7] It is perhaps only in the past few decades that such a production would be possible and that the radical mutability of gender implied by the phrase 'while you are a man' could be realized on stage.[8]

Thus the new gender world we inhabit has some unexpected implications for performing plays from the past, and especially for comedies. C. L. Barber argued that it is the comic genre, the 'temporary, playful reversal of sexual roles', that explains why 'there is so little that is queasy in all Shakespeare's handling of boys playing women, and playing women pretending to be men' (1963, 245).[9] I, on the contrary, would argue that it is precisely a certain level of queasiness that makes this

Figure 6.1 Georges Bigot as Orsino in a production of *La Nuit des Rois (Twelfth Night)* by the Théâtre du Soleil, Paris, France (1981), directed by Ariane Mnouchkine. Photographer: Martine Franck. Reproduced by permission of Magnum

kind of comedy possible. Comedy provides a safety net that allows the unfamiliar or the unacceptable to be presented in public, because the stakes are perceived to be lower than in tragedy. Consequently the outrageousness or unthinkability of some images – their potential for queasiness – can be excused as inconsequential playfulness. This allows greater free play than in work that is taken more seriously and is more closely scrutinized as a result. In *Twelfth Night*, images of deviant or defective masculinity can be presented in fun, in the carnivalesque, holiday spirit for which the play is famous, and anyone who objects too much might be thought of as approaching the ridiculous condition of Malvolio. The queasiness and the comedy are mutually supportive: not only does the comedy excuse the unease that transgressive acts can generate (and that seems potentially to have worried Barber), but the queasiness itself generates much of the comedy, the sudden bursts of laughter that erupt out of the *frisson* of shock or horror. To this extent the necessary laughs that are the currency exchanged for tickets at the box office are dependent on audience members, collectively, experiencing the titillation of momentary queasiness. But one of theater's ongoing problems, to which new solutions continuously have to be found, is that shock wears off. When social conditions change as rapidly as they have over the past 40 years, images of outrage quickly pass their expiration date, in which case the performers need to find new sources of surprise or the play can simply go flat.

In the case of Australia's Bell Shakespeare Company, based in the home town of the Sydney Lesbian and Gay Mardi Gras (which began in 1978 and is itself an important symbol of the change in Australian society since the 1950s), the excitement of the near-lesbian encounter of Viola and Olivia and the idea of a kiss between Antonio and Sebastian looked old hat by 1995 when David Fenton directed a production of *Twelfth Night*. The company had already created as much sensation as was likely with a kiss between the other Antonio and Bassanio in a 1991 production of *The Merchant of Venice* that had provoked some schoolteachers to walk out of the production in the first scene, taking their students with them. In the new present, the shock of transgression had to be found elsewhere than the relationship between Antonio and Sebastian. It found a location in John Bell's portrayal of Malvolio in the cross-gartering scene. Here the production generated riotous laughter, at the time, by bringing on Bell, the founder of the company and Australia's most established classical actor, wearing high heels and lacy suspenders. The customary cross-class-dressing where the sober servant appears in the dress of a flamboyant young nobleman had been replaced

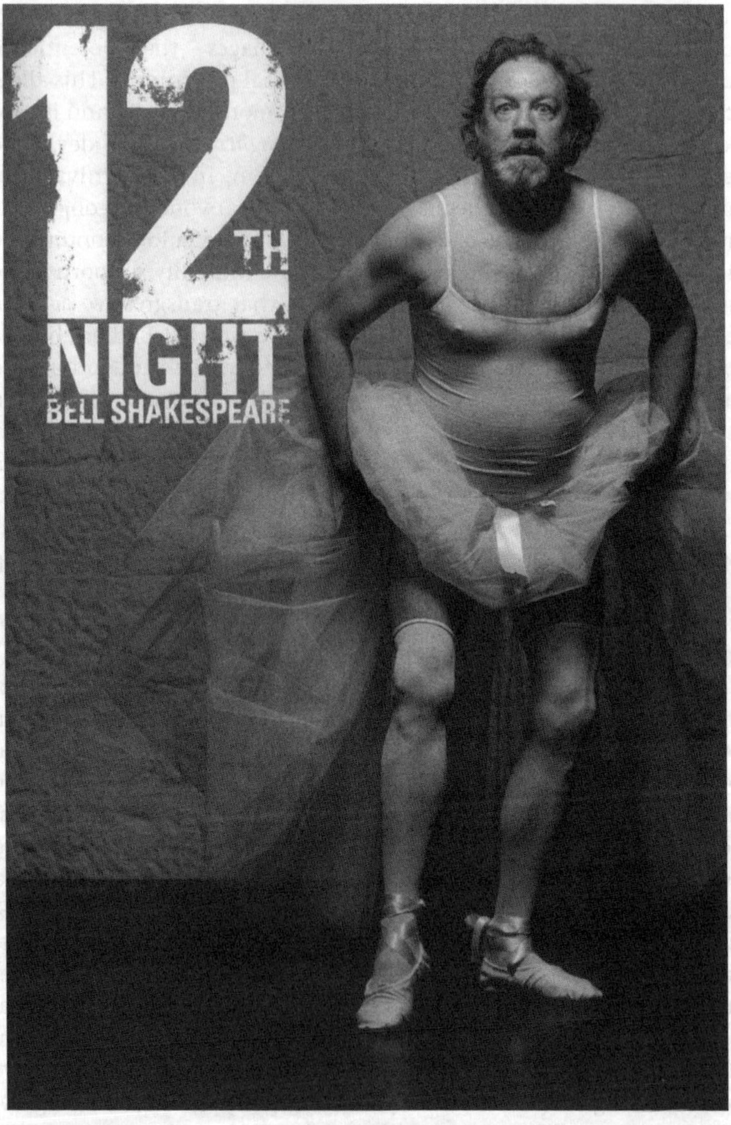

Figure 6.2 Bille Brown as Malvolio in an advance publicity campaign for a production of *Twelfth Night* by the Bell Shakespeare Company, Sydney, Australia (2004), directed by David Freeman. Photographer: Jez Smith. Art direction: Paul Clark. Reproduced by permission of Omee

by cross-gender transvestitism. It was that moment which most distinguished that production and, arguably, guaranteed its notoriety and success.

This image itself has now become dated. The play was staged again by the same company towards the end of 2004 in a new production by David Freeman, with Bille Brown as Malvolio. The publicity photos, created for the season launch a year earlier in 2003 and reproduced on the cover of the program, suggested that a similar approach had been considered. The play was illustrated by a shot of Brown caught in a moment of panic as if he had been taken by surprise while trying on a tutu (See Figure 6.2). The picture is rich, suggestive not only of the cross-gartering scene, but also the guilt-ridden secret life that is evident in many of the characters. However, by the time Freeman came to direct the show nearly a year after the photograph was shot, the thrill of that image had gone. In the production there was no hint of Malvolio cross-dressing, and the cross-gartered yellow stockings were just that.

Antonio's kiss is no longer seen as likely to spread contagion, physical or moral. There are surely other transgressive images that directors will find in *Twelfth Night* to generate nervous laughter in future productions, but if at some point in the future they run out there is a likelihood that the play will become tame and lose its power to intervene in the issues and debates of its present day. Plays do die. If our society continues to evolve in the direction it has been taking over the past 50 years, the gender play will certainly lose its *frisson* and much of its comedy. However, we also need to be aware of the possibility that the current rise of conservative politics and the revival of the religious right means that there is a new Malvolio, moralistic and Puritanical, waiting to take revenge on the whole pack of us. In that case there could be a revitalized role for plays like *Twelfth Night*.

Southern-crossed lovers

When Baz Luhrmann released his film, *William Shakespeare's Romeo + Juliet*, it was regarded variously as daring, sensational, a travesty of Shakespeare, but above all, popular because it was located in the present. While Luhrmann's achievements in this film are highly cinematic, it needs to be remembered that he began work as a director in live theater, achieving success in Australia with productions including *Strictly Ballroom* in 1988 (which he co-wrote as a stage work, and then filmed in 1992). For the Australian Opera he directed *La Boheme* and Britten's *A Midsummer Night's Dream*, both of which productions have toured internationally.

Luhrmann was trained in theater at the Australian National Institute for Dramatic Art (NIDA) in the mid 1980s, where he was exposed to a tradition of spectacular 'larrikin' productions, closely connected with NIDA itself, which dated back some 15 years to the early 1970s.

John Bell, who played Malvolio in the 1995 production discussed earlier, is an important figure in this genealogy of theater practice. He had a huge popular success with his 1970 production at NIDA of *The Legend of King O'Malley*, performed in a highly energized, vaudeville-based style. This production ostensibly dealt with the biography of an American-born confidence man who became a prominent Australian politician at the time of Federation in 1901, but it achieved much of its popularity because it addressed the topical issue of military conscription, which in 1970 was a lively and very current topic in Australia. The success of this play gave Bell and a group of colleagues the confidence to form a new, alternative theater company, the Nimrod, in 1970, devoted to revitalizing what was perceived as a largely moribund Sydney theater scene, considered a pale imitation of English theater. The aim of the Nimrod was to produce theater specifically for Australians, using two closely related strategies: the development and production of new scripts by Australian playwrights, and the staging of (mainly European) classics, especially Shakespeare, in ways that seemed appropriate to present-day Australian conditions. In practice, this meant a recourse to the popular traditions of theater that had flourished in Australia since the nineteenth century, such as melodrama, burlesque, and especially vaudeville and the circus. It also meant staging productions of classic plays that directly intersected with the concerns, the world and the time of the audience.

While at the Nimrod, Bell experimented with a range of approaches to the classics, and achieved success in a 1975 production of *Much Ado about Nothing*. Bell made the actors experiment with using extreme, exaggerated Italian accents as a rehearsal technique because he was concerned that their intimidation when confronted by Shakespearean language was restricting them both vocally and physically. A decision was taken during the rehearsals to perform in these accents, and the production proved popular and influential. Part of its success was due to the growing visibility and acceptance in Australian culture of the Italian immigrants who had arrived in large numbers after the end of World War 2, so a comedy by Shakespeare performed in Italian accents became a celebratory representation of a new Australia.

The first attempt to bring the qualities of irreverent energy and physicality into the world of Shakespearean tragedy was in 1979 with

Bell's production of *Romeo and Juliet*, starring the soon-to-be-famous Mel Gibson and Angela Punch in the title roles.

Unfortunately, there is little direct surviving evidence of the production, but some important features of its style can still be discerned. The casting of Mel Gibson as Romeo was a significant production choice; the first *Lethal Weapon* film was still nine years in the future, but as an actor he already had many of the qualities that would make him an action hero, a rugged and physical masculinity that reflected an Australian fantasy of ideal manhood. At the time Gibson was a year out of NIDA, and he had finished filming the first *Mad Max* movie, although it was not released until a month and a half after the opening night of *Romeo and Juliet*. (Indeed, the Sydney season of *Romeo and Juliet* was extended, and it transferred from the Nimrod's home base at Belvoir Street to the larger York Theater at Sydney University's Seymour Centre a week after *Mad Max* opened.) Nevertheless, as Bell has confirmed, Gibson's qualities as an active and overtly masculine actor were factors in casting him in the role of Romeo. Bell has said that Gibson's Romeo had his feet on the ground, that he was never effete, daydreamy or off the planet (Bell 2004).

At this moment in Australian history homophobia was a strong part of the accepted image of the Australian male – this was only one year after the first Sydney Mardi Gras. It seems that the production was setting out to dispel any perceived association between Shakespearean theater and the stereotype of arty homosexuality – Bell in his autobiography has acknowledged that the '"straight" acting fraternity' at the time was fairly homophobic (2002, 113). To achieve this, it reinforced the sense of vigorous and arguably homophobic masculinity in all of the male characters. This included Romeo himself, who often comes across as suspiciously sensitive even in productions that are otherwise emphatically macho. The apparent anxiety about homosexuality was reinforced by sexual taunts, including a moment of mock-sexual horseplay designed for comic effect between Mercutio (played by Drew Forsythe) and Benvolio (played by a very young and fresh-faced Michael Smith).

Part of Bell's overall approach was influenced by the successful Zeffirelli stage production in 1960 with John Stride and Judi Dench for the Old Vic. By contrast, it is clear that the later Zeffirelli film (1968) was not an important influence on this aspect of Bell's work, given its beautiful but extremely daydreamy Romeo (Leonard Whiting) who makes his first appearance holding a flower in his hand. Bell has said that he recalls hearing the observation that in the stage production Zeffirelli took the English theater world by surprise by doing the one thing that was most obvious: setting the play in Italy (2004). Of course traditional productions paid lip service to the location in Verona, but the performances, according to Bell, had been thoroughly English, with English voices, English physical reserve (with a focus on the play's poetic language rather than its physically exuberant situations), and a class hierarchy based on the English model of the time. What Bell found exciting in Zeffirelli's production was a willingness to take the Italian setting into the performances themselves, into the relationships between characters and into the presentation of street life, so that the actors didn't look and sound like English men and women in fancy dress but found a more open and emphatic, extroverted quality in both their speaking of the language and their movement and gesture.

That the conventional British approach was also current in Australia is evidenced by a full-length (though heavily cut) Australian Broadcasting Corporation television version directed by Oscar Whitbread, made in 1967 (the year before Zeffirelli's film). This is a thoroughly competent and largely unsurprising production featuring Sean Scully as Romeo and Helmut Bakaitis as Paris which provides Italianate architecture in the sets and traditionally Italian renaissance costumes; however, despite a promisingly energetic street brawl in the opening sequences, the performances quickly settle down into something that looks conventionally English. The most unexpected feature of the staging comes at the start of the final scene, where Romeo lingers over the dead body of Paris with surprising reverence and tenderness, suggestive of the kind of homoeroticism that Bell and Gibson seemed to want to work against.

Zeffirelli's breach with this tradition is very much what Bell carried over into his production at the Nimrod. Having achieved success with high-voltage comedy in *Much Ado*, this was a chance to transfer the technique into tragedy. Taking his cue from Zeffirelli's stage production, Bell aimed to make the young males in the play not aristocrats but street kids, 'bovver boys', using violent and vengeful body language. He went all out to make them a 'butch bunch of guys' (2004). However, there was a potential problem with a perceived ambiguity about the gender of Mediterranean men in Australia at the time: on the one hand, they seemed to perform a successfully heterosexual masculinity that was aggressive and pugnacious, ostentatiously muscular, and modern, but at the same time, they were seen as suspiciously feminized – emotional, volatile, flamboyant, and preoccupied with physical appearance. Bell wanted to emphasize the first aspects of the stereotype while avoiding the second, which were also easily associated with stereotypes of male actors – hence the need for a Romeo whose masculinity and heterosexuality were beyond question.

The costumes for Bell's Nimrod production were modernized but with an Italian feel, the young men wearing leather trousers and open shirts showing bare chests. The physicality of the production was so marked that one critic, H. G. Kippax, was moved to ask querulously, 'Why, among the young men, can nobody speak to anybody without slapping or punching or hugging him? Why is almost every cue to speak a cue to jump about? Why does social life in Verona look like a romp on Bondi beach?' (1979). Given the similarities between Sydney's Bondi beach and Venice beach in Los Angeles, Kippax's question and Bell's production both startlingly prefigure Luhrmann's approach some 20 years later. The prompt copy in the Mitchell Library confirms some of this crude physicality with notes for actors to grab their crotches while speaking bawdy lines.

Reviews of the time confirm the rhetoric of a new way of performing Shakespeare: one review praised the Australian vitality of the production which was 'certainly not typical of London or New York', highlighted the 'impetuosity and physical agility' of Mel Gibson, and described the minor roles as having been played with 'an exuberance not always polished, but which is never emasculated, as many of Shakespeare's characters seem unfortunately to be in other productions' (T. S. 1979).

There are many ways in which Luhrmann's film seems in accord with Bell's production decisions, most notably the testosterone-driven posturing and violence of the young male characters. Perhaps the most radical aspect of Bell's production also seems to have been an influence on Luhrmann. Bell was himself excited by and responded to a piece of scholarly commentary written by his former contemporary at Sydney University, Germaine Greer. In an article entitled 'Juliet's Wedding', Greer had written of this play,

> The extraordinary thing is that in a play which is, in itself, not a tragedy, in terms of its own structure not tragic, a character of true tragic dimensions emerges – young Juliet – and she herself makes of her co-protagonist also a hero, which by himself he would never have become. I believe that 'Romeo and Juliet' is a play written by a master poet, who had very little to learn about the medium of poetry, but who had not yet become a master dramatist. It is not a real tragedy, but it contains true tragic characters. (1979)

This paragraph, and especially the last sentence, clearly impressed itself on Bell in his thinking about the play – it was quoted in the program for the premiere season in Perth – though regrettably it did not result in a greater focus on the tragic character of Juliet. In practice, Bell responded more to Greer's insight that the play does not have a conventional tragic structure. This allowed him to think of it not as a star-crossed tragedy, as Zeffirelli had done in the film, but rather as a riotous and ribald comedy right up to the point where Mercutio is accidentally killed, an event that should ideally, according to Bell, come as a shock not only to the characters but also to the audience. In Bell's production, the interval was delayed until this point, a feature that has its equivalent with a fade to black at the same place in Luhrmann's film. Gibson, as well as resisting the traditionally effete characterization, has a good comic sense as an actor, and this enabled him, according to Bell, to perform some of Romeo's early scenes as a 'dopey teenager' which formed part of the production's more general comic horseplay in the first half (2004).

This radical view of the structure of the play lies clearly within the Australian tradition that Bell himself was consciously reworking and one that helped shape the treatment that Luhrmann brought to his film. Like Bell's, Luhrmann's reading of the play shows an initially comic vision of Verona, not only in the obvious sections involving Miriam Margolyes as the Nurse and Harold Perrineau's entertaining flamboyance as Mercutio, but also where the young men pose, show off and romp in a way that is recognizable as overdone and ridiculous, where Juliet's mother is a figure of pretentious fun filmed briefly in silent-comedy-style fast motion, and where the overall world of the play changes from a lighthearted bawdy romp towards darker, more serious and adult concerns at the moment when death and sex enter the action, almost simultaneously, for the first time. It is a strong dramatic structure to work with, and one that served Luhrmann well in the film.

Nevertheless, with the casting of the very boyish Leonardo di Caprio as Romeo, Luhrmann took a very different approach than Bell with regard to the performance of homophobia. Luhrmann's film was not afraid of the suggestion of homosexuality in the world of the play, or even in Romeo himself; the film places Romeo, while under the influence of drugs, in a men's toilet at just the moment before he first sees Juliet. The film seems to suggest that Romeo, perhaps influenced by his friendship with an overtly campy Mercutio who attends the Capulet ball in drag, could go either way, and that it is the sight of Juliet that sets him on the tragic path he will follow until the end. These features of the film suggest a much greater acceptance by audiences of sexual diversity. The shift from a ruggedly muscular to a boyishly pretty Romeo – an image that the Bell production could not have accepted at the time – parallels a wider shift in Australian representations of gender on stage towards less differentiation between masculine and feminine. It also allowed Claire Danes as Juliet greater prominence compared with di Caprio than Angela Punch was able to achieve alongside the more dominant Gibson.

The performances I have discussed in this essay have in common a desire to revitalize Shakespeare's plays by bringing them radically into the present day, and adapting or refocusing them so that they directly reflect current concerns, especially those dealing with the performance of gender and social changes regarding homophobia. However, this acknowledgment of the present when performing Shakespeare is not something that happens naturally or inevitably in theater practice; some productions are much more consciously concerned with present-day issues than others and the mere fact of liveness is not enough to make a performance presentist in any meaningful way. Here lies one of the differences between theater practice and theater scholarship. Whereas most scholarly criticism of work from the past can be seen as either presentist or historicist in its approach – and of course the work of some scholars combines both – much theater practice takes neither of these approaches seriously. There is very little genuine historicism in theater performance; theater has no real equivalent of those musicians who perform on period instruments and try rigorously to replicate original practice. However carefully researched a traditionalist production of a classic play might be, the historical data will normally be used as just one means of understanding the text more fully. Conversely, many modernizing productions introduce superficial references from the present, either inadvertently or as a way of amusing the audience, while preferring to leave unexplored any really significant parallels between texts from the past and concerns of the present. What interests me are those rarer examples of theater practice that successfully achieve the more difficult task of using the plays of Shakespeare to speak directly and urgently to us now.

Notes

Parts of this article were given at the annual meeting of the Shakespeare Association of America in Bermuda in 2005 and at the World Shakespeare Congress in Brisbane in 2006 in seminars led by Evelyn Gajowski and myself. I am indebted to the research project 'Marking Masculinities', funded by the Australian Research Council, and to my research partners Jonathan Bollen and

Bruce Parr, for whose contribution and collaboration I am very grateful. I am also very happy to acknowledge Jeremy Gadd, whose research into the video records of Australian theater practices within the 'Stage on Screen' project has been invaluable.

1. Neuschäfer and Serror (1984, 38).
2. The shock value of men kissing is considerable. When the law regarding homosexual acts was finally being changed in the Queensland parliament, there was a group of gay activists in the gallery watching the debate. After the vote was passed, one of the more progressive MPs invited the group for celebratory drinks (in a venue in Parliament House called the Strangers Bar). On the way to the bar there was a small, impromptu celebration which led to one of the tabloid newspapers the next day screaming all over its front page, 'GAYS KISS IN PARLIAMENT' (*The Sun*, 29 November 1990).
3. In the mid-1970s, I took part in an eclectic, high-concept production in Auckland by a politically active gay director in which the Antonio was presented as a Saint Sebastian martyr figure dressed in a loincloth.
4. I assume that in this line Sebastian thinks he is declaring his own virginity.
5. Stephen Orgel makes the point that the Elizabethan gender and sexuality system was relatively mutable, perhaps closer to what has (re)emerged in the past 40 years than to the way it was understood between about 1700 and the mid twentieth century (1996). However, it would be misleading to think of Renaissance and present-day concepts as identical.
6. Greif notes, for example, that in 1850 Ellen Kean's dress and manner 'preserved the womanly qualities in Viola's nature... in a style attuned to Victorian tastes', and that according to one critic, 'Mrs. Kean never for a moment forgets the modesty and reserve of her sex'; but even here 'there were some gentlemen of the press who would have liked Mrs. Kean to play Viola with even less vivacity' (1982, 80). On the other hand, Charlotte Cushman in 1846 was criticized because 'her male disguise suited her too well' (1982, 67).
7. Mnouchkine's first idea for *Twelfth Night* was to give it an entirely female cast, partly in the interests of gender equity, since male actors took all the major roles in the other two plays in the Shakespeare cycle, *Richard 2* and *1 Henry 4*. However, she abandoned this idea when she felt it didn't work in rehearsal. Perhaps, paradoxically, it takes male actors to play an explicit lack of masculinity on the stage.
8. Judith Butler's *Undoing Gender* (2004), argues that the complication and dismantling of the distinctions in our gender system are still proceeding.
9. I am interested in Barber's assessment of the play that was first published in 1959, the year before Trumbach dates the 'seismic shift' in ways of thinking about gender. Barber at that time reads *Twelfth Night's* 'fundamental distinction' as that of 'bring[ing] home to us... the difference between men and women'. Five decades later, my reading comes to exactly the opposite conclusion.

7

'My hand is ready, may it do him ease': Shakespeare and the Theater of Display

Michael Mangan

Prologue: the past is another country – and so is the present

In his introduction to *Shakespeare in the Present*, Terence Hawkes reclaims, in the face of historicist mistrust, 'presentism' as a critical strategy in Shakespeare studies. It must be, he argues, a theorized strategy, not a simple assumption or assertion that Shakespeare is our contemporary. It must be a strategy that 'will not yearn to speak with the dead [but will aim] to talk to the living' (2002, 4). And his words are heartening, since in performance theater is always and necessarily presentist. Hawkes recognizes this, and goes on to stipulate that

> placing emphasis on the present can't help but connect fruitfully with the current realignment of critical responses that stresses the *performance* of a play as much as its 'reference'.... Presentism thus highlights what has been termed drama's 'performative' function. (2002, 5)

Hawkes's broader thesis – that presentism makes it possible to reverse the chronology of causality, to ask questions about the influence of the present upon the past – resonates with the re-creative act of making theater, which has always needed to negotiate the influence of the present upon the past as well as *vice versa* in its search for what Milhouse and Hume call 'producible interpretations' (1985, passim).

In the theater, Shakespeare has been played in what used to be called 'modern dress' ever since the days of the first Globe, when the

Lord Chamberlain's men, like their colleagues in rival companies, played the parts of long-dead kings and earls while wearing the just-out-of-fashion cast-off clothes of the contemporary London aristocracy. In the late nineteenth and early twentieth centuries, following a spate of 'historically accurate' productions from Chronegk and the Meininger company onwards (productions which were largely designed to restore the Bard's intentions to center stage), the default design position became the historicized one. Consequently, to choose anything other than a basically Elizabethan costume and setting was always possible, but had the effect of making some sort of interpretive statement about the play's meaning. Theater design and scenography have moved on from there in more recent years, and the theatrical semiotics of the everyday has become more sophisticated. Modern dress no longer seems shocking. (Does it?) Even so, the point where the visual image intersects with the spoken text is still where the creative spark of meaning is most clearly seen to flash. With this in mind, then, I want to take a single, highly gestural, moment from one Shakespeare play and dress it up in some very modern-day clothes.

Kate's final speech in *The Taming of the Shrew* ends with the following advice to her 'sisters':

> Then vail your stomachs, for it is no boot
> And place your hands below your husband's foot.
> In token of which duty, if he please,
> My hand is ready, may it do him ease.
>
> (5.2.177–80)[1]

At which point, traditionally, she offers to do just that – to put her hand beneath her husband's foot. Let us experiment with a presentist reading of this dramatic *gestus* by way of an imaginary design suggestion. Let us place the scene in a contemporary fetish club – in London, New York, Los Angeles, or Sydney.[2] Let us give Petruchio all the leather regalia of a sadomasochistic 'top' – complete with a whip to crack and handcuffs hanging from his belt.[3] And let us give Kate (definitely 'Kate', the diminutive name by which Petruchio addresses her) a correspondingly submissive outfit – in rubber perhaps, or, if we are being completely stereotyped, with a hint of the maid's uniform about it. And let us imagine the look that passes between them as being the collusive look of two people playing (extremely well) the game of sadomasochistic submission and dominance, speaking to each other an erotic language of power and sexual role-play which they understand fully and the bystanders do not. And – if you wouldn't mind – now hold that thought, while I explain what I'm trying to do here.

Concept and etymology

The phrase in my title, 'theatre of display', is taken from Marjorie Garber's provocative, playful, and serious essay, 'Fetish Envy', in which she argues that 'fetishism is a kind of theater of display – and indeed that theater represents an enactment of the fetishistic scenario'. Concluding with the judgment that fetishism is 'foundational to theater itself' (1990a, 56), Garber focuses largely on questions of cross-dressing. This essay takes both a wider and a narrower approach to explore the implications of Garber's contention, asking questions both about fetishism as a 'theatre of display' and about the strategies of presentism as an approach to Shakespeare. It looks at the larger question of theater and the concept of fetishism, exploring the possibilities inherent in applying the notion to a particular play.

The concept, like many complex terms in cultural analysis, is sometimes quite strictly and narrowly defined; sometimes applied more broadly. (Perhaps it might be more accurate to say that there is both a strong and a weak sense of the word.) This is a consequence, in part at least, of the word's own complex and rather confused etymology, inherent within which is a series of intercultural contradictions, paradoxes and ambiguities. Its origins lie in eighteenth century imperial attempts (and failures) on the part of Western travelers to understand the cultures and religious practices of Central West Africa. The accounts of early Portuguese encounters with tribal Africans talked of their use of *feitiço* – a charm – and the West African pidgin term *fetisso* seems to be a later development of this. The word was employed as a pejorative term, to refer to the use of 'power objects', usually small figures which are seen as having the mystical – or magical – ability to protect their wearer from evil influences; they are imbued with spiritual potency, deriving from an animistic sense that they embody the spirit (at least in the case of the crucifix) of a deity. Linking this with their own ideas about witchcraft and magic, Western commentators inevitably interpreted this as evidence of the primitive and idolatrous nature of such African religious practices, as opposed to the presumed absolute truth embodied in Christian doctrine. During the nineteenth-century colonization of Africa, this contributed to the ideological construction of the African subject as a superstitious and inferior heathen who, in the words of the hymn, 'bows down to wood and stone'. In fact, these early explorers, traders, missionaries and proto-ethnologists consistently oversimplified and misunderstood the nature and variety of West African fetish beliefs and practices. Ironically, there is evidence to suggest that some of the tribal fetishes described by the early Portuguese adventurers were themselves constructed in imitation of crucifixes seen by tribesmen in encounters with even earlier Christians. The notion of the 'fetish', then, is surrounded by semantic and semiotic confusion from the moments of its first usage in European thought. It is a term which marks the failure of one culture to understand another, one indeed which 'is firmly anchored in the space between cultures, one of the most potent zones of misunderstanding', as John Mack points out (1995, 28).

Cultural theory

Over the last few years, the word has found its way into our mainstream cultural and critical/analytical vocabulary. Borrowed from anthropology, the word was inflected in significantly different ways by both Marx and Freud. In Volume One of *Capital*, Marx uses the term metaphorically, introducing the concept of commodity fetishism. He argues that

> when goods are produced for exchange on the market they come to be seen not only as articles of utility, with a 'use value', but also as inherently valuable objects with special 'mystical' qualities.... Marx describes this as fetishism because, as in religion, a human product... acquires a life of its own, and enters into relations both with other things of its kind, and with the human race. (quoted in Gamman and Makinen 1994, 28)[4]

Freud's rather different notion of sexual or pathological fetishism is closer to the way in which the word is now understood in everyday usage. Freud defines fetishism in terms of erotic arousal which becomes focused upon an inanimate object or a part of the body rather than upon a person. In his 1927 paper, 'Fetishism', he gives a psychoanalytic explanation of pathological sexual fetishism in terms of its subconscious origin in a disavowal of male castration anxiety:

> In every instance, the meaning and the purpose of the fetish turned out, in analysis, to be the same. It revealed itself so naturally and seemed to me so compelling that I am prepared to expect the same in all cases of fetishism. When now I announce that the fetish is a

> substitute for the penis, I shall certainly create disappointment; so I hasten to add that it is not a substitute for any chance penis, but for a particular and quite special penis that had been extremely important in early childhood but had later been lost. That is to say, it should normally have been given up, but the fetish is precisely designed to preserve it from extinction. To put it more plainly: the fetish is a substitute for the woman's (the mother's) penis that the little boy once believed in and – for reasons familiar to us – does not want to give up. ([1927] 1961, 1995, 152–53)

The implicit assumption, that sexual fetishism is an exclusively male attribute, was held by classical Freudian theorists in the teeth of evidence to the contrary. Oddly, the Lacanian psychoanalytic reaction, which in wider terms replaced the penis by the phallus and the anatomical/biological model of psycho-sexual development by the representational/symbolic model, largely left this assumption intact, attributed (like Freud) the ownership of desire to men. Recent work by feminist theorists, however, has all but destroyed Freud's phallocentric assumption. Developing, revising, and occasionally conflating these initial insights of Freud and Marx, cultural theorists, scholars, and critics have used the term as a way of exploring a wide variety of cultural and historical issues. This has resulted in a steady stream of books and articles about fetishism and cultural theory: fetishism and nineteenth century French and English literatures (Apter 1990; Schor 1988; Pike 1992; McLaverty 1981), fashion and fetishism (Kunzle 1982), fetishism and the imagination (Simpson 1982), fetishism and consumer culture (Cagle 1994), fetishism and Jean Cocteau (Gercke 1993), fetishism and Henry Fielding (Nickel 1992), fetishism as cultural discourse (Apter and Pietz 1993), the work of art as fetish (Bourdieu 1988), fetishism in Marlowe's *Edward 2* (Thurn 1990), Shakespeare as fetish (Garber 1990a, 1990b), fetishism in popular culture (Browne 1982), and, in the work of too many writers to list, fetishism and film theory from Laura Mulvey onwards (Mulvey 1993).

Across this range of work, the word has occasionally been used with a strictly Marxian inflection, more frequently with a strictly psychoanalytic one, and most often in the way that I intend it to be understood here: as something that brings together the socio-economic and the psycho-sexual, and that indicates and includes a broad continuum of sexual identities, orientations and behaviors in which the concept of power is foregrounded: from fixation on some kind of *objectum sexualis*, through the transgendered, to the sadomasochistic.

Foundational to theater itself?

It is in this context, concentrating on female-to-male cross-dressing in Shakespeare, that Garber contends

> that fetishism is a kind of theater of display – and indeed, that theater represents an enactment of the fetishistic scenario. Thus Freud's 'penis', the anatomical object, though understood through Lacan's 'phallus', the structuring mark of desire, becomes reliteralized as a stage prop, a detachable object. No one has the phallus... [The transvestite in Shakespeare is] not an accident of historical contingency but the necessary intervention that makes fetishism not only possible but foundational to theater itself. (1990a, 'Fetish', 47, 56)

What are we to make of this provocative claim? I find myself in a spirit of cautious agreement with Garber that there may indeed be something about the fetishistic gesture that *is* fundamental to theater, although my emphasis would be different than hers. She argues her case from a position which is rooted in Freudian/Lacanian theory and makes female-to-male transvestism the key to her argument. My own understanding would depend less on the isolation and foregrounding of female-to-male transvestism in Shakespeare and would turn less on the question of who, if anybody, has the phallus. It is more related to the broader sense of the word outlined above.

Similar points have been made before in a slightly different vocabulary: theater semioticians from Shakespeare himself onwards have alerted us to the idea that theatrical representation operates in a way which is essentially metonymic: the single bush stands in for the entire Forest of Arden, one man makes the imaginary puissance of a thousand soldiers, and so on. Metonymy is also the mode by which the classical sexual fetishism of the *objectum sexualis* operates, since it too maintains a focus upon the significant part (the foot, the knee) or associated item (the clothing) rather than attempting to encompass the whole. Yet metonymy is a weak term, and it omits what is surely the essential feature of performance, the influence of the audience in the process. Theatrical representation is more accurately described as a fetishistic process rather than a metonymic one, since the term more powerfully evokes the ritualistic investment of what happens on the stage with the psychic power which gives it the meaning in the first place. To the extent that the theatrical experience is essentially an erotic one, then it is a fetishized eroticism, in which the desiring that takes place between audience and stage is heavily encoded. Theatrical meaning depends upon displacement, the ways in which an object, or an attribute, or a process is singled out in some way and invested psychically with power, whether that power is seen as magical, ideological or erotic. This sounds, at first hearing, like the old idea of theatrical metaphor or symbol; but in fact it is not. With metaphor and symbol the tendency is always to look beyond the signifier to the signified; fetishistic displacement, in contrast, focuses more intently upon the signifier itself and attributes the power of the signified to it. This, I believe, is a quintessentially theatrical mode of knowing. But beyond that, the interpretation of meaning depends upon a series of sub-codes which are always culturally specific, and which may be local or even personal and secret. Fetishistic meaning thus effectively becomes a code in itself. It is the system – or series of systems – which governs the very structures and processes of displacement, and which makes possible the expression and interpretation of theatrical meaning.

In this broad sense, then, I would argue for the importance of the term in any consideration of theatrical representation. In a similar way, the relationship between Shakespeare the cultural icon, the product of the Shakespeare industry and a classical Marxian commodity fetishism seems uncontentious: his own quasi-magical transformation into an 'inherently valuable object with special "mystical" qualities' has been sufficiently written about. What happens, though, when we begin to apply this very 'present' notion of fetishism to our interpretation of individual plays?

Interpretive strategies

Different plays may invite, or elicit, different kinds of interpretive strategies, and it is unlikely that any single contemporary critical/theoretical position – presentist, psychoanalytical, deconstructive, new historicist – will find that it fits all plays equally well. (Psychoanalysis, to take a very crude example, has traditionally had a field day with *Hamlet* but has, on the whole, been less illuminating about *The Merry Wives of Windsor*.) As far as presentism is concerned, it may be that those plays that are most likely to stir us to respond in a presentist mode are those that we find most uncomfortable. Post-Holocaust Shakespearean studies, for example, have struggled with *The Merchant of Venice* precisely because of the ways in which that play makes us aware of our historical 'situatedness'. In terms of gender politics, *The Taming of the Shrew* has spoken to a generation of feminists and post-feminists in a very different way from that in which it spoke to their predecessors, precisely because it has thrown into stark relief the differences and disjunctions between past text and present structures of belief. And, of course, one consequence of this has been a fierce historicization of the play: an insistence (I have done this in some of my own previous writing on *The Taming of the Shrew*) that to understand it we have to read it in its contemporary context, to invoke Filmer's *Patriarcha* ([ca. 1630] 1949), *A Godly Form of Household Government* (Cleaver 1598), *An Homily of the State of Matrimony* ([1563] McDonald 1996), and other such contextualizing documents. But what would a presentist approach to this play look like: one which is 'informed by a heightened awareness of our situatedness', and which looks for ways in which this engagement with our historical specificity might inform our understanding of previous sexualities?

A theatrical sexuality

It is at this point that we return to the concept of fetishism. In terms of gender and sexual politics, fetishism, too, is a relatively new kid on the block. There seems to be something particularly presentist about fetishism itself. Its own 'situatedness' is to do with a style of sexual orientation and gender identity which has only comparatively recently been foregrounded and articulated. To reframe the Kate–Petruchio relationship in terms of an increasingly self-aware relationship between two people who are exploring, and eventually claiming, the sadomasochistic roles of dominant and submissive certainly gives us a producible interpretation of the play, and one which effects 'a recuperation of Kate as a woman with agency', as Taunton puts it, 'rather than as a victim' (1996). The centrality of role-playing to the fetishism of sadomasochism – that most theatricalized of sexualities – is matched by the centrality of role-playing in *The Taming of the Shrew*. This is not uncommon in Shakespearean dramaturgy, of course, but *The Taming of the Shrew* is one of the plays in which the concept is particularly relentlessly exploited and explored. Indeed, the main body of the play is *all* role-playing, since it is the 'pleasant comedy' played out for the supposedly therapeutic benefit of Christopher Sly. And within this metatheatrical framework are enacted familiar Shakespearean comic themes of disguise, imposture, and role-playing: lovers disguise themselves as schoolmasters, passing pedants impersonate wealthy fathers, masters and servants exchange places, and Lucentio cries, 'Let me be a slave to achieve that maid' (1.1.218).

Masters and slaves

This last point is particularly significant, on two levels. First, it reminds us of the shared vocabulary between the discourses of sadomasochism and of Elizabethan social relations. On the one hand, master/servant and mistress/maid relationships were part of everyday reality. On the other, the distinctly erotic overtones of slavery (which belong equally to the sonnet sequence and the contemporary fetish scene)[5] are to be heard in Lucentio's cry. Second, Lucentio's exchange of clothes with Tranio establishes an ongoing structural motif in the play. *The Taming of the Shrew* is, of course, structured according to comic conventions, but they are as much the conventions of master/servant comedy as they are of romantic comedy; these consist of elaborations and variations on the kind of *lazzi* which derive from Roman comedy and which were superbly exploited within the Italian *commedia dell' arte*. We are given the flavor of this with Petruchio's first entrance – a slapstick (sic) comic exchange between master and servant on the theme of beating and being beaten:

> Petruchio: Here, sirrah, Grumio, knock, I say.
>
> Grumio: Knock, sir? Whom should I knock? Is there any man has abused your worship?
>
> Petruchio: I say, knock me here soundly. (1.2.5–8)

The central conceit of the play is the structural transfer of these knock-about master–servant routines, which we first see played out between Petruchio and Grumio, to the romantic-comedy plot between Petruchio and Kate. Romantic comedy played out as master–servant routines sounds very much like a description of consensual sadomasochism.

Kate

A sadomasochistic reading of *The Taming of the Shrew* sees the play in terms of Kate's journey from the frustration of her actual societal role as an oppressed woman – symbolized by the genuine public humiliation of her father's open attempt to dispose of her on the marriage market, making her, as she puts it, 'a stale ... amongst these mates' (1.1.5) – to the point where she finds a paradoxical liberty in the submissive role-playing of a consensual sadomasochistic relationship with Petruchio. There are a series of key steps along the way. Kate's response to her initial humiliation is to claim the dominant role: tying and torturing her younger sister (making, as Bianca complains, a 'bondmaid' of her), then gender-bending by manifesting a physical superiority over the male suitors, beating and humiliating Hortensio. In Kate's interactions with Petruchio, however, not only does the power shift – so does the mode of Kate's discourse, as an element of playfulness emerges. This is evident even in their first meeting, which consists of an erotic battle of words between them. This is followed by a series of humiliation and denial games. These are stage-managed and controlled by Petruchio, but they contrast with the initial humiliation scene insofar as they are set up *as* games, small scenes in which Kate is cast as rebellious slave/servant to Petruchio. Reluctant at first, eventually Kate comes to understand that when power and dominance are played as games rather than inherited as societal and ideological necessities, a kind of freedom is achieved. And since 'one of sadomasochism's major givens', as Taunton points out, is that 'it is the submissive that is in control' (1994, 91), Kate joins in the game on terms that only *seem* to disadvantage her, accepting Petruchio in the role of master to her own submissive.

Petruchio

As with most readings of *The Taming of the Shrew*, this interpretation focuses on Kate, who is usually regarded as psychologically the more interesting figure of the lead couple. Petruchio, too, can be seen to grow into this relationship, however. If our first encounter with him is as the dominant master (in social rather than sexual terms) of Grumio, this is not entirely how he first enters into his wooing of Kate. He tells the audience that he intends his courtship to be a spirited one, based on role-playing; but the terms in which he describes his intentions show that he, too, has not yet worked out what his role will be. He will, he assures the audience,

> ... woo her with some spirit when she comes.
> Say that she rail; why then I'll tell her plain
> She sings as sweetly as a nightingale:
> Say that she frown; I'll say she looks as clear
> As morning roses newly wash'd with dew:
> Say, she be mute, and will not speak a word;
> Then I'll commend her volubility
> And say she uttereth piercing eloquence:
> If she do bid me pack, I'll give her thanks,
> As though she bid me stay by her a week:
> If she deny to wed, I'll crave the day
> When I shall ask the banns and when be married.
> (2.1.169–80)

The role with which he seems to be about to experiment is by no means a conventionally dominant masculine one: on the contrary, he seems to be preparing himself to tease Kate with his coy submissiveness. But in the ensuing battle of wits he discovers that this role will not work: it turns out that Kate is not attracted to submissive men, and Petruchio eventually claims the role of dominant, after all:

> And therefore setting all this chat aside
> Thus in plain terms: your father hath consented
> That you shall be my wife....
> Thou must be married to no man but me
> For I am he am born to tame you, Kate.
> (2.1.261–63, 268–69)

And from this moment on, it is his job to manage the 'scenes' – a task he does with gusto, and which leads to Kate's final acceptance, symbolized by the famous speech in which the moment with which we started, 'My hand is ready, may it do him ease', becomes a stylized gesture of a fetishized sexuality, marking the mutual consent of the playful sadomasochistic relationship.

Recuperation

I doubt if the reading which I am suggesting here is one that would gain unanimous support from those whom I see as allies in the field of gender-aware criticism. For some critics, radical as well as reactionary, the emphasis that queer theory has placed on sadomasochism in recent years has frequently been seen as a problem. For the reactionary critics, it is simply inappropriate, but for many radicals, it is at best a dilution and at worst a betrayal of the original impulses within the gender politics of feminist and gay criticism. And certainly a blanket application of queer theory to the Shakespearean *corpus* seems to pose as many problems as it solves. Even so, I would argue that such a reading of this particular play is not only producible but psychologically plausible, sustainable in terms both of the narrative and the language of the play, and generically apt in that it offers a comedically appropriate happy ending to the play – in terms, moreover, that do not depend upon an audience's implicit acceptance of an Elizabethan patriarchal model.

One side effect of a sadomasochistic *The Taming of the Shrew* might be to provide sadomasochism with the kind of cultural validation that comes from an alignment with the iconic (fetishized?) cultural figure of Shakespeare. This is, of course a common phenomenon in the cultural and political fields. Shakespeare, like the Bible, has been pressed into service by all sorts of causes. It is equally likely, though, that the equation could work the other way around, so that it is Shakespeare who is validated by the cultural cool of sadomasochistic discourse.[6] In recent years, Shakespeare enthusiasts have often felt that Shakespeare the misogynist (like Shakespeare the capitalist, Shakespeare the monarchist, Shakespeare the anti-Semite) has needed protection from the moral claims of a contemporary perspective. This 'recuperation' of his gender politics by way of a new mode of sexual discourse (albeit a controversial one)[7] sits comfortably enough within a tradition of criticism that seeks to rescue him from any apparent alignment with present-day reactionaries or with past barbarities. And while a purely textual scholarship may demand that the historicity of Shakespeare's position be allowed to speak unalloyed, any criticism that takes seriously the idea of 'producible interpretation' will tend to look for what we share rather than what separates us: few theaters wish to stage productions whose main point is how *irrelevant* a play is.

Questions

One of the differences between the academic and the stage director is that the director has to make choices and stick with them and their implications: to play a scene one way is to abandon the possibility of playing it another. Ambiguity is possible but its range is limited; even in the most 'open-ended' of productions, meaning cannot multiply endlessly. So there is always a question for the practitioner: what is being lost when we decide to adopt *this* interpretation rather than that one? In the case of this reading of *The Taming of the Shrew*, what is being lost is a cultural and historical specificity that informs the play throughout. It is the specificity that juxtaposes the story of Kate and Petruchio against the unyielding backdrop of *Patriarcha* (Filmer [ca. 1630] 1949), *A Godly Form of Household Government* (Cleaver 1598), and *An Homily of the State of Matrimony* ([1563] 1996) – texts in which domination and submission are not erotic games but theological imperatives and social absolutes. And so, having argued the case for such a 'queer' interpretation (or staging), I would like to conclude by raising a few questions about it. These questions arise from the memory that when Shakespeare plays overtly with the discourses of sadomasochism – 'Being your slave, what should I do but tend / Upon the hours and times of your desire?' (Sonnet 57) – the effect is rather different from what we have in *The*

Taming of the Shrew. The very fact that Shakespeare can 'put on' this voice in the sonnets serves to emphasize the extent to which, historically, the play is rooted in a very different kind of psycho-sexual politics. Does it matter that we lose that, if, in the process, we find a new and resonant meaning that takes its force from our own situatedness? Would it be possible to envisage a producible interpretation in which the relationship between historicism and presentism is not 'either/or' but 'both/and'? And if so, how? I cannot yet see it in production terms, but the suspicion is growing that presentism, this new kid on the block of Shakespearean studies, is most effective not as an alternative to historicism but as a dialectical partner to it. Might it be that the choice between speaking with the dead and talking to the living is a false one after all?

Notes

1. All citations of *The Taming of the Shrew* are from the Arden 2nd edition edited by Brian Morris (1989).
2. This is simply a mental experiment, an attempt to give visual form to an interpretive move. It is not a proposal for a physical staging, and any production which did engage with the ideas in this paper would have to do so in more subtle terms than I have offered here. The spirit in which the image is offered may be judged in terms of its origins – in the context of some studio work on the play with students in Aberystwyth in 2002 that chimed with Nina Taunton's work (1994, 1996). I already knew Taunton's interpretation, and had initially dismissed it; on rereading, however, it came to seem more and more resonant.
3. Petruchio's handcuffs may be a modern fantasy, but the whip was traditional enough. It can be traced back to Kemble's elaboration of Garrick's version of the play in the early nineteenth century. See Brian Morris (1989, 98–9).
4. Georg Lukacs extended the notion of commodity fetishism to include the way in which capitalism converts both people and objects into abstractions – the process of reification, which encompasses life in its totality under capitalism (1923, 1971). Both Marx's original formulation and Lukacs's later reinterpretation have become central concepts in cultural analysis, especially in the study of issues such as marketing and advertising techniques.
5. See, for example, Shakespeare's Sonnets 57 and 58.
6. Nina Taunton, after all, talks of her reading as providing 'a *recuperation* of Kate as a woman with agency rather than as a victim' (1996).
7. Since much of this essay has referred to the incorporation of sadomasochistic-fetish discourse into mainstream cultural discourse, it is perhaps salutary to remind ourselves, by way of balance, just how controversial this discourse still is in an age where sexual 'deviance' may continue to be demonized. Not only is sadomasochistic sexuality still prone, in the popular imagination, to confusion with sexual abuse, its legal status remains problematic in many

countries. In the U.K., for example, it was as late as 1990 that the high-profile police operation, 'Operation Spanner', led to the successful prosecution and subsequent imprisonment, for periods of up to four years, of 16 gay men for consensual sadomasochistic acts. U.K. law has not changed. See http://www.spannertrust.org/documents/spannerhistory.asp

8

'Through the Eyes of the Present': Screening the Male Homoerotics of Shakespearean Drama

Anthony Guy Patricia

For nearly three decades, studies of literature have been guided by the desire, as Stephen Greenblatt has famously described it, to speak with the dead.[1] This comment was, of course, made from the standpoint of new historicism, a mode of literary criticism that seeks to illuminate the past by exploring the dynamics of power and its exercise by those privileged enough to wield it over others, such as in the case of the colonized and the colonizers, men and women, and the monied and the poor, to name but three examples. While new historicist inquiries have, without question, enriched understanding of the past immeasurably, they also, by their nature, overlook what effects that understanding of the past can have on the present. According to Terence Hawkes, the aim of presentist literary criticism, in contrast to new historicism, is 'scrupulously to seek out salient aspects of the present as a crucial trigger for its investigations' (2002, 22).[2] Thus, the salient aspect of the present driving this study is my interest in – as, specifically, a gay man in the twenty-first century – the male homoerotics of Shakespearean drama.

On the phenomenon of homoerotics, Mario DiGangi's work focuses on such questions as the following: 'When is kissing an expression of sexual desire, of affection, or of a social bond? Under what circumstances might our ability even to distinguish these realms be frustrated? In a patriarchal culture, is intercourse always more 'sexual' than kissing? Is it more *erotic*?' His answers to these queries constitute an extended definition of homoerotics (1997, 11). Richard E. Zeikowitz, meanwhile, considers 'how bodies interact – literally, imaginatively, discursively'. Drawing on the work of Roberto Gonzáles-Casanovas, he posits a blending – rather than a strict differentiation – of the homosocial (social relations between men in all spheres), the homophilia (intimate same-sex friendships), and the homoerotic (romantic love between members of the same sex) to analyze fourteenth century texts like *Sir Gawain and the Green Knight* and Chaucer's *Troilus and Criseyde*, among others (2003, 3). Although I am interested in the questions DiGangi raises, my use of the term male homoerotics coincides more with that of Zeikowitz, and signals the potentiality of social, friendly, and romantic interactions between men that can include, for example, words conveying passion either emphatically or softly, a simple look or a touch, the sharing of an embrace or a kiss, or the enjoyment of a night of fully-fledged sexual intimacy.

Of course, we live in the here and now of the twenty-first century, and the dramatic texts of Shakespeare were first staged some 400 years prior. As such, I use critical analysis of contemporary cinematic texts that are based on Shakespeare's dramatic texts to bridge the distance between the late twentieth and early twenty-first centuries on the one hand, and the late sixteenth and early seventeenth centuries on the other, in as meaningful and productive a manner as possible. In particular, I consider Michael Radford's *The Merchant of Venice* (2004), Trevor Nunn's *Twelfth Night* (1996), and Oliver Parker's *Othello* (1995), each of which presents the male homoerotic elements evident in their respective Shakespearean dramatic texts as seamlessly and naturally as possible. Indeed, the argument developed in the pages that follow focuses on homoerotic moments and scenes that are as organic and necessary to these late twentieth and early twenty-first century cinematic texts as they are to the dramatic texts from which they derive.

Michael Radford's *The Merchant of Venice*

Tempestuous relations between Christians and Jews. The problematics of usury in a Christian and emergent capitalist society. Female agency, or lack thereof, in a patriarchal world. Love, money and family as influences on, as well as determiners of, marriage choices. Contractual, moral and ethical obligations. Justice versus self-righteousness. The state in opposition to the individual, and vice versa. The conflicts that propel *The Merchant of Venice* derive from a potent and intricate mixture of all of these dramatic motifs, elements and themes. However, Shakespeare also invested *The Merchant of Venice* with a rich and believable male homoerotic ethos that operates demonstrably throughout its five acts. This homoeroticism manifests in the text, for example, through Antonio's famous expression of sadness which, it turns out, derives from his almost single-minded apprehension in regard to his young friend and lover Bassanio; through Antonio's repeated willingness to sacrifice himself via his money and his body, as well as his staunch resolution to undertake any measures available to him, to assist Bassanio; and finally, Bassanio's own admission of love for Antonio. Without question, these and other homoerotic aspects of Shakespeare's *The Merchant of Venice* provide an inventive and insightful director such as Michael Radford with numerous opportunities to both represent, and to make present, male same-sex desire.

Immediately following the collage of anti-Semitic scenes that mark the opening of Radford's *The Merchant of Venice*, we see the merchant Antonio (Jeremy Irons) in the midst of a group of other Christian men in attendance at an evening mass. As the service ends, Antonio stares fixedly at a gondola filled with three men dressed in masks as if for a night of reveling as it drifts by on the nearby canal. Before long, one of the men lifts his mask and calls out from the shadows the name 'Antonio'. To this greeting, Antonio, his eyes still riveted on the craft slowly floating below, responds, 'Bassanio', as if seeking confirmation of the other man's identity. Bassanio (Joseph Fiennes) smiles at the older man standing on the quay, then drinks deeply from his goblet as a sort of silent toast to Antonio. This singular action on the part of Bassanio causes Antonio to smile briefly, but with unmistakable contentment, in return. Indeed, the lingering, almost intimate look Antonio and Bassanio share during these brief seconds surpasses recognition, friendship and camaraderie to encompass the affection, love and desire possible between one man and another. As such, from almost the very beginning of his cinematic narrative, Radford creates a plausible homoerotic context for the characters of Antonio and Bassanio. Of course, such a scene as that discussed above does not appear in Shakespeare's dramatic text. It exists, then, in Radford's cinematic text as a conscious and deliberate choice on the part of the director. That Irons and Fiennes play the scene with believable, but not overwhelming, homoerotic aspects also reflects a distinct determination on their part.[3] For director and actors alike, such a representation could not have been arrived at without serious consideration of the original drama.

Within the idiosyncratic temporal and spatial scheme of Radford's cinematic text, the 'I know not why I am so sad' scene with which Shakespeare's *The Merchant of Venice* commences takes place the next day and in Antonio's home (1.1.1–68).[4] Solanio (Gregor Fisher) and

Salerio (John Sessions) are eating and drinking heartily while Antonio paces the floor in front of a collection of large, intricately-paned windows set flush against one another. At one point, Antonio looks through the glass and spies a gondola containing a number of indistinct individuals fast approaching, while Solanio and Salerio speculate on the reasons behind Antonio's self-admitted sadness. When Antonio claims no concern whatsoever about the fate of his ships, Solanio suggests, 'Why then, you are in love', which causes Salerio, followed by Solanio himself, to burst into riotous laughter and Antonio to disavow such a notion decisively with the words, 'Fie, fie, fie' (1.1.46). But when Antonio turns back to the window, his attention is arrested by Bassanio, who rises to a standing position in the approaching gondola as it closes on the dock outside. At the same time, Salerio, who has come up behind Antonio and seen Bassanio for himself, says matter-of-factly, 'Not in love neither? Then let us say you are sad / Because you are not merry' (1.1.47–8). Antonio does not respond to this remark. Instead, he continues to look through the pane of glass at Bassanio. His gaze at the other man, in fact, becomes even more intense and, before the scene ends, Antonio smiles, as if the mere sight of Bassanio fills him, once again, with contentment and satisfaction.

The scene leaves the impression that Antonio's distress, in direct contrast to his disavowal, does indeed emanate from the cause of love, love for Bassanio, in particular, rather than having anything to do with the status of his ships or the merchandise they carry in their respective holds. Bassanio, in other words, means far more to Antonio than any kind of material goods. Meanwhile, the 'Fie, fie, fie' utterance stands as Antonio's admission of being in love with someone *and* it displays his disconcerted surprise at his friends' quick and unexpected discovery of that fact. Shakespeare's dramatic texts, as countless others have noted, are notoriously void of stage directions. Radford's *The Merchant of Venice*, however, with Antonio's significant and strategic gazes at Bassanio, allows audiences to both see and to understand the obvious implications inherent within the text: that it is Antonio's love for Bassanio that is making him a want-wit for sadness.

On the mechanics of moviemaking itself, Laury Magnus comments that 'while film's condensations can streamline its narration and make its action more symmetrical, more focused on the central characters, its substitutions of visuals for words can also cut to the chase too immediately, plucking the heart out of a character's mystery' (2007, 111). In regard to director Radford's depiction of the scene discussed above, Magnus finds 'this sort of visual oversimplification' in the manner in which the cinematic text presents 'Antonio's glimpse from the casement window of his beloved Bassanio seated below in a gondola, [because] it prematurely connects his sadness and its most likely cause; we see it emanating from what his eyes have lit upon and cannot have' (2007, 111). Magnus, it seems, would have preferred no excision of Shakespeare's lines from this scene which, according to her, when played in full, allow 'the audience to conjure both the ancient pride and the anxieties of the Renaissance venture capitalist' (2007, 111). What she does not say, of course, is that such a strategy would also serve to obscure, if not obliterate, the homoerotic nature of Antonio's attraction to Bassanio in the cinematic text. I would argue, however, that Shakespeare's dramatic text invites consideration of the possibility of the homoerotic nature of Antonio and Bassanio's relationship at precisely this point in both his dramatic text and Radford's cinematic text. As Shakespeare and Radford both make clear, Antonio's melancholy emanates more from concern about Bassanio than any concern about the fate of his ships.

Following the departure of Solanio and Salerio from Antonio's house, Bassanio's expression registers his mortification when his friend Gratiano (Kris Marshall) launches into his 'You look not well' admonition of Antonio (1.1.73). Before long, in fact, Bassanio – another example of improvised and inspired stage direction – throws his napkin at Gratiano, which startles him into ending his, more-than-likely unintended, impertinence. Upon Gratiano's leaving, Bassanio shakes his head ruefully and apologizes to Antonio for his friend's rude behavior: 'Gratiano speaks an infinite deal of nothing, more than any man in all of Venice' (1.1.114–15). Thus Bassanio betrays not only his awareness of Antonio's sadness, but also his sensitivity and understanding of the other man's dilemma. We may suspect, in addition, that Bassanio knows that he himself is the cause of Antonio's melancholy, hence his careful and solicitous treatment of him in this regard. In any case, Antonio merely gazes at Bassanio for some moments before saying, 'Well', with a questioning lilt to his voice (1.1.118). After a brief pause, the two men rise from the table and walk side-by-side into Antonio's bedroom. There, Antonio requests that Bassanio tell him that which he promised to speak of earlier.

Reflection at this point allows for the realization of just how extraordinary these moments are in Radford's cinematic text. First, according to Shakespeare's *The Merchant of Venice*, this scene takes place outside and on a street in Venice, not in Antonio's house. Second, Radford extends the pause between Antonio's 'Well' and his 'tell me…' lines far beyond what the comma between the two in the actual text seems to suggest in terms of pacing. Of course, during this lengthy break, Antonio and Bassanio leave the dining room for Antonio's bedroom, where their conversation continues. This brings us to the third and final point: that this discussion does, in fact, occur in a place long-associated with closeness, intimacy, privacy, and sexuality between individuals. And, in this case, the individuals in question happen to be two men: Antonio and Bassanio. Despite knowing that members of the same sex routinely shared beds in Shakespeare's day,[5] the implied homoerotics of this scene, as Radford presents it, could not be any clearer.

Nevertheless, Bassanio, who has positioned himself on the other side of the room from Antonio and, more significantly, next to the ornate, canopied bed draped with rich, red-velvet coverings, evinces a curious mixture of repentance and guilt on his youthful face. He paces and removes his cloak as he speaks. By the time he says, 'To you, Antonio, / I owe the most, in money and in love', he is lying in Antonio's bed (1.1.129–30). Antonio's next words are delivered as he, himself, walks toward the bed. Indeed, he smiles and strokes Bassanio's shoulder when he states, 'And if it stand, as you yourself still do', then he, too, sits on the bed, right next to Bassanio and with his back pressed against the headboard. Though still fully clothed, neither seems the least disturbed by the fact that he is in the same bed with another man. Antonio merely explains to Bassanio that he can 'be assured / My purse, my person, my extremest means / Lie all unlocked to your occasions' (1.1.136–38). We ought not to fail to note, furthermore, that when Antonio speaks the words 'my person' here, he smiles broadly at Bassanio, an action which only serves to underscore the bodily intimacies these two men have shared, and continue to share, with one another. So encouraged, Bassanio rises to his knees on the bed and proceeds to tell Antonio about the rich and beautiful heiress in Belmont, Portia (Lynn Collins).

Upon hearing of Bassanio's attraction to, and desire for, Portia, Antonio drops his eyes away from Bassanio's face and swallows deeply. These actions do not, however, indicate either dejection or despair. In fact, Antonio merely – and not surprisingly – falls into thought here, and without doubt he is thinking about how he can best help his friend and lover in the current circumstances. He soon reminds Bassanio of the fact that his fortunes are tied to the sea at the present moment. After contemplating the situation for a short while longer, Antonio leaves the bed, and Bassanio's side, for a desk situated at the other side of the room. After hastily scribbling a note of authorization, Antonio suggests that Bassanio investigate what Antonio's credit can do in terms of securing sufficient funding for Bassanio's venture 'to Belmont, to fair Portia' (1.1.181). By this point, Bassanio has also left the bed and walked to where Antonio stands at the desk. For this kindness and generosity, Bassanio first kisses Antonio's hand. As Antonio smiles, Bassanio places his hand gently upon Antonio's cheek, cups his chin in his fingers, then kisses Antonio full on the lips. And Antonio returns the kiss from Bassanio with his eyes closed in obvious pleasure and contentment.[6] Depicting two men kissing in this manner not only confirms the nature of their relationship as homoerotic, but also makes such a homoerotic relationship unavoidable and palpable through visual representation.

Later, during their visit with Shylock (Al Pacino), the moneylender agrees to loan Antonio 3,000 ducats on the condition that, should he fail to repay the money according to the term limit of the bond, Antonio will forfeit a pound of his flesh to Shylock. Bassanio's horror at the imposition of such a caveat registers immediately upon his face, and he tells Antonio – 'You shall not seal to such a bond for me!' – both highly significant indicators of how much Bassanio cares for Antonio, despite his selfish desires (1.3.146). But Antonio counters with the confident statement: 'Why, fear not, man, I will not forfeit it' (1.3.148). Nevertheless, when Antonio assents to 'seal unto this bond' with Shylock, an obviously distressed – and guilty – Bassanio averts his eyes.

In Act 2, scene 8, of Shakespeare's *The Merchant of Venice,* Salerio reports to Solanio on Bassanio's departure from Venice for Belmont and fair Portia. Radford, however, shows us this leave-taking, rather than providing the information secondhand. The scene begins with Bassanio reaching out to embrace Antonio while a heavy rain falls and lightning flashes. After Bassanio jumps aboard his ship, Antonio tells him: 'Be merry, and employ your chiefest thoughts / To courtship and such fair displays [ostents] of love / As shall conveniently become you there' (2.8.43–5). Upon receiving such counsel, Bassanio blows Antonio a kiss from the boat as it starts to pull away from the dock. Antonio, in turn, 'catches' Bassanio's kiss between his clasped hands and then presses them against his lips. He closes his eyes as if savoring the kiss, opens them again, and then raises one hand in farewell to Bassanio as the multi-manned craft carrying him pulls away and into the ever-flowing canals of mighty Venice. Once again, no stage directions in Shakespeare's dramatic text call for the exchange of air-kisses on the part of Antonio and Bassanio. Yet, without question, this scene, in all of its particulars, fits perfectly within the context of Radford's cinematic text. It serves, in fact, as nothing less than a pointed reminder of the homoerotic nature of Antonio's and Bassanio's relationship, even as Bassanio heads off to claim a rich and beautiful heiress for himself in Belmont. In another, similar, improvised departure from Shakespeare's text, Radford shows us a portion of the wedding of Bassanio and Portia. This scene lasts only a few seconds, but in that brief amount of time, Bassanio's face never quite loses its stricken quality, suggesting, yet again, that his thoughts are almost exclusively with his lover, Antonio, in serious danger in Venice, rather than with Portia and the marriage at hand.

Reasoned words on the subjects of killing and love, directed toward Shylock, mark Bassanio's arrival at Antonio's trial in Venice. Later, when Portia, dressed as the young lawyer Balthasar, inquires as to whether or not Antonio can pay the debt owed to Shylock, Bassanio leaps from the crowd to kneel at the feet of the Duke (Anton Rodgers), then passionately insists that he himself will 'tender it for him [Antonio] in the court' or he 'will be bound to pay it ten times o'er, / On forfeit of my hands, my head, my heart' which, as evidenced by his smile, offers Antonio nothing if not some measure of comfort (4.1.204 and 206–07). Later still, as the attendants strap a bare-chested Antonio to the chair in which he will give up a pound of his flesh to Shylock, Antonio says, 'Give me your hand, Bassanio', which the latter does immediately (4.1.260). Antonio clutches Bassanio's hand as best he can, given the straps securing him to the chair, and kisses it while trembling with fear. Bassanio proceeds to embrace Antonio, who tells him 'fare you well', with fatalistic resignation (4.1.260). Gratiano then has to restrain Bassanio from attempting to free Antonio. Several moments of tense, heart-stopping drama follow, as Shylock comes as close to slicing into Antonio's chest with his knife as he ever will before Balthasar/Portia intervenes by calling a halt to the proceedings. Even more time elapses prior to Shylock's unwitting legal downfall and Antonio's release from the straps binding him to the chair of justice/vengeance. Throughout the remainder of this stunning denouement, Bassanio remains standing behind Antonio – more like a husband or a lover than a mere friend or disinterested spectator – supporting him figuratively and literally by his position at his back and, more significantly, by the placement of his hands on either of an exhausted Antonio's shoulders.

Despite the continual sensitivity and attention to the male homoerotics of *The Merchant of Venice*, Radford's cinematic text significantly missteps in this regard not long before the closing credits scroll. Portia says,

> It is almost morning,
> And yet I am sure you are not satisfied

Of these events in full. Let us go in;
...
And I [we] will answer all things faithfully.
(5.1.293–97)

Bassanio slowly follows her into the house in Belmont as if he is in a daze. Furthermore, he quite clearly and deliberately 'forgets', or 'ignores', Antonio, as he walks past him and after Portia. Then, the last time we see Antonio in the movie, he steps toward an open window through which the rays of the rising sun can be seen, without saying a word or betraying any kind of emotion. Given Radford's penchant for creating scenes that do not, technically, exist in Shakespeare's *The Merchant of Venice*, as well as for depicting stage directions that make logical sense in tandem with the context – and particularly the homoerotic context – of the dramatic text, such an ending of his cinematic text seems rather odd. Scrutiny of Shakespeare's dramatic text shows that Antonio, and therefore the homoerotic, remain very much a part of its concluding fabric. We do not read of any mention of exiling him from Belmont, and we know, too, that Bassanio foresees absenting himself from Portia and her estate from time to time. We have more than sufficient reason to suspect that Bassanio will be in Venice, and in the arms of his beloved Antonio, during the course of his wanderings from home. Would that Radford had created a scene or set of scenes for the end of his version of *The Merchant of Venice* that capitalized on these elements and was as attentive to the homoerotic as the rest of his cinematic text so demonstrably and consistently is.

Trevor Nunn's *Twelfth Night*

Twelfth Night stands as one of Shakespeare's most delightful, enjoyable, and accomplished comedies. Its plot of 'midsummer madness' (3.4.48)[7] includes, and makes the absolute best of, a portentous shipwreck, a cross-dressed woman in mourning for her dead brother, various counts, countesses, seamen and servants alike suffering from the illness of unrequited love for the 'wrong' person, drunken revels, an expertly fabricated duel of honor, and a key case of mistaken identity that only exacerbates the overall gleeful mayhem. Given its form as comedy, furthermore, *Twelfth Night* allows its audiences the pleasure of witnessing first-hand, vividly imagining, and vicariously experiencing several different modes of human existence in a completely non-threatening manner – chief among them, those dealing with gender and sexuality. In regard to the characters of Antonio and Sebastian, for instance, Shakespeare presents us with a wholly poignant romantic courtship that takes place, most significantly, between two men. Thus the relationship between Antonio and Sebastian can be understood as exemplifying the male homoerotic. All of the instances that form Antonio's and Sebastian's story in *Twelfth Night* – including Antonio's desire to function as Sebastian's servant in order to remain close to him, the fact that these two men have spent the whole of three months both day and night in each other's company while Sebastian recovered from the trauma of a shipwreck in which he lost his beloved sister, and Antonio's putting himself at significant risk by following Sebastian to Illyria – testify to the loving and intimate nature of their partnership. Trevor Nunn, another inventive and insightful director, vividly dramatizes these textual aspects of *Twelfth Night* and, once again, makes present a coherent and plausible vision of what early modern male homoerotics may well have been like.

On a dark night wracked by a powerful storm, a ship bound for Messaline makes her way through treacherous seas. Two young twins, both dressed exactly alike in rather exotic and androgynous outfits – complete with veils covering their faces – entertain a company assembled in the ballroom with a lively ditty. A bearded man attired in the livery of a seaman stands at the edge of the crowd, his unsmiling gaze riveted upon the two performers. Voice high jinks soon reveal that one of the twins is, in fact, a man, and the other a woman. Before their true gender identities are exposed, however, disaster strikes as the vessel runs into submerged rocks, tearing fatal holes into its hull. Chaos reigns on the deck of the ship when the twins (who, the narrator tells us, are brother and sister) finally arrive there. Before long, the sister is swept off the deck and into the sea, despite her brother's attempt to hold onto her in the violence of the wind. Seconds later, the brother is prevented from hurling himself into the ocean by none other than the seaman who lately observed the performance of the twins with such peculiar intensity. But the brother struggles blindly against the seaman, escapes his well-meaning grasp, and dives into the roiling waters below in search of his sister. Brother and sister manage to find one another under the surface of the sea, but the current rips them apart and separates them for good. Both reach the stormy surface, but neither can determine the whereabouts of the other. Then we see the seaman throwing himself off the sinking ship in order to save the brother while, elsewhere amongst the roiling waves, the sister receives assistance from the captain. And the gasping screams of this terrified young woman bring the heart-rending scene to an end. So commences, with flair, panache, and high drama (if not melodrama), Nunn's superb cinematic production of *Twelfth Night*.

Some time later, at a ship-building yard, one man walks quickly away while another man chases after him: 'Will you stay no longer?' the latter asks plaintively (2.1.1). The former not only refuses to remain at this location, but also insists that he will not reveal to the other man his destination. Upon a bit of reflection, however, the determinedly reticent man confides to Antonio (Nicholas Farrell) – recognizable now (thanks to a closer camera shot of both characters) as the bearded seaman from the ill-fated ship at the beginning of the cinematic text – that his name is Sebastian (Steven Mackintosh) – also recognizable at this point as one half of the brother and sister performing duo the seaman took such note of prior to the vessel's destruction in the storm – and that his father was Sebastian of Messaline, of whom he is sure Antonio knows of. A tearful Sebastian proceeds to tell Antonio of his sister Viola, who was drowned the night Antonio saved Sebastian from the ravages of the sea. Antonio's face evinces the distress he feels for the grieving Sebastian: 'Alas the day!', he says as he moves to sit next to Sebastian (2.1.16). Sebastian's feelings overwhelm him as he continues to recount his story, and he bursts into full-blown tears and buries his face in Antonio's chest. For his part, Antonio wraps the other man in his arms while closing his eyes in shared anguish. Shortly thereafter, when a horse-drawn carriage arrives, Sebastian wipes his face with his hand, then leaves the safety and comfort of Antonio's arms, and resolutely makes his way across the green toward the conveyance.

Antonio hurries after Sebastian. 'O good Antonio', Sebastian says over his shoulder, 'forgive me your trouble' (2.1.25). When Antonio catches up with Sebastian he grabs his arm, forcing him to stop and face him. 'If you will not murder me for your love', he pleads, 'let me be your servant' (2.1.26). Sebastian tells him not to wish for such an arrangement, then turns again and walks to the carriage. When situated in his seat, Sebastian looks at Antonio for a moment or two, then sighs and reveals that his destination is the court of Count Orsino. As the vehicle pulls away, Antonio's expression displays a mixture of concern for Sebastian's welfare and dismay that Sebastian has left him. Antonio calls upon God's beneficence to protect Sebastian, then softly proclaims that he, too, would venture to Orsino's court were it not for the many enemies that await him in Illyria. Anyone familiar with Shakespeare's *Twelfth Night* will quickly realize that here Nunn has excised two significant lines of Antonio's following Sebastian's departure: 'But come what may, I do adore thee so / That danger shall seem sport, and I will go' (2.1.35–6). Of course, Antonio's adoration of Sebastian comes across visually in the cinematic text via his continuous looking at (which the audience sees taking place onscreen) and his overall deferential and solicitous treatment of the other man. The elimination of the last line makes even more sense because it creates a tangible sense of surprise when Antonio does, in fact, show up in Illyria and reunites with Sebastian.

Thus, Nunn's *Twelfth Night* depicts the male homoerotic in much the way textual analysis of Shakespeare's dramatic text suggests is possible. Indeed, homoeroticism quite literally pervades the representation of the scene with Antonio and Sebastian discussed above. Evidence of such an assertion appears, for example, in the manner Antonio observes Sebastian throughout their moments together in the shipyard – with a potent mixture of tenderness, compassion, understanding, love and desire; in the open and solicitous manner of Antonio's addresses to Sebastian; and, perhaps most of all, in Antonio's longing to remain nowhere but in Sebastian's company and service. At the same time, however, confirmation of the male homoeroticism also appears in Sebastian's behavior and actions: in, for instance, the tearful admission of his true identity and the revelation of the loss of his sister; in his willingness to bury his face in another man's chest – to be held by another man, in other words – in his profound bereavement; and in his decision to disclose, finally, the terminus of his journey to Antonio.

In line with contemporary interpretations of *Twelfth Night*, Nicholas R. Jones writes, Nunn's

> Antonio displays an obvious longing for Sebastian. ... This potentially gay relationship, however, is doomed from the start by cluelessness on Sebastian's part, who senses something odd in Antonio but seems never to have considered the possibility of a man desiring another man. (2002, 27)

Jones proceeds to describe Antonio as closeted by necessity, having 'to live a cycle of intimations and unspoken rejections, a hard fate made memorably visual by the sad-sack countenance that Nicholas Farrell brings to the part' (2002, 27). While it is true that Nunn's *Twelfth Night* is attentive to, and respectful of, contemporary interpretations of the dramatic text, particularly in regard to sexual orientation, there is no reason to characterize Antonio and Sebastian's potentially gay relationship as doomed. Sebastian is not clueless about Antonio's interest in him, and he most definitely does have an understanding of men desiring other men. Serious doubts arise, after all, that the three months Antonio and Sebastian have spent day and night in each other's exclusive company have been platonic to the point of emotional, affective, and physical celibacy. Being of a higher class than Antonio, it is possible that Sebastian's circumspection as regards his feelings for Antonio is the result of his upbringing rather than naïvete or lack of interest. Furthermore, the sadness that Antonio (as projected by Farrell) exhibits in the cinematic text always and only results from the fact he feels deeply for Sebastian in his suffering for the loss of his sister. It is not the product of Antonio's imprisonment in the closet where all he can ever do is pine without any real hope for a relationship with young men like Sebastian.

As in Shakespeare's dramatic text, we do not see Sebastian again until he arrives in Illyria proper. At this point in the cinematic text, Nunn creates a scene with intriguing, though short-lived, suspense: Sebastian, while walking through the streets of the city, acts as if he is being followed. His self-defensive movements seem justified when the camera shows us a man dressed in the vague habit of a parson trailing behind Sebastian. Within moments, this oddly-clothed individual catches sight of Sebastian among the throng of the marketplace and, as the tension-inducing music surges, he rushes toward him, removing the hat and glasses he has donned to disguise himself as he does so, thus revealing none other than the seaman Antonio.

'I could not stay behind you', Antonio admits to Sebastian, who is surprised to see him but, nevertheless, says with a bit of a laugh in his voice, 'My kind Antonio', then throws himself into an embrace with the other man (3.3.4 and 13). For as long as they hug, Antonio's eyes are squeezed tightly shut, signaling just how much it means for him to be in Sebastian's arms. Once they part, Sebastian, with a look of happiness on his face, thanks Antonio for seeking him out, then suggests that Antonio accompany him on a sightseeing tour of Illyria. That is when Antonio confesses that he is a man wanted by Count Orsino and his men and, therefore, dares not walk about too openly for fear of capture. Sebastian's expression upon hearing this revelation registers his concern for Antonio's welfare, as does his sincere verbal exhortation for Antonio to keep himself well-concealed so as to avoid discovery. 'You shall find me', Antonio says while putting the glasses and the hat of a parson back on, 'at the Elephant', then he takes Sebastian's hand and places his purse into it (3.3.38–42). When a puzzled Sebastian asks Antonio why he has given him his purse, Antonio explains that he wants Sebastian to have enough money to purchase anything he desires, should he find something that strikes his fancy, but exceeds his own means which, Antonio suspects, are 'not for idle markets' (3.3.46). As evidenced by his smile, Antonio seems, in fact, to be very happy that he can give such a gift of himself to Sebastian. In any case, Antonio starts to walk away after explaining his motives in regard to the giving of his purse, but he stops after only going a few feet and turns back to Sebastian. He reaches out and touches Sebastian with both hands and says anxiously, 'To th' Elephant', to which Sebastian responds with a laugh: 'I do remember' (3.3.48). Hence, this scene plays out in Nunn's *Twelfth Night* as Shakespeare's text makes possible, but with one noteworthy exception: when Antonio actually leaves the area, Sebastian shakes his head in a manner that implies he thinks Antonio's behavior has been excessive, odd, or both. This seems incongruent with the way the balance of the scene is played, which is with an unselfconscious attendance to the underlying homoerotic attraction between Antonio and Sebastian on the part of the actors playing these two characters.

When we next see Antonio, he comes upon Viola dressed as Cesario (Imogen Stubbs) as s/he parries with Sir Andrew Aguecheek (Richard E. Grant) in the sword fight Sir Toby Belch (Mel Smith) and Fabian (Peter Gunn) have expertly engineered between them. Shocked by what he sees happening, Antonio leaps on top of the stone wall separating the orchard where the duel is taking place and the road and yells: 'Put up your sword' (3.4.255). In the surprise of his arrival, all desist from their activities. Antonio, as he enters the orchard proper, says, 'If this young gentleman / Have done offense, I take the fault on me', then he takes Viola/Cesario's weapon as his own and places the 'young gentleman' behind him in order to protect and defend him properly (3.4.255–56). Clearly, Antonio believes that Viola/Cesario is his beloved Sebastian. Moments later, Antonio proclaims to Sir Toby that he is 'One, sir, that for his love dares yet do more / Than you have heard him brag to you he will' (3.4.259–60), then begins to parry with Sir Toby with the sword he appropriated from Viola/Cesario. Within seconds, however, Orsino's officers arrive on horseback and proceed to surround and arrest Antonio. As he is being bound in the chains of a prisoner, Antonio looks at Viola/Cesario and says: 'This comes with seeking you' (3.4.273), meaning Sebastian, of course, then asks for some of the money that was in his purse. An extremely confused Viola/Cesario offers to loan Antonio money for his kindness which, in turn, baffles and enrages Antonio, who asks incredulously, 'Will you deny me now?' (3.4.288) before using both of his bound hands to knock Viola/Cesario's bag, and all the coins it contains, to the ground. Then Antonio allows himself to be led away quietly by Orsino's men. Antonio's anger, however, flares again when he is brought before Viola/Cesario and Duke Orsino (Toby Stephens) himself a short while later. 'A witchcraft drew me hither', Antonio says with obvious anguish when questioned by the count about his unfortunate presence in Illyria. 'That most ingrateful boy there by your side', he yells, 'His life I gave him.... For his sake... [faced] the danger of this adverse town' (5.1.64, 68, 70, and 72). When Orsino asks Antonio to explain when Viola/Cesario came to the city, Antonio responds: '[Yesterday]... and for three months before.... Both day and night did we keep company' (5.1.83 and 85). Of course, for Orsino and Viola/Cesario, this is an impossibility because s/he has been serving him for the past three months, an intelligence which only confuses Antonio further.

In the particulars discussed in the preceding paragraph, Nunn's *Twelfth Night* follows Shakespeare's dramatic text closely. This means, of course, that Viola's disguise as Cesario has proven so effective that no one recognizes her for what she really is, least of all Antonio. Of all the characters in *Twelfth Night*, Antonio ought to know the difference between his beloved Sebastian and Viola/Cesario – between a man and a woman. Alas, however, he is unable to tell the difference and, as a result, he suffers a great deal of distress when Viola/Cesario (whom he thinks of as Sebastian) cannot help him nor acknowledge their past relationship. And it bears repeating that, given all his efforts and sacrifices on Sebastian's behalf, Antonio has more than a right to feel both angry and betrayed at this point – feelings that Nunn's cinematic text depicts masterfully and believably, and without losing sight of the homoeroticism at the heart of Antonio's relationship with Sebastian.

The arrival of the Countess Olivia (Helena Bonham Carter), sends the scene in a different trajectory entirely that, ultimately, leads to the story's denouement. Indeed, her new husband – the real Sebastian – soon appears, and does so with apologies to Olivia for hurting her kinsman, Sir Toby. After kissing his wife, Sebastian takes note of, first, Orsino, and then the shackled Antonio. The second he recognizes him, Sebastian runs toward Antonio (leaving Olivia behind, significantly), saying – 'Antonio.... my dear Antonio!' – immediately prior to throwing his arms around the other man in a happy greeting (5.1.202). 'How have the hours racked and tortured me', he gushes, 'Since I have lost thee' (5.1.203–04). If nothing else, this moment in the movie reconfirms the homoerotic nature of the relationship between Sebastian and Antonio despite Sebastian's very recent marriage to Olivia. A still confused Antonio inquires tremulously: 'Sebastian, are you?... How have you made division of yourself? ... Which is Sebastian?' (5.1.205, 207, and 209). The emotional and affecting reunion of the twins, Viola and Sebastian, follows, separated by the shipwreck at the beginning of the cinematic text.

Like Radford's *The Merchant of Venice*, Nunn's *Twelfth Night* displays continual sensitivity and attention to the male homoerotics evident in its Shakespearean source text. However, like Radford's cinematic text, Nunn's cinematic text also significantly missteps in this regard in its final treatment of Antonio. Indeed, Nunn presents a collage of scenes immediately prior to the scrolling of the credits. Most prominent among these images are those that depict the double wedding celebration of the couples Sebastian and Olivia, and Orsino and Viola. At the same time, we are also made privy to the silent departures of Feste, Malvolio, Sir Toby and Maria (Imelda Staunton), and Antonio from the Countess Olivia's (and now, presumably, also the Count Sebastian's) mansion. It is, of course, Nunn's depiction of Antonio's departure that raises concern in the present context. When we see him, Antonio appears utterly alone on the path leading from the estate. Given the evident fog and dampness, it cannot but be a raw and inhospitable time of day. He pauses long enough to bundle himself further into his coat as defense against the cold. Thus fortified, Antonio trudges on his way, without looking back at the house where, presumably, his lover Sebastian remains with Olivia in wedded bliss. In its specificity, such a depiction of Antonio's fate comes across as the cinematic equivalent to a slap-on-the-face directed toward the cinematic text's queer viewers. In Shakespeare's dramatic text of *Twelfth Night*, there is no mention of Antonio's departure from Olivia's domain, and although I disagree with Alan Sinfield's notion that Antonio, Sebastian, and Olivia would live and love together in some kind of harmony within the expansive confines of the latter's residence,[8] I do not believe, either, that the marriage of Sebastian and Olivia signals the death knell of Antonio and Sebastian's relationship. With his penchant for inventiveness, I feel that Nunn could have included a scene or scenes in his concluding collage that depicts Antonio and Sebastian not only embracing as the former prepares to depart, but agreeing to meet in Messaline, perhaps, where they, once again, enjoy all of the emotional, affective and erotic pleasures that two men can share with each other during the time that they are privileged to be together. As it is, the conclusion of Nunn's *Twelfth Night*, despite its overall excellence, leaves its queer audience with a distinct longing for what could have – indeed, should have, been.

Oliver Parker's *Othello*

In life we do not discover everything about the people we are involved with on that journey all at once; we learn about them, and they us, bit by bit as time, experience and, sometimes, determination allows. We come to know Iago, Othello, Desdemona, Cassio, and all the other *dramatis personae* that appear in Shakespeare's *Othello* in a comparable though dramatically compressed manner. Therefore, we may be content, for example, to accept the fact that Iago is acting as deliberately malicious in the opening scenes of the tragedy simply because he has been passed over by Othello for promotion to the rank of officer in the military service. It seems a logical consequence, in fact, that Iago would retaliate for being treated in such a disrespectful manner by denigrating both Cassio and Othello, following the latter only to do him an equal, if not greater, wrong. Beyond vengeance, however, something unexpected and extraordinary occurs when Iago continues his verbal manipulation of Othello in Act 3 of the dramatic text. A significant part of Iago's elaborate fabrication of proof of Desdemona's marital indiscretion(s) includes not only representing Othello's wife as a wanton, but also depicting himself as Cassio's bed partner, and thus, as the apparently willing recipient of another man's amorous physical advances. As the highly visceral images Iago creates here resonate in the minds of readers, the realization begins to dawn that, perhaps, something else entirely has been going on in *Othello* – at least in regard to the sexual dynamics at work in the drama. Indeed, for queer readers of *Othello*, the exhilarating possibility that Shakespeare might not be privileging heteronormativity as much as was first thought begins to manifest at this point, and soon demands a complete reassessment of the dramatic text guided by the thesis that Iago's hatred masks a profound love for Othello that encompasses the homosocial, the homoerotic, *and* the homosexual. To his great credit, Oliver Parker does not flinch or shy away from these facets of Shakespeare's text in his cinematic text of *Othello*.

Parker's *Othello* begins in Venice and in the rather disturbing gloom of night. Gondolas furtively skirt the waterways of the city, and we first encounter Iago (Kenneth Branagh) with Roderigo (Michael Maloney) as they witness, in stealth, Othello's (Laurence Fishburne) marriage to Desdemona (Irene Jacob). After bride and groom kiss, Iago launches into his complaint about Othello's promotion of Cassio (Nathaniel Parker) instead of himself to the position of lieutenant in the military organization in which they serve. Though Shakespeare only mentions it in his dramatic text, Parker actually shows us Cassio's elevation in a ceremony that Iago remembers in his mind's eye; it includes Othello's giving of an ornate knife to Cassio, as well as the embrace of the two men as Cassio is welcomed into Othello's service. The following moments include Roderigo and Iago's sadistic taunting of Brabantio (Pierre Vaneck) about the absence and elopement of his daughter. When we again see Iago, he is standing next to, and looking very intently at, Cassio; when Cassio turns suddenly, Iago winks at him, then smiles. In and of themselves, of course, a hug between two men observed by another man, and a wink and a smile between one man and another, could be understood as purely platonic actions. But, given that textual analysis of Shakespeare's *Othello* clearly establishes Iago as what we would term in the twenty-first century a bisexual, if not an exclusively homosexual, male, his observations and gestures in the early moments of Parker's cinematic text demand further consideration. Hence, Iago's remembrance of the embrace Othello and Cassio shared suggests that Iago understands he will never again experience such an intimacy with the general because of Cassio's selection as Othello's right-hand man. That we later learn of Iago's night spent entwined in the same bed with Cassio transforms his wink from the merely sly, to the sly *and* the homoerotic. Although Iago loves and desires Othello, he is not at all immune to, or incapable of noticing, Cassio's attractiveness, as this scene attests. This, in turn, ties into his later jealousy of Cassio's daily beauty (*Othello*, 5.1.19–20).

The homoerotic nature of Iago's character becomes even more explicit as Parker's *Othello* continues. For instance, a portion of what corresponds to Shakespeare's Act 2, scene 1, involving Iago and Roderigo, takes place underneath a large cart at night during the celebration of Othello's and Desdemona's marriage on the island of Cyprus. While Iago and Roderigo talk as they lie next to one another on the ground, a male and female couple enjoys rather energetic and noisome sexual relations in the cart directly above their heads. Significantly, as Iago says (in reference to the relationship between Desdemona and Cassio he is in the process of fabricating), 'An index and obscure prologue to the history of lust and foul thoughts' (2.1.244–45),[9] he moves his face slowly, and ever closer, to that of Roderigo. Indeed, Iago's actions here become so intimate that it seems as if he is about to kiss Roderigo full on the lips. Alas, however, Iago does not kiss Roderigo, he merely continues speaking: 'They met so near with their lips that their breaths embraced together. Villainous thoughts, Roderigo! When these mutualities so marshal the way, hard at hand comes the master and main exercise, th'incorporate conclusion' (2.1.245–48). Although he does not, in fact, kiss Roderigo, it is nevertheless intriguing that Iago allows their 'breaths to mingle' just as he has suggested Desdemona's and Cassio's have done in an illicit sexual encounter. Furthermore, when he says the words 'hard at hand', Iago slowly and deliberately places his right hand on Roderigo's thigh, then continues to move that hand until it cups Roderigo's testicles and penis. For his part, Roderigo is either so distraught about the fact that Desdemona does not love him that he fails to notice the touch and/or location of Iago's hand, or being groped by another man in such a manner is so commonplace an occurrence for him that the sensation no longer registers upon his consciousness. The former supposition is, by far, more likely. But, in either case, the homoeroticism Parker depicts here cannot be overlooked or dismissed – regardless of the fact that Iago is only ever using Roderigo for his own ends. That Iago *might* consider Roderigo an extraneous sexual partner in addition to his dupe only adds another layer to the overall maliciousness of his character, while simultaneously confirming the non-normative nature of his erotic interests and desires.

As in Shakespeare's dramatic text, the male homoerotic reaches its peak in Parker's *Othello* during the depiction of Othello and Iago's bonding in Act 3, scene 3. This scene takes place upon the battlements of a castle on Cyprus and it includes the exchange of a blood vow between the two not mentioned in Shakespeare's dramatic text. First, Othello cuts a gash in his palm with his knife, and Iago follows suit immediately after. Then they clasp their bleeding hands together in complete solidarity with one another, and Othello says, 'Now art thou my lieutenant' (3.3.495). At this point, both men are on their knees and, significantly, they embrace. First, we see this embrace happen from a distance, then the shot changes to a near close-up of Iago as he is held in Othello's arms. The look on Iago's face is one of almost painful, yet at the same time exquisite, relief. It is as if he cannot believe that he is, once again, being held by his beloved Othello. 'I am your own forever', Iago says, and it is as if each word is being ripped from the very depths of his soul; then he squeezes his eyes shut, as if to hold back his tears (3.3.496). Arguably, a scene of this kind might well present a same-sex union or wedding between Othello and Iago, had such ceremonies taken place in early modern England. And Parker's cinematic text thus both capitalizes on, and makes vivid and real, the homoerotic potentiality inherent within this portion of Shakespeare's dramatic text.

However, Parker offers one additional homoerotic moment in his *Othello* that warrants attention. In the penultimate scene of the cinematic text, after the deaths of Desdemona, Emilia and finally, Othello himself, an understandably incensed Lodovico (Michael Sheen) forces Iago, who is on his knees and bleeding from his wounds, to gaze upon the heinous outcome of his deeds: 'Look on the tragic loading of this bed. / This is thy work' (5.2.374–75). And Iago does look at the three lifeless bodies spread before him. Then, in silence, Iago forces himself upward, onto the bed, and lays his head in the crook of Othello's leg. Though undeniably grotesque, this singular action of Iago's reveals nothing if not the fact that his attachment to his general lingers, even in the chaos of destruction and the finality of death.

U.S. films, supposedly reflecting the society-at-large they seek to entertain, all too often and for far too long have either ignored the male homosexual or portrayed him in the most offensive and stereotypical manner possible. Such representations both emanate from and serve to perpetuate the irrational homophobia employed to maintain the dominance of heterosexuality within our patriarchal culture.[10] Radford's *The Merchant of Venice*, Nunn's *Twelfth Night*, and Parker's *Othello* thus serve as significant correctives to oversight, ignorance, inaccuracy, and injustice, among other negatives. In fact, these movies allow gay men like myself to connect with their history in a way that informs their present. In other words, they can see for themselves that they are not, nor have they ever been, the freaks or abominations others, in their fear, have sought to condemn them as. They can see that they are not alone, and they can see that they are as human in their wants, needs, and desires as any other group of people.

Singularly and in tandem, Radford's *The Merchant of Venice*, Nunn's *Twelfth Night*, and Parker's *Othello* function as cinematic exemplars because they demonstrate how plausibly and effectively the male homoerotics of Shakespeare's dramatic texts can be represented on contemporary movie screens. In fact, we ought not to lose sight of the fact that the filmmakers of these recent productions felt compelled, not only by the source material, but also by an understanding of sexuality in early modern England that continues to gain depth, nuance and significance to render the male homoerotic visible and integral. In a very real sense, Radford, Nunn and Parker bring what has been buried or overlooked for centuries as regards male same-sex relations into the present in a manner that leaves no room for further avoidance, equivocation or rationalization. It can only be hoped that future cinematic texts of Shakespeare's dramatic texts are as attentive as presentist literary criticism to their respective male characters, such as Antonio and Bassanio, Antonio and Sebastian, and Iago and Othello, who happen to desire and love other men.

Notes

1. 'I began with the desire to speak with the dead' is Greenblatt's first sentence of his first chapter, 'The Circulation of Social Energy', of his book, *Shakespearean Negotiations* (1988, 1).
2. I wish to acknowledge my debt to Hawkes for also providing me (unknowingly of course) with the title of this piece. In the Introduction to his *Shakespeare in the Present*, he writes:

   > the critic's own 'situatedness' [in the present] does not – cannot – contaminate the past. In effect, it constitutes the only means by which it's possible to see the past and perhaps comprehend it. And since we can only see the past *through the eyes of the present*, few serious historians would deny that one has a major influence on their account of the other. (2002, 3, emphasis mine)

   Along similar lines, I would like to thank Evelyn Gajowski for offering me the unexpected privilege of making a contribution to this collection of essays.
3. In '*The Merchant of Venice*: Shakespeare through the Lens', one of the special features on the DVD version of Radford's cinematic text, Jeremy Irons comments: 'He [Antonio] finds himself very happy in the company of young men... ah, particularly one young man [Bassanio], who is sort of everything he'd like to be'. However, a short while later, Irons insists: 'I didn't play Antonio gay'. Rather, he portrayed Antonio as merely a very great friend of Bassanio's – nothing more, nothing less. Since, as I argue in these pages, both Shakespeare's dramatic text and Radford's cinematic text evidence an unmistakable male homoeroticism between the characters of Antonio and Bassanio, Irons's remarks here prove ironic in the extreme.
4. All quotations of Shakespeare's *The Merchant of Venice* are from David Bevington's edition as it appears in the Bedford/St. Martin's Texts and Contexts series, edited by M. Lindsay Kaplan (2002).
5. On this point, see Alan Bray's 'Homosexuality and the Signs of Male Friendship in Elizabethan England' (1994), especially pp. 42–4.
6. Magnus notes:

   > Fiennes's star power makes it easy to overlook Bassanio's mindless initial prodigality, his careless reliance on Antonio's generosity, the grubby materialism of introducing Portia as an answer to his bankrupt state, and his willingness to risk not his own fortune (which he has already squandered) but his friend's. One even forgives the kiss on the lips that he bestows somewhat too knowingly upon Antonio. (2007, 114)

   Hopefully, what requires forgiveness for Magnus is the calculated quality of the kiss, rather than the fact that it occurs between two men. In either case, she fails to take into account the possibility that Antonio and Bassanio do, in fact, have an affective, emotional and physical relationship. Doing so, I would argue, might alter her interpretation.
7. All quotations of Shakespeare's *Twelfth Night* are from David Bevington's edition as it appears in the Bedford/St. Martin's Texts and Contexts series, edited by Bruce R. Smith (2001).
8. I refer here to Sinfield's 'How to Read *The Merchant of Venice* without Being Heterosexist' (2006a, 65–6).

9. All quotations of Shakespeare's *Othello* are from David Bevington's edition as it appears in the Bedford/St. Martin's Texts and Contexts series, edited by Kim F. Hall (2007).
10. See Eve Kosofsky Sedgwick's discussion of the irrationality of homophobia in her introductory chapter (1985), especially note 1.

9
Estranging Bedfellows: Early Modern Cinema Today

Douglas E. Green

Scene 1: another part of the forest

> Placing emphasis on the present can't help but connect fruitfully with the current realignment of critical responses that stresses the *performance* of a play as much as its 'reference': that looks at what the play *does*, here and now in the theatre, as well as – or even against – what it *says* in terms of the world to which its written text refers. Presentism thus highlights what has been termed drama's 'performative' function: a feature that always operates concurrently with, and perhaps as a modification of, its referential function.
>
> –Terence Hawkes (2002, 5, Hawkes's emphasis)

Let's begin with a winter's tale, one that has been repeating itself, with variations, for ten years on frigid Saturday mornings about a half mile from downtown Minneapolis. In a chilly room with no windows, five non-traditional students – four middle-aged white women and one 20-something African-American man – are putting on a selection of scenes from *Cymbeline*, all of them focused on Belarius, the foundling princes he has raised as his own sons, and their cross-dressed sister Imogen. The students have been working on these scenes for months. Though I know the scenes they have chosen, I have no idea what to expect.

The set looks like a 1960s commune on an outing at a state park. Someone has set up a tent on one side of the well of the lecture hall we have moved to for the day. There are beer cans and cigarette butts strewn about, as well as copies of Herman Hesse and Marcuse. 'Aquarius' is playing in the background. Darrin steps downstage, sporting an Afro wig, to give Belarius's lines about how the boys' royal blood is manifesting itself. For me, at least, Belarius and *Cymbeline* will never be the same again.

Nor will my sense that, as Hawkes's presentist might say, the 1960s have influenced Shakespeare. Or that, to be more exact about this case, second-millennial students' impressions (and in a few cases memories) of the 1960s have influenced these Shakespearean scenes: Belarius's response to Cymbeline's injustice has been to set up a countercultural anti-court. But as Darrin's witty wig suggests, he and his fellow students sensed that Belarius has been 'playing' this anti-courtly part and that now, as his putative sons' 'natural' aspirations emerge, he is realizing the game is up. Like baby boomers turned stockbrokers, these Shakespearean aristocrats-in-rustic-clothing seem poised to return to courtly ways.

Unlike Darrin, all of the women in these scenes are cross-dressing. Two are playing Imogen's brothers; the oldest of the women, who anticipates a temporary separation from her spouse and one of her kids when she goes east for graduate school, is playing Imogen. Fiona simultaneously makes us feel Imogen's discomfort in her new role as Fidele and suggests that she is having fun making her character squirm; the others are playing to the hilt the brother's ineluctable attraction to their sister – and suggesting some confusion on their character's parts about what they are feeling.

And of course there is that quintessential border-crossing, that linguistic and temporal transvestitism that occurs when insecure twenty-first century American students – in some cases compounded by the insecurities of their belated return to college – speak Shakespearean verse convincingly in their own accents and voices. Between early modern text (is any 'school' edition really that?) and postmodern students, an exchange, too easily taken for granted, has occurred – the kind that performance best affords. I am tempted by but resist the old romantic jargon: Do they inhabit Shakespeare's verse or does the verse inhabit them?

Scene 2: 'Prithee unpin me here'

> All restorations face one major problem. Reaching backwards, they can't afford to examine the position in the present from which that manoeuvre is undertaken.
>
> –Terence Hawkes (2002, 2)

When we compare the famous 'willow' scenes in the 1965 Olivier/Burge film of *Othello* and the more recent Parker *Othello* (Burge 1965; Parker

1995, 2000)), each Shakespearean film seems to function as a palimpsest of past and present texts. These scenes raise issues – or can be used to raise them – of current and enduring interest about the play's performance history, especially the shift from boy-player to adult woman actor, and about the history of gender and sexuality. Considering the two versions together may also shift our view to the changing conventions of cinema, the ways in which they have constructed gender and sexuality, and the ways in which Shakespearean constructions and inscriptions of gender and sexuality interact with cinematic conventions. The conjunction of Shakespeare and film provides a nearly perfect instance of intersection between present(s) and past(s) that allows us to question our assumptions about both.[1]

The juxtaposition of the 'willow' scenes from the Olivier and Parker films tells us something about the staging of womanhood and perhaps something about the history of sexuality, too.[2] Combining elements of the first Quarto of 1622 with the text of the First Folio of 1623, Olivier and National Theater Director John Dexter, who first mounted the production, have excised the most famous speech in the scene as preserved in the Folio: Emilia's Shylock-like indictment of men as the cause of evil in women. I have not met a student (or a Shakespearean scholar) who has not wondered why, especially since the production is *not* religiously following the first quarto: at what effect was Olivier aiming in this 1960s film? Whatever he aimed at, the decision certainly has the effect of making Barbary's 'song of Willow' the central feature of the scene between the two women (4.3.28). Barbary and the woman of the song's narrative join the women of this Shakespearean scene as lovers scorned and abused; Emilia and Desdemona share their victimization by 'these men, these men' (4.3.60). When the camera pulls back to reveal Maggie Smith and Joyce Redman dwarfed by the enormous set, we feel the smallness and helplessness of two women caught in the web Iago has woven with, ironically, Othello's help. The emphasis, at least in my view, is on female victimization, woman as the emblem of suffering and sorrow. Except perhaps for one line: maybe it is just wishful thinking on my part, but when Maggie Smith says, 'these men, these men', I hear her trying to capture in that line – taken from the Folio but moved to the end of the scene – some of the criticism of Emilia's excised speech. There is a hint of accusation and not just resignation.

In Parker's version, Irene Jacob's Desdemona sounds more resigned to me; she can afford to be because Anna Patrick's superb Emilia delivers an indictment tipped with the sting of experience. Patrick's version of Emilia's famous speech is also, to my mind, the first real instance of camaraderie between these two women. Before that, Patrick gives us an Emilia who seems astounded and a bit exasperated by Desdemona's blind good faith – among the Emilias I have seen, only Zoe Wanamaker's in Trevor Nunn's version is more embittered, largely because Ian McKellan's Iago is even more sadistic than Branagh's. Once Desdemona is a fellow-sufferer at the hands of a husband, this Emilia sympathizes. Hence the feeling of conspiratorial good will – underscored by the intimacy of the introduction of a bath and a goodnight kiss.

Though I love Maggie Smith's performance as Desdemona and though I certainly think her the stronger actor, Parker has come nearer the spirit of the scene – and the play: in other words, I think that Olivier's elision of Emilia's speech reflects his underlying vision of women in this play (and maybe beyond it) as absolutely helpless, as emblems of grief that arouse pity and fear in us. They are like Barbary and the woman in her song. They are like Desdemona in her final lines, when Emilia asks 'who hath done this deed?': 'Nobody. I myself. Farewell. / Commend me to my kind lord' (5.2.123–25). Interestingly, Parker cut Desdemona's famous last words. But Parker has not erased the affecting sadness of the willow scene; rather, he has restored, particularly through the strong presence of Patrick's Emilia, the sense that though these women may not win, they do recognize and at least resent what the men have thrown at them. They, too, are like Desdemona in the last scene, the Desdemona struggling against Othello, desiring even one more night of life: 'Kill me tomorrow, let me live tonight! ... But half an hour! ... But while I say one prayer!' (5.2.80–3). The heroine's fate may be the same, but the two versions of the willow scene suggest very different ways of meeting that fate: the difference between resignation and resentment (perhaps too strong a word), between abject suffering and resistance to submission, between unwitting victimization and self-knowledge, however ineffective.

Lest I sound simply anti-Olivier or, worse, as if new is better than old, a rather self-defeating position for a Shakespearean, Parker's scene fails miserably in one area: the intrusions of the wistful Othello among the reeds at the water's edge. Though I may disagree with Olivier's notion of what these two women are talking about and how they are talking, Olivier and Company got one thing right: this is one of Shakespeare's best fourth acts, one of his best 'rests' before the denouement (as they used to be described), and it is so because for one moment in this play so thoroughly dominated by the world and relations of men and by the relation between men and women, we have two women utterly alone with each other. Here, in isolation, the women articulate what the audience recognizes with tragic irony that other characters need to hear. Desdemona tells her story in song; Emilia constructs an etiology of woman's fall that counters the misogynistic account of the fall of man by placing the blame squarely on the example of supposedly superior men – in the speech excised from the Olivier/Burge film (4.3.84–103). Later, Desdemona's voice will fail to prevent the murder and will die telling what is, at least literally, a lie. Emilia will tell the truth – shrewishly in Iago's eyes – and die for not 'charm[ing] thy tongue' (5.2.183). Shakespeare's disjoining the clear truth-telling voices of the willow scene and the constraints on women's speech in every other scene – with the possible exception of Desdemona's performance before the Senate (1.3.180–83, 248–59), where she creates a version of love that neither she nor anyone else can live up to – exposes the very problem of the female voice in patriarchal culture: the men at best are not listening – or not until it is too late – and at worst are silencing women. Shakespeare's women can and do speak, but to what end? Who *hears* them?

The willow scene, a moment of great intimacy between women, provides an answer: They hear each other. 'Dismiss me?' Emilia asks, echoing her mistress and wondering why Othello would require his wife be alone before his arrival (4.3.14–18). Similarly, Desdemona's 'prithee unpin me' and 'unpin me here' (4.3.21, 34) – conflated by Parker ('Prithee unpin me here') – remind us of the intimacy between mistress and maid or lady-in-waiting. The willow song articulates the women's sad perspective on relations with men, a state akin to the no-win situation in which each of these loving and loyal wives is caught. Whether we feel, as Olivier seems to, that Shakespeare creates women as hapless victims or even sees women essentially as suffering, at least in this play, or whether we, like Parker, find the women more actively trying to cope with and even questioning their situation, struggling to come to terms with it, there is no doubt in my mind that inserting shots of Othello distracts us from the women's plight and their encounter, however we see it.

Are these interpolations meant to be what Desdemona is imagining? Are they meant to remind us that Othello is suffering and troubled too, as if we needed reminding? In this case, though the shots can be variously interpreted, they detract from the one unique feature of this scene: its unhurried focus on the interaction between the two central female characters – the one moment when their concerns take center stage instead of being sandwiched between the comings and goings of men. If Olivier has to enforce his interpretation by cutting Emilia's proto-feminist speech, Parker undermines the focus of the scene by intruding Othello upon it in ways that distract us from the women, from what they are saying and feeling and thinking.

Though undoubtedly a case can be made for the interpolations and though viewers not familiar with the play may be untroubled by them, my student-readers – non-traditional undergraduates, mostly women, ranging from their late 20s to their late 50s – have consistently questioned Othello's atextual intrusion here. Sometimes they are not sure why it bothers them. But in nearly every class someone has suggested that this is the women's scene and he does not belong there. Certainly, one may feel that Othello and even Iago may be on the minds of Desdemona and Emilia as Desdemona sings. But introducing Othello as if he were the ghost of King Hamlet goes a bit too far, does it not? Parker nearly undoes the solidarity between women he recovered by restoring Emilia's speech. Fortunately for Parker, the fact that Emilia's speech follows the 'song of Willow' and the sighed 'these men, these men' may save the scene: her speech is too wry and witty about husbands to overlay it with wistful images of lovelorn men. So the scene ends intimately: Emilia sits on the bed, she smiles and Desdemona smiles back, and, after exchanging goodnights, Emilia kisses her mistress.

That kiss brings me to the boy-players who originally performed women's parts in Shakespeare's day, the ones we love to talk about in cross-dressed comedy, but generally eschew in discussions of tragedy – the ones even *Shakespeare in Love*, that playful pop romanticization of old Queen Bess's England, has to get around. But like Cleopatra refusing to 'see / Some squeaking Cleopatra *boy* my greatness / I' th' posture of a whore' upon the Roman stage (*A&C* 5.2.219–21), Desdemona's 'unpin me here' comes daringly close to unmasking the great illusion of English Renaissance tragedy, to revealing the absence of women on the stage. Around this matter there has been a good deal of debate and theorizing by critics such as Rackin (1987), Greenblatt (1988), Jardine (1989), Traub (1992), Howard (1994), Orgel (1999), and others – much of it focused on the effects, specifically the erotic effects, of this all-male mode of production in comedy. How conscious was the audience of the cross-dressing in the theater? Though some consciousness now seems obvious in the comedies, how near the surface can the convention come in tragedy without breaking the illusion – if illusion-making is what Elizabethan and Jacobean theater is all about, if illusion-making meant the same thing to them as it does to us, and thus what, if any, relation there is between 'playing' and illusion? How variable was the audience response to the boy-player and how various were the members of the audience, in particular how many women were there and of what classes? And do the demographics matter? How different or similar were the conceptions of boy and woman – in other words, how alike are their gender categories and ours? Was the effect homoerotic and does that mean what it does to us?

Now film by itself does not automatically raise these issues; if anything, it solidifies the tradition of women playing the female parts that came to dominate public theater in England during and after the Restoration, further erasing the theatrical practices of early modern England within and for which Shakespeare wrote. But for students of Shakespeare familiar with those practices, watching a film like Olivier's or Parker's can produce some curious realizations: Maggie Smith's 'unpin me here' suggests undressing, but the conventions of stage and film within which Olivier was working (on the verge of collapsing entirely at the time of this film) tend to avoid nudity. From our vantage point, there is a certain reticence about and high stylization of the body in both the high-culture theater of Olivier's era and the Hays Code that governed the Hollywood studios of Olivier's prime. Though the bedroom scene in his 1948 *Hamlet* must have seemed remarkable for its explicit sexuality, today students and other viewers tend to find it mannered and formal. Similarly, in the 'willow scene', Maggie Smith's Desdemona signals her disrobing, rather than actually doing so, as might have happened had Polanski directed an *Othello* akin to his *Macbeth* of the 1970s, once notorious for its nude sleepwalking Lady Macbeth (1971). So here we students of Shakespeare are reminded that the representation of gender is a matter of conventions, both in Shakespeare's day and in Olivier's. Though both conventions point toward the body of the actor playing the woman's part, the effects are, I think, quite different. We might ask ourselves whether or how it matters that neither the Renaissance boy-actor nor Maggie Smith can be 'unpinned'. We might ask what it says about gender codes and construction in each period – as well as our own.

In contrast, Parker exposes the female body: here we are firmly in the world not only of having blacks be blacks, but of letting men be men and women be women. But that is not all. As anyone who witnessed the birth of *Star Wars* in the late 1970s knows, film can make impossible fantasies reality – or at least make them appear real. So in Parker's film, we see Cassio in bed with Desdemona as presumably Othello sees her in his mind's eye, prompted by Iago. We see interpolated bedroom scenes between Othello and Desdemona too – and even a hint of *ménage a trois*. No reticence about the body here – no all-male conventions or residual Hays Code to contend with. Our conventions focus on the body of the actor – the female and increasingly the male body. Thus Emilia is pouring Desdemona's bath and seems peeved and/or suspicious about Othello's command that Desdemona dismiss her.

Here's where, as I've suggested elsewhere (Green 2002), the contemporary film's encounter with academia may come into play: I am absolutely convinced that in the traitor scene of his *Henry 5* Branagh is making use of contemporary new-historical accounts of bedfellowship, and here I think Parker is influenced by his Iago, who has a gossipy speech about sharing a bed with Cassio, as officer-soldiers might well have done. Starting with Alan Bray in the late 1970s and early 1980s, historians of sexuality have been looking at the common early modern practice of sharing a bed with a companion of the same sex. There were certainly practical reasons – warmth and preserving virginity (and thereby marriageability and the whole system of inheritance) among the foremost. But then there are the more speculative yet nonetheless reasonable ones: controlling the presumably riotous sexual impulses of the young, providing a 'safe' form of intimacy (these are more problematic since clearly any sexual relations, especially sodomitic ones, would have been officially frowned upon), allowing for some choice about whom one is intimate with both before and after marriage (in other words, spouses might be arranged, but bedfellows can be chosen). At any rate, Emilia here seems to be asking, 'Why does Othello want you to dismiss me? That usually signals conjugal relations, but you two haven't exactly been getting along lately. I don't trust him'. And because we know so little about how these relationships worked, she may be adding, 'Why doesn't he just have me leave when he gets here – as he usually does?' In other words, I think it is possible that Parker is suggesting that the two women regularly sleep together and that this dismissal might be a departure from the norm. This would be part of the intimacy of mistress and lady-in-waiting, along with dressing or (if this scene is believable) bathing when their spouses are not demanding their company in bed. Oddly enough, the ahistorical addition of bathing to this scene – to signal intimacy – is indeed what makes me think that Parker has some such historicist notion of bedfellowship in mind. Forget unpinning, here Irene Jacob's back is washed by Anna Patrick.

I am not claiming that the intimacy here means that Desdemona and Emilia are lovers, although such an interpretation might wreak some fruitful havoc on this play, as did the lesbian Princess Hamlet in a Cincinnati Shakespeare Festival production I saw a few years ago at the annual meeting of the Shakespeare Association of America in Cleveland

(Minidakis 1998). Interesting as such reinterpretations are, they seem more like adaptations than the play itself. Nevertheless, the heightened intimacy of Parker's scene, with its emphasis on the body and touch, suggests – through a certain homoeroticism – an intimacy (even a love) different from that of the marriage, a refuge from the war that Othello has ironically moved from the martial field to the marital bedroom even as he has announced how marriage and cuckoldry have undermined his generalship among men: 'Othello's occupation's gone' (3.3.357). Parker gives us in this scene an instance of the lesbian continuum of Adrienne Rich's famous 1980 article about 'compulsory heterosexuality' (1993). Emilia's critique of husbands and marriage even smacks of Rich's descriptions of female marriage resisters and other critics of the institution.

But I would not want to take the argument too far. Emilia's speech starts with a rejoinder to Desdemona's unbelievably naïve claim that no woman would ever betray her husband by committing adultery. Emilia could just laugh, but her wry response – 'who would not make her husband a cuckold to make him a monarch?' (4.3.75–7) – focuses on adultery as an expression of loving one's husband enough to risk damnation. In a scene played differently, the line could make one wonder: did Emilia sleep with Othello in a presumably unsuccessful effort to get Iago a promotion? In this film, it suggests to me Emilia's unfortunate fidelity to Iago, her concern for him, even though here she makes light of the lengths to which she would go – or has gone if we remember the purloined handkerchief that is causing so much grief. So there was no need to bring Othello or Iago into this scene: in the final exchanges between Emilia and Desdemona 'these men, these men' are all too present. Parker should have remembered that less is more, but I think that the fear of bringing the female intimacy in this scene too close to lesbianism has scared him into using the image of Othello here in much the same way that the woman is used in buddy movies of the 1970s like *Butch Cassidy and the Sundance Kid*. Whether out of 'ambivalence' toward his own directorial or his actor's instincts or in an attempt to control an 'unruly cinematic text' (Gajowski 2005) by bringing in the phantasm of the husband, Parker forestalls the potential homoeroticism of the female intimacy he has so daringly underscored. But even if his scene falls short of a private moment between women, it certainly offers an alternative to the scene as mere interlude before resuming the action and even to the Olivier/Burge version of the scene as an emblem of feminine pathos. In its focus on the female body, Parker's scene simultaneously erases, recalls, and transforms the same-sex intimacy prompted by Desdemona's textually conflated request: 'prithee unpin me here'.

Scene 3: the function of film clips at the present time

> Meanwhile the complexities of affective time will continue to proliferate in ways not mapable in terms of 'successive revolutions', revealing a fundamental incommensurability between subjectivity and historicity. To this extent, the very notion of a 'historicized subject' of early-, mid-, or post-modernity is a contradiction in terms. Perhaps this is one of the reasons why Shakespeare continues to be 'timeless': not because he 'transcends' History but because we were never early modern.
>
> –Linda Charnes (2000b, 65)

As Laurie Osborne has noted (2002), the use of film clips in class has affected our very experience of the text: when we focus on the 'willow scene', that section takes on an interpretive prominence that may obscure or overwhelm or reshape other possibilities. And given the at-home feeling we all have about film and video in this culture, these clips may naturalize what is in fact an arbitrary interpretive choice on our part – just as surely as Cleanth Brooks's choice of a metaphor made that one seem, when I was in college, the key to a particular Donne poem. I am not denying that stage performances can have a similar effect, can reshape the way we experience a text we return to or remember. But once seen they can only have that effect memorially; film can keep affecting us – we can come back for more. So when we show a clip – and even more certainly when we show more than one of the same or different scenes – we are constructing our own film, our own primitive hypertext. Our path through Shakespeare may never be quite the same again.

And those clips come from films and videos, as we have seen, shaped by a particular mode of production and by their historical and ideological contexts. But records though they are of the past, they are far from transparent – not least because they are always screened in new contexts, often pedagogical ones. Our seminars and conferences and classes re-play Shakespeare in ways that reveal at least as much about us and the reasons for our 'investment' in Shakespeare as about the historical playwright who lived in early modern England or his work or the reception of his work. All the way back in *Political Shakespeare* (Dollimore and Sinfield, 1985b), Alan Sinfield emphasized the functions of

Shakespeare at the present time: 'Shakespeare is one of the places where ideology is made' (1985, 132). Sinfield's interest in the reproductions of Shakespeare has in the two intervening decades played second fiddle to recovering the early modern, but the ghost of presentism has returned to haunt the once-new historicism.

Crossed-dressed boy-players, the Hays Code, homoeroticism at the Globe (Shakespeare's and Mark Rylance's), Shakespeare on and in film – we can approach early modern manifestations of gender and sexuality, terms that are really ours and not theirs, only through our own ideological perspectives on these and other cultural categories. Needless to say, the categories themselves are hardly as neat as we make them out to be. For instance, in Hatcher and Eyre's film evocation of the moment when gender and performance realigned themselves with biology on the aptly named Restoration stage, Billy Crudup's Ned Kynaston gives up playing Desdemona and takes on the role of Othello. *Stage Beauty*'s choice of *Othello* is telling, because in this new era Kynaston – formerly the 'most beautiful woman on the London stage' – must face the irrelevance of his own understanding of man and woman, as well as of same-sex and heterosexual desires, both onstage and off. Interestingly, in the play's final scene, his Othello is not the oversized, bombastic black villain of Tom Wilkinson earlier in the film, but a vulnerable and self-doubting black outsider. It is no accident the filmmakers give us a feminized depiction of the black man as the precursor of modern realism, because Hatcher's screenplay reflects, though sensitively and rather self-consciously, a U.S. literary tradition and ideology at least as old as Harriet Beecher Stowe's Uncle Tom and Mark Twain's Jim. But the depiction is not a simple one. This traditionally feminine vulnerability is played off the racist stereotype of Othello as a black sexual predator – indirectly but clearly articulated by Brabantio (1.2.62–81). Indeed, race, gender, and sexuality move center-stage as Kynaston and Maria take up their new parts. Given the complexities, it is little wonder *Stage Beauty* offers this theatrical moment as the harbinger of modernity.

Presentism is not ahistorical; it is not the other of history but the condition of history. In this sense, *Stage Beauty* is not merely an exercise in imaginary stage history and/or in imaginatively 'historicizing' sexual ambiguity and gender bending, though it certainly seems to be both. The film, however anachronistically, also leads us to inquire into the complicated intersection of race, gender, and sexuality in our past(s) and present(s) – U.S., British, Restoration, historical, literary, Shakespearean. The 'clip' from the final scene of *Othello*, with which

Stage Beauty culminates, is of course not authentic, but it creates an impetus to reinterpret, to reinvent, our past and, in so doing, to re-create our present and ourselves. This impetus is presentism: an attitude toward historicism, a self-consciousness not just about history but also about the impossibility – and the inevitability – of our making history.

Notes

1. What follows has grown out of an address to student and faculty participants in an undergraduate Shakespeare colloquium at St. Olaf College, 'Winter Will Power' (Northfield, MN, 16–17 February 2001), sponsored by the St Olaf and Carleton English and Theater Departments, that also served as the basis of a position paper ('Shakespeare in Love: Sexuality, Cinema, and the Literature Classroom') for the 2001 SAA (Shakespeare Association of America) Workshop on Shakespeare and the Moving Image: The Pedagogy of Film. In March 2003 at an RSA (Renaissance Society of America) session on Genre, moderated by Heather Dubrow, I treated some of the same Shakespearean material in a paper entitled 'Desperately Seeking Desdemona: Film, Gender, and Shakespearean Tragedy', which led me to reassess some of my earlier claims in light of film theory and the growing body of literature treating Shakespeare on film. However, my overall sense of the significance of the willow scene (4.3) remains indebted to Eamon Grennan's article in *Shakespeare Quarterly* (1987). References to Shakespeare's plays are taken from the second Riverside edition (1997b) .
2. Though I am not focusing on it here, I must mention the image of Olivier as Othello (Burge 1965). In his performance, as contrasted with Fishburne's (Parker 1995), we see a bit of the contested stage history of the play: the matter of Othello's race, who can and should play the part, and how. Whether or not Olivier's version is meant to be sympathetic and/or veristic (and folks still fight about it), this black-face performance reminds us that our *Othello* – that of the black actor playing out the history of the black man's encounter with Europe (and vice-versa), which is further shadowed by the particular history of slavery in this country – is decidedly *not* the version that has so long reigned on the stage. Indeed, for every Ira Aldredge, the great black nineteenth-century Shakespearean of whom Errol Hill has written so eloquently (1984), for every Paul Robeson or James Earl Jones or Laurence Fishburne, there must be dozens or hundreds of artificially darkened Othellos. And even the degrees of blackness were contested – witness the tawny North African of Anthony Hopkins in the BBC production (Miller 1981) vs. Olivier's 1960s evocation of the Negro. The facts and implications of these performance choices and conditions are still being worked out and debated by theater and film historians and Shakespeare scholars. And as not-so-distant radical biracial productions like Janet Suzman's in South Africa remind us (1988), such choices will likely remain significant for some time to come. The significance of this play in the West – its place in shaping and reflecting our troubled history of race – is crystallized in seeing Olivier and Fishburne juxtaposed. See also the brief discussion of Billy Crudup's

feminized Othello in *Stage Beauty* (Eyre 2005) at the end of this essay. Among the many works, in addition to Hill's, that have influenced my thinking on race in *Othello* are those of Karen Newman (1987), Martin Orkin (1987), Stephen Greenblatt (1988), Valerie Wayne (1991a), Jyotsna Singh (1994), and Barbara Hodgdon (1998).

Part IV

Uncivil Unions

10
Uncivil Unions

Linda Charnes

> Any sociological system theory that treats 'truth' functionalistically…carries an immense potential for cynicism.
>
> –Peter Sloterdijk

> We only hate gays because it's in right now. Hating gays, hating evolution…it's the new Age of Enlightenment.
>
> –Karen, *Will and Grace*

In *A Critique of Cynical Reason*, philosopher Peter Sloterdijk argues that one of the most enduring effects of the Enlightenment has been 'a mania for identity': an obsession with being 'a formal somebody'. As distinct from earlier eras, in which social order, gender, class, and even religious affiliation 'identified' their bearers through external mechanisms, the post-Enlightenment mania for identity is largely an internalized phenomenon: 'As bearer of our social identifications [it] is, so to speak, programmed into us' in our youth (1987, 73). Prior to the nineteenth century, identities were arguably functions of traditional social structures that both organized and performed people's identifications for them. If, for instance, one happened to be born a duke or a peasant, the conscious adoption of that identity was unnecessary since it was essentially a by-product of a position that had real, objective social existence. Like the Buddhist prayer wheel that, when physically turned, 'objectively prays' for its user (irrespective of what he or she may be thinking), a term that designated a social position fulfilled its purpose without the need for its bearer even to think about it.[1] Duke, peasant, tinker, prince, even wife, conveyed social identities that superceded individual ones. Christopher Sly, in the Induction to *The Taming of the Shrew*, asks the Lord what to call the 'woman' who is presented to him as his long-suffering wife. The

Lord tells him, 'Madam'. 'Alice Madam or Joan Madam?' 'Madam, and nothing else, so lords call ladies' is the Lord's answer.[2]

Of course, the very fact that the Lord perpetrates this nasty trick reveals his own excessive self-consciousness about 'being a Lord' and his anxiety about men who (like the pesky 'new man' or even a lowly drunken tinker) do not know their place. There have always been exceptions to the rule, people at odds with their social designations (and especially among more 'outcast' groups, such as 'bastards' and 'unclaimed women'). The 'givenness' of traditional identities was contradicted, if not undermined, across several categories in early modern England, the most obvious example of which was Queen Elizabeth herself, who turned the generic role of 'woman' on its ear, refusing to give way to the subordinate and reproductive requirements of that primal baptism 'Madam Wife'.[3] In Shakespeare's plays, excessive self-consciousness is usually the central dilemma, as figures as different as Richard 2, Malvolio, Katherina, Christopher Sly, Edmund, Othello, Olivia, and Hamlet, among many others, have illustrated. In general however, Sloterdijk's point about post-Enlightment subjectivity holds true, since it describes less a social category than an awareness of degree: the radical *internalization* of a *desire* for social identity, a process that is the result of the 'years of apprenticeship in inwardness' that every child undergoes as s/he is programmed into the gender system (1987, 72). This 'apprenticeship in inwardness' operates largely unconsciously, laying the groundwork for subjective conditions that will manifest themselves only later: 'in becoming aware of oneself, men and women discover a spontaneity of feeling constituted in such and such a way: I like her; I don't like him; those are my impulses, this turns me on; those are my wishes' (1987, 72). If earlier eras did not require (or permit) one to *decide* to be a duke or peasant, contemporary Western culture teaches people to aspire (whether up or down) to any social identity they please. This is not to be understood merely as a desire for social mobility, which was fairly rampant in Shakespeare's day (and in Shakespeare himself). 'Betterment', however, was still understood more as a structural commodity – an objective social position achieved through, say, service or marriage – than as a psychological property or a quality of inwardness.

Here I should differentiate between how I am using the terms *identity* and *identification*, since in the remainder of my discussion they will overlap but are not synonymous. By identity, I mean a fixed and presumably 'permanent' social *and* psychological entity that is the end result of decisions having already been made with regard to a vast range of preferences, occupations, and sensibilities: choices made to the definitive exclusion of other choices. If one 'has' an identity one is, so to speak, finished or 'decided'.[4] By identifications, I mean something less fixed and more mobile: tendencies and affiliations that may be no less programmed, perhaps, but have not yet been permanently 'decided upon': affiliations that are still (to use the lamentable new-age phrase) 'in process'. Which presents us with an interesting paradox: despite our contemporary 'mania for identity', we live in a culture whose commerce and economy depends less upon identity than it does upon identifications. The myth (or maybe the reality) of 'spontaneity of feeling', the ability to be persuaded now this way and now that, to be perpetually changing one's mind along with one's options, drives the consumer marketplace. A fixed or permanent identity would bring to a halt the endless metonymic slide of consumer desire for the marketed 'changes' in subjectivity that keep us buying ever new products and services. Not for nothing is the Makeover – the 'renovation' of our personalities, our bodies, our homes – the new great U.S. spectacle. Our new cultural apotheosis, both sublime and fleeting, is 'the Reveal', whose epiphanic thrill lasts only until the next makeover.

Despite, however, the fungibility of so many categories of identity (for instance, a 'gangsta rapper' who is also a clothing mogul, an ex-housewife who controls a product empire), there is still one category that has been frozen in abreaction, subjected to a backlash of identity mania, and that is gender. The 2004 elections saw 11 states, including the usually liberal Oregon, ratify amendments to ban gay marriages; and in June of 2006, Congress voted on whether or not to pass a Federal Marriage Amendment, which would ban same-sex marriages in the Constitution (it was taken off the table, but presumably only for the nonce). In July 2006, even the New York Supreme Court decided that banning same-sex marriages was not an unconstitutional infringement upon civil rights. The recent elevation of heterosexual marriage to the status of apotropaic fetish is contradicted by an increasing acceptance of homosexual unions in daily life and in the realm of entertainment. Many of the same Americans who are against same-sex marriage 'in principle' enjoy consuming sentimental fantasies of gay civil unions (as in popular entertainments such as *Four Weddings and a Funeral*, and in *Will and Grace*), or even in 'grittier' versions (as in *Brokeback Mountain*). Domesticated homosexuals in film and television are not threatening, as long as their most passionate commitments are to decorating their homes (and ours), styling our hair, and cooking for their fondly indulgent heterosexual friends. We readily hand over to presumed gay 'expertise' many of the same domestic arts most associated with married life. The recent campaign, therefore, by activist anti-homosexual legislators against full legal rights for gay unions is bizarre in a culture that now, more than ever before, embraces queer eyes for the straight guys. We could call this disjunction a textbook case of 'cynical idealism': cynicism expressed by and through, rather than expressed against, an idealist fantasy.[5] Even as our culture plays endlessly with gay identifications, when it comes to legalizing same-sex marriage and the benefits therein, a majority of Americans continues to insist that heterosexual gender is the one 'true' identity category that transcends time, place, and politics and, lest we forget that, must be protected by constitutional law. If we have a mania for any identity, it seems to come down to this.

Although many people readily concede a difference between biological sex and social gender codes, there remains a stubborn undercurrent of 'rock bottom' gender binarism, making it arguably the most successful holdout from pre-Enlightenment, and premodern, political economy. Among all the other shifting identities offered to us by the mania for identity, the early modern patriarchal doctrine of 'gender complementarity' seems to have stuck. With women earning money in the workplace, and new reproductive technologies increasingly available, gender complementarity increasingly seems a fantasmatic specter cut loose from its former economic and even reproductive necessity. Free-market capitalism no longer requires traditional heterosexual roles in order to sell us things we do not need. Thus the recent hysteria about constitutionally legislating marriage as a 'sanctified' heterosexual institution reveals that the formerly 'self-evident' truth of the heterosexual norm is under historic pressure and must now be redeployed, even if only *ritualistically*, for tradition's sake. The major argument articulated against homosexual marriage is functionalistic: opponents claim that *only* traditional marriage serves and protects the interests of children, and that the *only* purpose of marriage is the procreation of children. In today's culture, however, this is demonstrably untrue; consequently, the deployment of a crudely functionalist argument masquerading as a values-discourse carries, as the epigraph to this essay says, a 'tremendous potential for cynicism'.

While such arguments are certainly reactionary and further a conservative agenda tied to election-year politics, I believe that the current movement to 'protect the sanctity of marriage' reflects something more than just 'idealism' about families, sex and marriage, something more amorphous. The obsessive focus on gay marriage is the field upon which many of our cultural anxieties about history, and what it should mean, are being played out. 'Tradition', G. K. Chesterton said, 'means giving votes to the most obscure of all classes, our ancestors. It is the democracy of the dead. Tradition refuses to submit to the small and arrogant oligarchy of those who merely happen to be walking about' (2000, 207). The most politically powerful argument against gay marriage – one that unites religious and secular platforms – is less that it goes 'against nature' (although this is the stance of religious conservatives) but that it goes against history and tradition: that the two-parent, heterosexual family is the last bulwark against *historical* (not necessarily biological) discontinuity. We cannot, the argument goes, let those who 'merely happen to be walking about', try to alter 'the democracy of the dead'. Despite the fact that most polls indicate a steady 50 percent divorce rate, and philandering is estimated to occur in somewhere between 50 to 70 percent of households, the family-values brigade continues to insist that marriage between a man and a woman is a condition mandated by divine fiat.

Even the most casual observation, however, suggests that the biggest threat to the 'sanctity' of marriage and the family comes not from gay unions but from *within* the existing institution. Such denial of the obvious would border on delusional were it not, as I think it is, substituting for other anxieties. In a society that disavows class differences, no longer officially endorses open displays of racism or sexism (even Mel Gibson had to apologize for his anti-Semitic rant), and considers itself 'pluralistic', gender identity has become the main vehicle which sustains every other 'mania for identity'. U.S. nationalism, which frequently seems to outweigh all other identities, is modeled on our views of what it means to be a man – to be 'Ram tough'. Yet marriage is the only social institution to which the word 'sanctity' is regularly attached, the only one whose doctrine requires us to sign up for a 'metaphysical mortgage' (Sloterdijk 1987, 357). As a socio-economic political institution presented as a sanctified one, marriage bears a structural similarity to the same 'negative hallucination' that for centuries underwrote the doctrine of the divine right of kings.[6]

On the Shakespearean stage, the cultural force of the 'negative hallucination' – of seeing what is *not* visible while refusing to see the obvious – is most vividly played out in *Twelfth Night*, which is all about multiple gender identifications that must, by Act 5, be transformed into single identities, no matter how dubious that transformation may be. The characters, if not the audience, has to agree to be 'convinced' by the rapid conclusion that everyone has what he or she really wanted all along. While the play's conclusion self-consciously privileges traditional biological sexual identity, its preceding acts thematize a mania for gender cross-identifications. Critics have often remarked that Olivia's attraction to Cesario seems partly based on her desire to retain class superiority, and that it 'balances out' her subjection as a female by letting her keep her superior status as an aristocrat relative to a servant. Orsino's rationale for sending Cesario as his ambassador uses the logic that nature, 'in her bias', will better enable penetration of Olivia's resistance through the appeal, the supposed intimacy, of 'likeness'. But the question of what constitutes attraction of *any* kind is at the very heart of the play; is beauty seen in the eye or in the mind? The 'mistaken identities' effect a complete separation between gender as performative and bodies as biological 'givens'. Orsino's moodiness, his performative subjection to the pangs of Petrarchan love, effeminize him (as his attendants nervously point out when they ask, 'Will you hunt, my lord?'). Olivia's manipulation of her household and her self-bestowal and selection of Cesario are clearly masculinizing traits. When she and Cesario engage in their banter, it is not possible to say who plays more fully the 'woman's part'. Is Olivia attracted to Cesario's feminine appearance? If so, her sexual attraction may be based on lesbian desire; if she is attracted to Cesario's haughty swagger and wit despite his feminine appearance, the attraction would be heteroerotic – an attraction based on performative gender rather than biological signifiers of sex. In other words, we are left to wonder if Olivia has a queer eye for the straight guy, or a straight eye for a queer guy. Or given the play's artificial 'cure' of its biosexual mismatches, does the question of queer or straight make any sense at all when talking about what makes a couple 'companionate'? At the play's end, the two most 'companionate' couplings are unquestionably the most homoerotic: that of Cesario and Orsino, which can be publically ratified because of the 'body beneath', and that of Sebastian and Antonio, which cannot be ratified for precisely the same reason.[7]

In 1634, John Milton, in 'The Doctrine and Discipline of Divorce', conflated the religious and civil realms by arguing that 'In God's intention, a meet and happy conversation is the chiefest and noblest end of marriage' (2003). The Protestant notion of companionate marriage offered an alternative to the harsh Pauline view of the institution, which saw it as a way for men simultaneously to subjugate women and to mortify their own sexual urges by strictly limiting them to the reproductive confines of marriage. In Milton's view, 'meet and happy conversation' encompasses not only the socially appropriate but the pleasurable as well, and privileges a mode of engagement that has little directly to do with how the genitals are used. This is not to say that Milton would have supported homosexual marriage – clearly he would not have; but he recognizes that intellectual and emotional companionability is the one 'fit' that matters above all others, a fit not in any way guaranteed by biologically different sets of genitals. Acknowledging that many couples are childless, Milton avers that it is 'God's intention' that the 'noblest end' of marriage is an ideal friendship; and if 'meet and happy conversation' is the chief and noblest aim, then procreation must be considered subsidiary to that aim. In other words, while sexuality may be bracketed by Milton's version of companionability, reproduction is as well. The dominant value in companionate marriage is not reproduction but an ideal friendship. If this is the standard by which marriage may be judged, Olivia will surely find herself unsatisfied by marriage to smug and passive Sebastian, who lacks Viola's masculine wit, humor, and vitality. By the play's end, proper sexual arrangements have been restored, but at the cost, at least in the case of Olivia, Sebastian and Antonio, of a companionability based not on binary sexual oppositions but on multiple gender identifications.

That gender is fluid and operates independently of biological sex is something that Shakespeare, and perhaps his audience, understood. The fact that male and female 'parts' were all played by male actors underscored the theatricality of gender as a performative rather than a 'natural' category. Although the Judeo-Christian doctrine of 'gender complementarity', with its system of binary oppositional traits assigned to men and women, proferred an ideological fantasy of absolute gender difference, it could not effectively police the 'spillover' of characteristics between male and female sides of the balance-sheet. As many scholars have pointed out, effeminized men and masculine women prominently figure as recurrent themes in Renaissance drama.[8] Despite the gender experiments on the early modern stage, however, marriage as a cultural institution was still *by necessity* the union between a man and a woman because it was the only route to 'legitimate' procreation. Lacking the technologies of contemporary science and medicine, sexual intercourse between a man and a woman was the only way to induce pregnancy and guarantee offspring. With legal procreation forming the entire basis for the hereditary disposition of property, as well as social and political position, marriage between a man and a woman was an indispensable mechanism of biological and cultural transmission. Its relationship to the actual 'gender' of its participants may have been anything but 'straight', but the requirement of biologically different bodies went unquestioned.

With social status, political alliance, economic stability, and the transmission of property all dependent upon the production of legitimate offspring whose bodies contained the bloodlines of both parents, marriage between a man and woman in Shakespeare's time was not the idealist fantasy it has become today. Rather, it was a concrete system of relations upon which *all other forms of social commerce depended*. Precisely because there was only one route to reproduction, the particularly heightened discourse that we now call 'family values' was not necessary in Shakespeare's day. Certainly marriages were administered through the church, Protestant or Catholic; and yet, the foregrounding of its unchallengeably primary function – as the mode for the organization and transmission of monies, titles, properties and estates, made the 'metaphysical mortgage' a by-product, the ideological icing on what nearly everyone understood to be a pragmatic cake. By contrast, today's discourse of 'family values' floats a raft of sentimentalist fictions in which all family relations are imagined solely to be warmly benign. In early modern England in general, and in Shakespeare's plays in particular, any talk of 'family values' would have to include fraternal competition and rivalry, murderous resentment about birth order; suppression and oppression of wives and daughters; and seething distrust between parents and children.

Paradoxically, therefore, although traditional marriages were far less idealized in Shakespeare's time than they are today, they were also less *functionally* cynical. Sloterdijk argues that 'any sociological system that treats 'truth' functionalistically... carries an immense potential for cynicism' (1987). I would add, however, that any sociological system that treats truth functionalistically, whilst aggressively disavowing that it does so, displays not cynicism *per se* but 'cynical idealism'. This unholy twist on cynicism is, according to Sloterdijk, an inevitable by-product of post-Enlightenment culture, which continues to insist upon traditional moral codes formerly enforced by religion while no longer believing in their universalist or essential foundations. The social critique that has always been implicit in cynicism – its rebuke of idealist hegemonies – is, under cynical idealism, defanged, recruited now for the propagation of the very benefits that accrue to such hegemonies. Cynical idealism is 'enlightened false consciousness' (1987, 5), or 'cheekiness that has changed sides' (1987, 110). Although Sloterdijk sees this mutation in the history of cynicism strictly as a post-Enlightenment phenomenon, Shakespeare's plays frequently illustrate a similar dialectic between cynicism and cynical idealism. *Twelfth Night* is a clear example of the latter, while *Measure for Measure* has the (arguable) virtue at least of standing by its frank cynicism, of not even gesturing toward a supremacy of ideals – which raises for us an interesting but troubling question: which is better (or worse), cynical idealism or cynicism straight-up?

In *Measure for Measure,* the functionalistic truth of marriage strictly as social management is thrust upon the characters whether they like it or not. Marriage in the play is the primary delivery-device of both 'discipline and punishment', a Foucauldian instrument if ever there were one.[9] Claudio and Juliet, commonlaw spouses despite her lack of dowry, have a companionate (insofar as it is self-chosen) marriage but lack the imprimatur of state and church. When the Duke sets up his shell-game, they are among the first to be subjected to the crushing power of the state apparatus – channeled now through Angelo, the perfect scapegoat. The aim clearly is to censure, by harsh example, the very *idea* of unsanctioned enjoyment of each others' bodies and their conception of offspring not 'officially' recognized by the church. Throughout the play the biggest perceived threat to the authority of state power is sexual commerce that does not return profit to the Duke's coffers. Represented by the shutting down of 'the houses', this reasserted sovereignty over bodily communion may reinforce the laws, but it interferes with Viennese citizens' ability to conduct financial, and sexual, commerce. At stake is not the sanctity of marriage but the status of Law and of citizens' relationship to it. 'Legitimate' marriage becomes the litmus of compliance with sovereignty. Everyone is forced into the same disciplinary straitjacket by the play's end: Lucio, for gossiping about the 'Duke of dark corners', is condemned to be married 'to a punk'; Angelo, to the woman he has grievously abused (and clearly does not love); and the Duke literally 'takes' Isabella, whose *only* desire for a sanctified union is explicitly non-sexual: to be a nun. In this play, Marriage is Marriage for the same reason that Law is Law: not because it makes sense in every particular circumstance but precisely because it does not have to make sense – it is Law. As Slavoj Zizek puts it in his discussion of Pascal's separation of belief and habit, law has 'a constitutively senseless character':

> we must obey it not because it is just, good or even beneficial, but simply *because it is the law* – this tautology articulates the vicious circle of its authority, the fact that the last foundation of the Law's authority lies in its process of enunciation ... obedience out of conviction is not real obedience because it is already 'mediated' through our subjectivity – that is, we are not really obeying the authority, simply following our judgement, which tells us that the authority deserves to be obeyed in so far as it is good, wise, beneficent. (1989, 37)

In other words, we do not obey the law because its principles make sense to us, or because we 'agree' with it: such subscription would be consent, not obedience. Rather, we obey it because we must, irrespective of what we think; furthermore, the foundational authority of Law is founded in its 'incomprehensible' character, which is its 'positive condition' (1989, 37). Law is most Law when it makes no sense to us but we obey it anyway. In *Measure for Measure*, the Duke's aim in leaving Angelo to impose the lapsed law is not to convince his subjects of the law's validity but to translate a picayune set of 'strict statutes' into a Law of shock and awe. In *Measure*'s world, companionability, as a criterion of choice unto itself, is a threat to the state, for it prioritizes the subjective experience of volition. In a state where Law is Law, what people really want from each other is beside the point. Seen in this light, the Duke's 'seizure' of Isabella – despite his lip-service to her 'willing ear' (5.1.529) – exhibits perfectly that 'kernel of irrationality' needed to turn marriage into Marriage.

Shakespeare repeatedly approaches the complex issue of companionability through disruptive and unauthorized cross-identifications: of gender, class, and even race. In his world there is no ideological platform for either interracial, or same-sex marriage. There is, however, a stage for it. There is arguably one play in which a 'same-sex' marriage takes place; but it can occur only through the 'homosocial' triangulation provided by a woman (Sedgwick 1985). If Antonio, silent and unaccommodated, drops out of the marriage picture at the end of *Twelfth Night*, his predecessor finds himself factored into its embrace. At the end of Act 5 of *The Merchant of Venice*, Portia, having finally arrived at the 'truth' of Antonio and Bassanio's desire when Bassanio gives her ring away to 'Balthassar', realizes that the *only* way to secure her marriage to Bassanio is to make accommodation within it for Antonio. The second ring exchange, in which Portia instructs Antonio to hand the ring directly to Bassanio on her behalf, includes Antonio in the ceremonial 'loop' of desire. By incorporating Antonio into the symbolic structure of her marriage, not only does Portia acknowledge the futility of forcing either of them to 'choose' against his desire but she manages to cobble together a 'companionate' marriage, albeit a crowded one.

The conclusion to the play gives us a mixture of destabilized sex and gender arrangements. Both Antonio and Bassanio display traits from the 'female' side of the 'complementarity' ledger – Bassanio is effeminized by his need to borrow funds, both from Antonio and then from Portia; Antonio is self-effeminized by his own martyrdom and his passive willingness to embrace it: 'the weakest kind of fruit / Drops earliest to the ground' (4.1.114–15). For Portia, however, femininity is obviously a masquerade. After delivering her orthodox performance as a poor 'unlearned girl' in Act 3, she shuffles off its girlish coil with dispatch, running to prove that, in terms of gender, she can swagger and swear oaths like any bragging jack. The three-way marriage that ends the play includes two male bodies with feminine personalities and a female body gendered male (of course, metatheatrically all three actors are sexed male). Unlike *Twelfth Night*, which makes no accommodation for its Antonio, *The Merchant of Venice* acknowledges that triangulation within the geometry of a circle provides stability: that a ring with three legs makes a sturdy platform on which to stand. In Shakespeare's plays the formation of a union that includes both companionability and sexual reproduction seems to demand some kind of 'same sex' partnership within the institution of marriage, even if it takes three people to pull it off. The incorporation of a homoerotic union into a heterosexual marriage is the only 'cure' for the fetish of what Peter Stallybrass calls 'the body beneath' (1992), that tyrannical arbiter still being used to police 'legitimacy' in marriage today.

If it is true, as Zizek has argued, that we are all 'secretly believers' irrespective of *what* we believe, then to greater or lesser degrees we all maintain an investment in 'irrational' epistemologies – that is to say, in Belief itself (2002). The uneasy co-existence of new reproductive technologies with a 'post-secular' reinvestment in conservative religious or 'moral values' that insist that 'families' should appear in only one form, is *truly* an uncivil union. In the contemporary U.S.– with its wealth, growing population, doctrine of free choice and supposedly equal rights – the continued insistence that body parts, rather than desires, are the only legitimate ground of sexual companionability, and the rejection of more flexible and ultimately more humane definitions of what may constitute a 'family', are unparalleled acts of cynical idealism. If there is any threat to 'marriage' that comes from outside the existing institution, it comes not from homosexual marriage but from the new reproductive technologies. When it comes to sexual reproduction, bodies – hetero- or homo-sexual – can be entirely divorced from their biological functions and yet 'reproduction' can still occur. The really threatening truth is not that same-sex marriages may disrupt heterosexual marriage but that many people no longer have to be married to an 'opposite sex' partner to have, and successfully raise and support, children. If male and female genitals working in concert within the confines of a marriage are no longer the only 'delivery devices' for the ingredients of reproduction, the idealist fantasies used to enforce heterosexual marriage come under threat; for the clear implication is that heterosexual marriage itself may now be – for the first time in history – not the lynchpin of civilization but a 'lifestyle choice' based *purely* on desire and volition. And this is not a bad thing. To privilege desire and volition is not in any way to denigrate heterosexual unions or marriages, which (one could certainly argue) can only gain strength by being 'uncoupled' from reproductive necessity. It is simply to remove the ideological bullet of Nature from the legislative shotgun. Once we acknowledge that the 'truth' of marriage can no longer be treated 'functionalistically', we might have to temper our cynical idealism, and allow that the ethical and *spiritual* right of companionate marriage should be available to any couple, straight or gay, not on the basis of their body parts, but solely as a matter of Will and Grace.

Notes

1. On the Tibetan prayer wheel and the 'objectivity of belief', see Zizek (1989, 34).
2. All references to Shakespeare's plays in this essay are to *The Norton Shakespeare* (1997c).
3. In his discussion of Saul Kripke's work on 'descriptivist' and 'antidescriptivist' signifiers, Zizek argues that a name or a title may be originally assigned as a descriptivist term, one that denotes objective properties, but that over time such a word may come to mean something else, something 'anti-descriptivist' that remains constant no matter how the properties of the original object may change. When such a term carries forward its original meaning despite superficial changes, it is said to have conveyed a 'primal baptism'. The example Zizek gives is 'gold', which began as a term for an element with a 'glittering yellow color'. Now we use the term much more portably; however, it remains tethered to its 'original substance' (1989, chapter 3 passim).
4. For a more complete discussion of how I use the term 'identity', see my introduction in *Notorious Identity: Materializing the Subject in Shakespeare* (1993).
5. This term was coined by Peter Sloterdijk in the introduction to his seminal work *A Critique of Cynical Reason* (1987, passim).
6. On 'negative hallucination', see Zizek (2002).
7. The phrase, 'the body beneath', is taken from Peter Stallybrass's essay 'The Body Beneath: Speculating on the Boy Actor' in *Erotic Politics: Desire on the Renaissance Stage* (1992).
8. Critics who have remarked on this are too numerous to list. A few who have influenced this essay are Lisa Jardine (1983, 1989); Leah Marcus (1986); Jean Howard (1988); Janet Adelman (1992); Marjorie Garber (1992); Madelon Sprengnether (1996); and Dympna Callaghan (1999). There are many others whose work over the last 20 years has been fundamental to our understanding of Shakespeare and gender.
9. See Jonathan Dollimore's classic essay, 'Transgression and Surveillance in *Measure for Measure*', in *Political Shakespeare: Essays in Cultural Materialism* (1985, 1994).

11

'A Local Habitation and a Name': Presence, Witnessing, and Queer Marriage in Shakespeare's Romantic Comedies

Arthur L. Little, Jr

> I do not think [canceling out the right of gay people to marry in Massachusetts] is an appropriate response...certainly not to the threat that millions of people are threatening to commit love.
>
> –Barney Frank[1]

> To claim that a right to engage in such conduct [i.e., homosexual sexual acts] is 'deeply rooted in this Nation's history and tradition' or 'implicit in the concept of ordered liberty' is, at best, facetious.
>
> –U.S. Supreme Court Justice Byron R. White[2]

> Let me not to the marriage of true minds
> Admit impediments.
>
> –William Shakespeare[3]

Why are there so many *possible* queer marriages in Shakespeare's plays? My question may seem a bit 'facetious', a sordid comedic gesture, since our culture so insistently performs the very real *impossibility*, and indiscretion, of queerness, most especially of queer marriage, since queer marriage can only body forth in the imagination, at least here in the liberalism of U.S. imperial culture, as a mockery[4] – a reaction (in all its attendant abjection) – to the institution of heterosexual marriage, both presently and historically. Indeed, queer marriage, like homonormativity more generally, is read as a mockery of history, of national culture itself. But what happens, and I am posing this as a serious and urgent question, to the signifying insignificance of queer marriage in an era in which so many of us (however we feel about the matter) are part of an industrialized late capitalist world (however we feel about the matter) that takes gay marriage seriously? To ask my opening question in a contemporary U.S. that has become very jittery about the possibility of same-sex (queer) marriage does seem to show me accepting Evelyn Gajowski's invitation to foreground the look of Shakespeare, or what Shakespeare could look like, in the present. And to a very real degree... *I do.* Presently, after all, only two states have legalized same-sex marriage; 20 states have passed anti-gay marriage constitutional amendments; 43 states, statutes restricting marriage to one man and one woman; the federal government, the 1996 Defense of Marriage Act; and stalled, at least for now, is an effort to pass the Federal Marriage Amendment that would effectively ban all gay marriages and civil unions in the U.S.[5]

Presentism does indeed seem to be a relevant strategic move here – presentism as an act of not only consciously reading through the present but insisting on its engagement with the deep meanings/enunciations of the Shakespearean example. In trying to make his case for presentism, Terence Hawkes has argued that 'the present ranks, not as an obstacle to be avoided, nor as a prison to be escaped from... it's a factor actively to be sought out, grasped and perhaps, as a result, understood' (2002, 3).[6] And while Hawkes himself is not invested in any affinities between presentism and queerness, it is not surprising that presentism, according to Hawkes, 'finds itself inevitably predisposed to engage sympathetically with those "inverting" tendencies that have lately begun to undermine some of the inherited priorities governing our perception of Shakespeare's plays' (2002, 4–5). There is something more than rhetorically apt about Hawkes's '"inverting" tendencies' and the broader cultural reading of the proclivities (the tendencies) of inverts.[7] It is important to note too the already well-wrought link between queerness and 'the present'. Queerness has been conceptually understood, perhaps more accurately – suspected – to work literally and symbolically as a sign of immediate, unbounded, and undisciplined gratification, the *maintenant.* Not coincidentally, queerness is characterized by its adherence to the present, to presence, whether we speak of queer*ing* history – the Renaissance, the Middle Ages, etc. – or of locating queers *in* history.[8] They both announce themselves as acts of presence, something we can do to history now with our current intellectual investments in the case of the former; and, in the case of the latter, discover queerness (at least in part) through the kind of identitarian understanding of sexuality through which we understand ourselves.

Expectantly, juridical discourse aligns the language of queerness, of sodomy, with the present; this is especially evident in the language of queer marriage (haunted by sodomitical acts), where heterosexual marriage, dominated as it is by discursive strokes to tradition and children, is situated in the past and the future, respectively. Nowhere is all this more evident than in the various legislative and judicial documents surrounding the issue of gay marriage (and sodomy) in the U.S. As the *New York Times* reported on the now notorious 1986 sodomy case, *Bowers v. Hardwick*, the U.S. Supreme Court 'looked to history' to substantiate its case not only against sodomy but against homosexual sexual expression. The Court's opinion invoked 'ancient roots', 'the history of Western Civilization', 'Roman law', 'the Western Christian Tradition', 'Henry 8',[9] and 'the common law of England' during the Reformation. In short, homosexuality was to be made suspect because it belonged so thoroughly to the present. To recognize it as anything else would be 'at best facetious', to recall the epigraph by Justice White, a shrewd or trivializing bit of comedy.

The argument that heterosexuality belongs to history (and biology) and homosexuality to the present (and cultural engineering) is underscored nowhere as much as it is in the debates around queer marriage as may be found in *A Proposed Constitutional Amendment to Preserve Traditional Marriage*, a 53-page document in which the word 'tradition' appears almost one hundred times, often as a qualifier to the words 'marriage', 'family', and 'institution'. While the document marks heterosexuality as historical, it situates homosexuality and same-sex marriage at the site of 'activism', using the word (or its cognates) more than 30 times in reference to them. When conceding anything to homosexuals, the Court allows for gay persons to love but forges a distinction between love – think immediate gratification – and the business of heterosexual marriage, that is, reproduction. To say nothing about the document referencing or alluding to individual families themselves as genealogical or historical entities, the document mentions children, the future, nearly 70 times.[10] Marriage is, in the most encompassing official terms, about children. As Lee Edelman has put it in his highly cogent polemic, '*queerness* names the side of those *not* "fighting for the children", the side outside the consensus by which all politics confirms the absolute value of reproductive futurism' (2004, 3). In short, according to dominant (legislative and judicial) discourse, queer love has only presence, only sodomitical indulgences – it has no future and no past.[11]

Queer marriage in Shakespeare is a question of the present, of presentism, but it is not, I want to argue, only about the present (the temporal) but the ontological (as opposed to what is absent). If the law of the father in Shakespeare's romantic comedies is a kind of historical authority standing in opposition to the present of the unbridled desires of young lovers, then the driving dramatic force of these plays not only flaunts the father's absence but confronts the audience with questions of what is actually theatrically present, that is, male bodies (boys and men). And it is not surprising that presentism as a predisposition finds itself, as Hawkes has shown, emphasizing the *performance* of the play, what the play does.[12] Hawkes pushes to decipher here something beyond recitation, something beyond recovering performance in any narrow historical sense. Following the work of Robert Weimann, Hawkes distinguishes between *playing* and *acting*.[13] Hawkes insists that 'playing, as distinct from acting, evidently embraced a far broader spectrum of activity, both on the stage and in the audience, than appears to modern eyes' (2002, 5). Schematically, the locus of acting is in adherence to the script; of playing, the performer marking himself as literally present, as distinct from the script he recites or the character he evokes. 'The essence of playing' ('a much older practice'), according to Hawkes, 'lies in [an actor's] symbiotic relationship with the audience' (2002, 111). I argue in this essay that where Shakespeare's romantic comedies *act* out heterosexual desire and heterosexual matrimony they *play* with queer desire and queer marriage, and not in spite of the rather schematic nature of my argument, I insist too that Shakespeare's queer marriage plays take full advantage of what is often the ambivalent relationship between acting and playing. Putting aside the issue of heterosexism in much of Renaissance studies, what Jonathan Goldberg and Madhavi Menon call 'compulsory heterotemporality of historicism' (2005, 1616), presentism and queerness do indeed seem to go together, and from the viewpoint of 'traditional' values, any kind of serious endorsement of same-sex marriage – treating it as something other than 'facetious' – would betray the history and rituals of heterosexual marriage to be nothing less or more than a culture at *play*. And not surprisingly, comedy (which privileges playing over acting) emerges, technologically (logistically) and ideologically, as the genre of choice.

In romantic comedy, Shakespeare deals his most extended and most theatrical challenge to heterosexual marriage and insists upon marking out a space for the possibility of queer matrimony.[14] It is important that we attend to these queer marriages in Shakespeare not only because homoeroticism in Shakespeare is so often wrapped in tropes of marriage but because doing so shifts us away from the psychologizing of queerness, a less fruitful enterprise for helping us understand Shakespeare's staging of queer marriage through his staging of compulsory heterosexual marriage. In other words, a discussion of Shakespeare in the present shifts us, not that these are in any way mutually exclusive, from the psychoanalytically nuanced subject to the public sanctioning and witnessing of homosexuality as cultural and institutional category.

It is worth making more playing-performative and less acting-consequential Bruce Smith's word 'yielding', when he argues that 'all of Shakespeare's comedies and tragicomedies end with male friendship yielding place to heterosexual love' (1991, 72): comedy foregrounds and makes fodder of the inevitability of this yielding even as it seemingly gives in to it. Kathryn Schwarz has argued in her discussion of 'what we already know about comedy' that 'socialized desire is an ordering impulse forcibly acted out. Yet that explicitness does a kind of generic damage, revealing that comic conclusions may not have the power to govern or dispel the excesses of comic plots' (2000, 211). Something always seems to be leftover, not quite contained, and if we remind ourselves of Herbert Blau's observation that 'the erotic capacity of theater is not of secondary importance [and that] it's right there, in the bodies' (1982, 289), then it becomes easier to grasp how *playing* bodies propel the queer marriage plots of Shakespeare's romantic comedies. And while it is worth keeping in mind Judith Butler's argument that the performative nature of heterosexuality reveals it to be 'not only ... a compulsory law, but ... an inevitable comedy' (Schwarz 2000, 223), I am interested in the way Shakespeare exploits the heterosexual performative as a way to stage at least the possibility of queer marriage. In other words, returning to Smith's above reading, Shakespeare's romantic comedies end not only with the reifying and presumed stability of heterosexuality but with Shakespeare's audience being coerced into witnessing the end of queer desire and queer marriage.

Shakespeare's romantic comedies are not only deeply aware of the theatricality and seriousness of compulsory heterosexual marriage but of the *use* of this compulsion to make knowable the possibility of queer marriage. Andrew Parker and Eve Kosofsky Sedgwick have argued that 'marriage itself [is] theater ... [it is] a kind of fourth wall or invisible proscenium arch that moves through the world ... continually reorienting around itself the surrounding relations ... of the possibility and impossibility of a given person's articulating a given enunciatory position' (1995, 11). Marriage is of course performative (performed), essentially the enactment of a ritual to bring realness (culture recognition and value) to parties entering an 'artificial kinship' arrangement. There is no apparent difference between such 'artificial' arrangements and those same-sex unions that historians and others in the past especially have labeled as 'artificial kinships' in order to distinguish them in their essence from (the performative nature of) heterosexual marriage. As John Boswell has argued, those who called such same-sex unions *artificial*, 'never considered the possibility that [they were ceremonies] of same-sex union in some deeper sense' (1994, 271).[15] Marriage is theatrical too in the sense that it is *witnessed*. As Parker and Sedgwick have argued, paying particular attention to 'the role of witness in constituting the space of the speech-act', 'Like a play, marriage exists in and for the eyes of others... Like the most conventional definition of a play, marriage is constituted as a spectacle that denies its audience the ability either to look away from it or equally to intervene in it' (1995, 11). And marriage performs not only a particularized set of rites but a whole history of cultural citation. As Didier Eribon has observed, 'The performative utterances of a wedding ceremony... [must draw into its ambit] the entire set of all preceding marriages and also the institution of matrimony... [for the] ceremony to have any meaning at all' (2004, 115). To recall Hawkes, it is our 'modern eyes' that both prevent us from and enable us to theorize what it means to witness queer marriage in Shakespeare's romantic comedies (whether we speak of our present moment or Shakespeare's). From this vantage it is easy to argue that we are complicit, and that Shakespeare's challenge to our heteronormative witnessing of marriage is as much a part of some of Shakespeare's plays as the stories his actors en*act*.

Beginning with *Twelfth Night* and moving on to *As You Like It* and, most extendedly to *A Midsummer Night's Dream*, I offer these three plays as the three most elaborate dramatizations of queer marriage in Shakespeare, and our being made witnesses to it. I begin with *Twelfth Night*, the most queerly discussed of these three plays, but as is true of Shakespeare's other queer marriage plays, queer scholarship seems to have either not noticed or has been reticent about the way the play uses the stage to grant cultural location to queer marriage. Like the other two romantic comedies being discussed here, *Twelfth Night* toys (borrowing from 5.1.384) with both male and female same-sex matrimonial coupling, and, as iterated, queer desire in these plays is thoroughly enwrapped in issues of queer marriage. In *Twelfth Night*, Olivia does not simply desire Viola (in the guise of Cesario) but pushes Cesario/Viola to marry her. One could argue, I imagine, that this is all a matter of convention, even though as Richard Rambuss cautions us, 'Too often interpretation desists at the point of such a determination, as if the status of being conventional would make a discursive construct or a sentiment any less thick with significance' (1998, 1–2).[16] Of course, with Viola's brother Sebastian taking Cesario/Viola's place, the trick of theater quickly shifts a near same-sex marriage (for Olivia) into a heterosexual one. But it is important, I think, to notice how Sebastian becomes the convenient heterosexual stand-in for Viola who has been the dramatic object of Olivia's passions and matrimonial fantasies. More complex still is the coupling of Orsino and Cesario, since the unqueering of their possible marriage depends not upon the substitution of one character for another but, suspiciously, on one character's sartorial change. It is less true that 'Orsino settles for a marriage with his male page' (Charles 1997, 140) than that Orsino gives up his male page and settles for Viola. If only visually, the playgoers have experienced, through its presentation, the attachment of Orsino and Cesario. And as has oft been noted, the ending of the play resists any easy heterosexualizing, since the play ends with Orsino referring to Viola as Cesario, as matrimonial plans are made: 'A solemn combination shall be made / Of our dear souls. ... Cesario, come – / For so you shall be while you are a man, / But *when* in other habits you are seen, Orsino's mistress and his fancy's queen' (5.1.376–77, 378–81, emphasis added): the audience *witnesses* (Shakespeare toying with the possibility of) two men conjoined in marriage.[17] This moment can only be limited to its *apparent* facetiousness, I think, by closing it off from the way *Twelfth Night* uses sex-gender to paradigmatically queer desire and exploit the relationship between queer desire and queer marriage.[18]

As a way of further underscoring the strategic and serious staging of and playing with these possible queer marriage couples, Shakespeare forces a kind of queer conflation in which desiring and being desired, female and male, and homosexuality and heterosexuality are inextricably dramatically intertwined. After all, it is quite arguable that even after all these variously laden cultural positions are 'corrected', the audience finds itself witnessing a woman (Viola) having successfully courted a man (Orsino), and that that reversal of traditional sex-gender roles opens up a possible space for queer desire and marriage, a theatrical space where it becomes more than a comedic interlude to stage the desiring woman and the desired man. If women can desire and men can be desired (in a world where we *already know* that men desire and women are desired), then far from being an odd phenomenon, the sex-gender story of *Twelfth Night* stages and makes known the cultural logic of queer marriage. In other words, from the vantage of this reading (even though I would insist that what I am offering here is 'more' than a reading), the sex-gender crossing *acted* out in *Twelfth Night* more importantly *plays* out the precarious yet prevalent place of queer marriage, at least on the romantic comedic stage.

In the end, then, this seemingly heterosexually invested play offers no heterosexual refuge from queer marriage. In fact, heterosexual matrimony, at least as played out in the dramatic vertebrae of the play, Orsino's desire to wed Olivia, gets indicted in the very opening lines of the play – 'If music be the food of love, play on, / Give me excess of it, that, surfeiting, / The appetite may sicken, and so die' (1.1.1–3) – as already exhaustively superficial, overwrought, and over*played*.[19] And, moreover, when put in terms of the elemental (3.1.58),[20] the play does all but make explicit (through its toying with a kind of *elemental* metatheatrics) its trafficking in fantasies of male–male matrimonial coupling. It should not prove surprising that the most endearing articulation of same-sex romantic affection comes from Antonio, a character who is ultimately not recuperative or locatable in the play-world's heterosexual matrimonial demands. Criticism has a tendency to understand desire without grasping marriage's implication in the same. It is not only queer desire that 'is not erased by the successful disruption of gender boundaries' (Charles 1997, 141) in *Twelfth Night*, but the possibility of queer marriage as a kind of symbolic expression and sanctioning of these desires that 'continues to *haunt* the subject despite the performance of the most fantastic of love's imaginings' (Charles 1997, 141, my emphasis). The denouement does far more cultural work than stage 'a critique of binarism, a *parodic* subversion of the dichotomies between male and female, homo- and hetero-sexual' (Charles 1997, 140, emphasis added). Rather, I would argue, it stages the refusal of compulsory heterosexuality to grant space to or even finally acknowledge the possibility of other formal kinship relations.[21]

In *As You Like It*, queerness breaks through the bounds of regulated passions and becomes a sign itself of the impossibility of successfully regulating passions. Touchstone's confession about his own passionate past reveals as much:

> I remember, when I was in love I broke my sword upon a stone and bid him take that for coming a-night to Jane Smile; and I remember the kissing of her batler, and the cow's dugs that her pretty chapped hands had milked; and I remember he wooing of a peasecod instead of her, from whom I took two cods, and giving them her again, said with weeping tears, 'Wear these for my sake'. We that are true lovers run into strange capers; but as all is mortal in nature, so is all nature in love mortal in folly. (2.4.43–52)

Swords, stones, kissing, dugs, peasecods, cods, and *weeping* intermingle in his bestial, heterosexual, and homosexual erotics of *folly.* Like *Twelfth Night, As You Like It* plays too with the possibility of both male and female same-sex marriage coupling: Orlando and the suggestively named Ganymede and Rosalind and Phebe. By the time Phebe enters the game and unhesitatingly offers herself in marriage to Ganymede, homosexuality and queer marriage seem uncontainable. In the metatheatrical universe of Shakespeare's play, all the world is a stage (2.7.130–31), and in this context I would add to Frances E. Dolan's observation about the play that 'despite disguise and disruption, each person miraculously ends up in a heterosexual union with someone of the same social standing' (2000, xliii), that the artifice suggested by Dolan's ironic use of the term 'miraculously' is precisely the artifice that Shakespeare both stages and critiques. After all, however much under-realized, this play's most demonstrative coupling (as in *Twelfth Night*) is a same-sex one, here, Celia and Rosalind, whose love is described by one character as 'dearer than the natural bond of sisters' (1.2.266).[22]

As You Like It goes further still by staging a marriage, what Bruce Smith calls a 'mock-marriage' between Orlando and Rosalind as Ganymede (1991, 146), but 'mock' is too overly determined a term because it has the effect of erasing what Rosalind in effect stages, a same-sex union that *could* be read as signaling the mockery, the theatrical game, that is heterosexual matrimony when put up against the far-reaching disruptive coupling of Celia and Rosalind that poses a threat to the (patriarchalist) realness of heterosexual matrimony.[23] It also risks that we might miss seeing how this wedding, in effect, realizes a same-sex marriage for Ganymede, who would (were the classical-meet-Shakespearean fantasy to play itself out) find himself married not to Orlando but Jove. (Same-sex uniting is not unavailable, as is made evident by Rosalind's question to Celia about the author of all those love verses about Rosalind being affixed to trees: 'Is it a man?' [3.2.176]). Furthermore, the play steps beyond the boundaries of the story and into thick space of the theater and its conventions when just before this queer ceremony Orlando accepts Ganymede's invitation to think of him as *truly* ('very very') his Rosalind and tries to give him a kiss; Rosalind's response, 'Nay, you were better speak first', prevents the staging of a seeming same-sex kiss, one that at one and the same time makes the audience complicit in Ganymede's flinching away from such a kiss and underscores the way the 'very very' materiality of Shakespeare's theater trades in just such same-sex smooching (4.1.6–72). Shakespeare openly 'knows' that his audience does not want to see such a true same-sex kiss. It would be somewhat misdirected, I think, to debate what side of all this

Shakespeare comes down on rather than to note how such a moment as this foregrounds the interplay between theater and witnessing that truly becomes the subject of Shakespeare's queer marriage theater.

In any event, a couple of scenes after Ganymede and Orlando's marriage, the queer matrimonial narrative delivers a serious coup, albeit in the context of comedy (and arguably only in the context of comedy could Shakespeare do so), when Oliver (Orlando's brother) delivers Rosalind a bloody napkin from Orlando, whose arm has been partly mauled by a lioness (4.3.137–55).[24] As an iconographic reversal, it is Orlando, it is Jove who bleeds, calling up at once images of sodomitical consummation and a role reversal (if not deconstruction) in which Ganymede becomes the penetrator of Jove, Rosalind of Orlando, one woman of another woman, and a boy of a man. Shakespeare's iconography of queer marriage demands a kind of equivalency, one found, not surprisingly, in Orlando's own poetic wooings when he writes about 'some of violated vows / 'Twixt the souls of friend and friend' (3.2.130–31).[25] In *As You Like It* we should note images of manliness and femininity: Orlando is both, Rosalind is both, they are each husband and wife. Even though the play ends with the play-world looking forward to the predictable and patriarchically sanctioned nuptials of Rosalind and Orlando (among other heterosexual couples), their impending marriage remains oddly and irresolutely set in relationship to the titillatingly playful courtship between Orlando and Ganymede. Once queer marriage is granted a real viable presence in Shakespeare's play we come to hear differently the oft-emended speech near the end of the play, where Hymen, the god of marriage, says:

> Then is there mirth in heaven
> When earthly things made even
>   Atone together.
> Good duke, receive thy daughter;
> Hymen from heaven brought her,
>   Yea, brought her hither,
> That thou mightst join his hand with his
> Whose heart within his bosom is'. (5.4.106–13)[26]

Mirthful playing does allow the performance of evenness, the marital conjoining of 'his hand with his', as Shakespeare's *deus ex machina* Hymen outdoes the *deus ex machina* Venus in John Lyly's *Gallathea* (1583–85) (Lyly 1976), who ends that play by effectively making it possible for the two main female characters to marry.[27] At times, at least, there is something refreshingly funny and inspiring about queer marriage in Shakespeare.

Heterosexuality (and heterosexual marriage) becomes something of a ruse, an aggressive bit of heterosexualizing metatheatrics, made emphatically and repeatedly evident by Rosalind's epilogue that begins with her further destabilizing of her sex by pointing out that 'it is not the fashion to *see* the lady the epilogue' (Epilogue 1, emphasis added). Her command to the audience, however – 'I charge you, O women, for the love you bear to men, to like as much of this play as please you; and I charge you, O men, for the love you bear to women (as I perceive by your simpering none of you hates them), that between you and the women the play may please' (Epilogue 11–16) – quickly reassures her audience that she is quite aware of their heterosexuality, that what happens in the theater stays in the theater (so to speak). But immediately following this reassurance, Rosalind goes from being the 'lady' she announces herself to be at the beginning of the Epilogue to the performing boy, who despite his subjunctive, 'If I were a woman', manages still to engage in a homoerotic seduction, 'I would kiss as many of you as had beards that pleased me' (Epilogue 16–17). 'If', of course, is no casual word in *As You Like It*,[28] as Touchstone has said fewer than just 100 lines before the Epilogue: 'All these [types of lies] you may avoid but the Lie Direct, and you may avoid that too, with an If... Your If is the only peacemaker. Much virtue in If' (5.4.95–101). And when Ganymede/Rosalind finally says that he is sure the men in the audience will bid him farewell for his 'kind offer' (Epilogue 18–21), a bit of a tease, s/he allows them to participate in and distance themselves from the homoeroticism in the theater they have not only witnessed but experienced. 'The epilogue's suggestive reference to a sexual transaction between the men and women in Shakespeare's audience', does echo, as Phyllis Rackin has argued, 'the multiple marriages that have just been depicted on stage and also [does imply] that the relation between the play and its audience is a kind of sexual transaction or marriage' (1987, 36), but more than this still, the (queer) marriage possibilities here between Rosalind and her audience have more a mimetic resonance than the metaphorical one suggested by Rackin's language.

Unlike *Twelfth Night* and *As You Like It*, *A Midsummer Night's Dream* does not rely on cross-dressing – sex-change and sex misapprehension and misrecognition – as a kind of strategically efficient metatheatrical device for staging (the possibility of) queer marriage. While like *Twelfth Night* and *As You Like It*, *A Midsummer Night's Dream* articulates queerness in relational – female and female, male and male – terms, it also comes closest to imagining a kind of queer subjectivity or queer body and of locating compulsory heterosexuality – the fiction of heterosexuality – in dominant culture's utilitarian (heterosexualizing) theatrical exploitation of the body itself. The play-world of *A Midsummer Night's Dream* insists not only on heterosexual marriage as inherent in the very structures of a healthy society but that heterosexuality itself is attached to the originary body, which in its originariness is always already a healthy body. Joane Nagel has put it this way in her thinking about our present subject-sex position:

> The gendered and sexualized body is a *major location* for the social construction of men and women, masculinity and femininity, and male and female sexuality. The body is an instrument of *performance* and a site of *performativity.* Gender and sexuality are both performed and performative – conscious and unconscious, intended and unintended, explicit and implicit.[29]

A Midsummer Night's Dream is the play, I am arguing, that most suspects that the erasure of queer marriage depends less upon the kind of straightening out one can do, say, by changing Viola into Sebastian or vice versa or by changing Ganymede into Rosalind, than a kind of violent distortion of the elemental body itself, made especially evident through Hippolyta, Titania, and Bottom. The main thrust of the play's heterosexual marriage imperative is of course the four lovers, and Shakespeare stages these four lovers to 'miraculously' end up in heterosexual pairs. When filtered both through the state's demand (in and outside the play) for heterosexual marriage and through the play's highly metatheatrical constructedness, no Shakespeare play succeeds more than does *A Midsummer Night's Dream* in trafficking in the possibility of queer marriage.

Kathryn Schwarz argues in one of the most provocative readings of the play I have come across, 'There is something innately parodic about *A Midsummer Night's Dream,* something that tempts alternative readings. The poster-play for the argument that Jack shall have Jill lends itself readily to other couplings and to second, skeptical looks at heterosexual happy endings' (2000, 204–05). Rather than join a critical consensus that argues that the play ends with an affirmation of heterosexual love and marriage, I am arguing (as Schwarz has suggested) that *A Midsummer Night's Dream* is *about* these regulatory practices, about the disruption of homosociality through the compulsion of heterosexuality. The demand that Jack shall have Jill plays out with, through, and against the male actors onstage, *this* community not only of homosociality but of homoeroticism. From this perspective, heterosexual marriage rites get subsumed by a culture of queerness. The theater of *A Midsummer Night's Dream* is haunted by the regulatory coerciveness of heterosexual matrimony. The play asks what to do with all that erotic energy, those friendships that the demands of heterosexuality and of heterosexual marriage have made excessive, transmogrified into a form of cultural waste. To put this historically (as Valerie Traub has done): 'As England was transformed into a modern, civil society, friendship was recast as a noninstrumental affinity: "rational, objective, universal", and for the most part irrelevant to...public affairs' (2004, 342).[30] In *A Midsummer Night's Dream*, we become witnesses to this process through which the heterosexuality evacuates out the homoerotic, a kind of passionate athleticism, from the homosocial.[31]

It is almost possible to miss Lysander's lines (a few moments into the play), when he says to an insistent Demetrius, who is arguing with him for the right to marry Hermia, 'You have her father's love, Demetrius; / Let me have Hermia's: do you marry him' (1.1.93–4). After all, Demetrius does have the blessings of Hermia's father. Lysander's words are, arguably, quite facetious. I want, however, to trouble these lines, take seriously precisely their signifying insignificance, because the possibility of queer marriage – of same-sex erotic and civil union – has both a theatrically substantial and constitutive place (location and a name) in the deep texture and presence of *A Midsummer Night's Dream*, this play that seems episodically so comprehensively driven both by a push toward and the imposition of heterosexual marriage. At the level of its performative meaningfulness, Lysander's proposition to Demetrius underscores quite succinctly the threat of 'deviant' erotic and civic behavior and why for a proper heteronormative (and patriarchalist) culture to work, its habits and practices must be so carefully finessed, so *judiciously* orchestrated; after all, it is safe to assume that Athens signals the originary site of Western law for early modern audiences as well as contemporary ones. In any event, Lysander's proposition to Demetrius does more than simply raise the specter of queer marriage – a naughty bit of facetiousness to be sure – but signifies at the same time the dangers it presumably poses to the Athenian social order.[32] Not only would Demetrius by marrying Egeus, Hermia's father, marry another man but he would also, in effect, marry the parent of his sexual interest instead of the child herself, hinting at some link in the process between homosexuality and incest.

With his quip, Lysander performs his heteronormative and natural right to Hermia; his possession of her seems safely guarded against the kind of linguistic slippage that could (to anticipate my later discussion of Bottom) transmogrify a paternal love into an erotic one. In other words, queer marriage upsets not only one's sexual identity and one's originary heterosexual body but patriarchy and its reliance on a particular understanding of familial arrangements and relations. Lysander's quip too must be understood contextually, the way it counters the kind of paternal fatalism being offered up by Theseus: 'To either die the death, or to abjure / Forever the society of men' (1.1.65–6). In other terms still, the characters find themselves in this predicament because of a potentially unchecked paternalism, one that is obviously itself in need of being regulated. Unchecked, paternalism has a way of literally destroying femaleness, and unchecked femininity poses a serious threat to paternal arbitrage. Patriarchy relies for its rationale on the arbitral rights and privileges of the father. As Theseus says to truant Hermia when she argues that Lysander is really as fine a person as Demetrius, 'In himself he is; / But in this kind, wanting your father's voice, / The other must be held the worthier' (1.1.53–5). Left unregulated, marriage becomes socially and politically lethal, potentially poisonous (to evoke Puck and his love juices), capable without a moment's notice of performing a slippage (legal or otherwise) between arbitration and arbitrariness.

But Lysander's proposition is only symptomatic – as quips or jokes so often reveal themselves to be – a release of a social and political pressure that frames the play. A more serious specter of same-sex marriage – same-gendered marriage to be more accurate – is Theseus's own upcoming marriage to Hippolyta, his Amazonian war bride. Says Theseus just before the entrance of Egeus and the four lovers: 'Hippolyta, I wooed thee with my sword, / And won thy love, doing thee injuries; / But I will wed thee in another key, / With pomp, with triumph, and with reveling' (1.1.16–19). What Theseus proposes to do, of course, is to move his relationship with Hippolyta from war to, say, the realm of comedy. But already more is going on here. From a patriarchalist viewpoint, the Amazonian warrior is a usurper of male prerogative (an issue that will come up a few times in this play); she is seen as a castrator of the male body, as a thief who has taken possession of man's penis, if not, indeed, his phallus. From this perspective, somewhere in Theseus's having 'wooed' Hippolyta, his having *wood* her – some amalgam, some tricky linguistic melding of courtship, military conquest, and rape – of having done her 'injuries', survives the very strong suggestion, a kind of male bravado, in which Theseus prides himself on being well on his way to having effectively *re*-castrated his Amazonian prize. In short, part of what Theseus must do, and his being the conqueror assures him of his movement in the proper direction, is feminize Hippolyta, move her from the battlefield to the bedroom – 'to bed ... to bed' (5.1.366–70), by *returning* her to her originary heterosexual body.

The courtship – the stay of four days – is literally and figuratively performative: Theseus already possesses her, and the pomp, triumph, and reveling may be understood to function as a kind of surplus or excess. But I wish to suggest quite the contrary. With the story of the four lovers providing the audience onstage and off with the necessary *diversion*, Shakespeare's theatrically and materially thick play deploys romantic comedy as a kind of feminizing mechanism. (My use of the word *deploy* here is meant to have militaristic connotations.) Comedy, in other words, will re-socialize Hippolyta, re-equip (or, perhaps, un-equip) her body as properly female and heterosexual.

Of course, more is at stake than making Hippolyta's body ready for heterosexual marriage. Theseus's own heterosexuality is intricately and intimately bound up with that of Hippolyta's body. Unlike the Amazon's, Theseus's wooded sex is not marked by ambiguity; he gets to act here as a kind of non-variable (sexually speaking); he is not going to play the female object of Hippolyta's manly desires. From the perspective of Theseus's patriarchalist Athens, it is the potential threat to the heterosexuality of the male body that most necessitates a response to the ambiguity, the transgressive qualities, of the Amazon's sexual and gender identities. It is not enough that Theseus has conquered her on the battlefield. As in many other Shakespearean instances (the first scene of *Titus Andronicus* and the final scene of *Henry 5* come most readily to mind), it is necessary to perform, to make ritualistically exacting, the transition from one kind of social or political identity to another. (In *A Midsummer Night's Dream*, romantic comedy takes the place of hacked limbs or a coy but non-negotiable courtship.)

Theseus's sexual banter in the opening speech, the moon 'lingers my desires ... Long withering out a young man's revenue' (1.1.4–6), is far more purposeful than playful, since the *stay* of four days which will bring in another moon only adds to the ritualistic and symbolic import of his male prerogative, his wood, and stages his refusal to engage in a same-sex/gendered marriage with Hippolyta. In the same instance in which Theseus pushes for the heterosexualization of Hippolyta's body (and the fortifying of his own), he also civilizes her, re-socializes her in the ways and mores of Athenian society. In terms of both sexual identity and race, she becomes a subject to be made over.[33] Notwithstanding any of my remarks here, Theseus remains throughout the opening scene – and indeed throughout the play (when Shakespeare ventures to bring him back into it) – in a rather assured position. He has already conquered Hippolyta before the play opens, so his insistence upon a kind of performative rejection of queer marriage, like the possibility of Demetrius's marriage to Egeus, remains no significant threat – really – to what seems to be the play's overdetermined heteronormativity.

But this is Athens and Theseus – not Shakespeare's play. Theseus and his Athens want to secure heteronormative and patriarchal order, and what is evident from the start is that unregulated female bodies give rise to the possible transmogrification of male homosocial bonds into queer marriages, whether these marriages are cast in terms of a man marrying a masculinized woman (as would be the case of Theseus and Hippolyta) or a man marrying another man (as in the case of Egeus and Demetrius). And if Athens and Theseus can pride themselves on so quickly shifting potentially queer marriages into straight ones, of leaving male control fairly confident, the second act challenges the first not by continuing with the subject of same-sex male marriage but by re-investing in the subject of queer marriage through an exploration of same-sex female marriage, exposing in the process fantasies of sex, gender, sexuality, and race that seem so assuredly in place in the patriarchalist world of Athens.[34]

Titania's presence challenges the assurance of Theseus and Athens, and her body is certainly more erotically and socially dangerous than Hippolyta's. If Hippolyta as Amazon may be said to have *mimicked* maleness too effectively,[35] Titania plays her opposite in that her passions and activities are so thoroughly committed to a society of women. Where Hippolyta may fancy herself entering (to some extent) into a same-sex/gendered marriage with Theseus, Titania imagines herself (despite her lawful and nominal marriage to Oberon) in a fully realized erotic and social communion with her now dead votaress. Of the two forms of homoeroticism, female-female eroticism is the more dangerous, the play seems to suggest, since it remains the most outside male social regulatory agencies. As Valerie Traub has argued, 'Titania is psychologically threatening precisely to the degree that she upsets the homosocial "traffic in women" formally negotiated by Egeus and Theseus in the opening scene' (2002, 68).

The opening lines of the second act waste no time in giving the lie to the ease with which the first scene (especially the first two thirds of it) seems to regulate sex, gender, and sexuality. Puck and the Fairy's expository conversation catches the audience up on the story of Titania and Oberon before the stage entrance of this queen and king of fairydom.

When the queen and king do enter, they immediately engage in a squabble of jealousies, accusing each other of having serious amorous interests in other partners, Oberon for Hippolyta and Titania for Theseus. However read, their expressions of jealousy cannot be taken at face value, since we have already learned from Puck the real source of their contention. It is not so much their heterosexual flirtations as it is Titania's queer marriage – a marriage she insists on continuing to recognize (even though her spouse is dead) and Oberon insists on erasing. Not only has the enacting of the heterosexual marriage imperative not succeeded in thwarting or displacing queer erotics, Titania and the votaress have managed to finagle it into their own reproductive fantasies. As Puck tells the story, Titania has in her possession and dotes upon a child born to her votaress just before the votaress dies – 'a lovely boy, stolen from an Indian king...so sweet a changeling' – and Oberon wishes to take possession of the boy for his own purposes (2.1.18–31). As Titania herself tells the story:

> His mother was a vot'ress of my order,
> And, in the spicèd Indian air, by night,
> Full often hath she gossiped by my side,
> And sat with me on Neptune's yellow sands,
> Marking th'embarkèd traders on the flood;
> When we have laughed to see the sails conceive
> And grow big-bellied with the wanton wind;
> Which she, with pretty and with swimming gait
> Following – her womb then rich with my young squire –
> Would imitate, and sail upon the land,
> To fetch me trifles, and return again,
> As from a voyage, rich with merchandise.
> But she, being mortal, of that boy did die;
> And for her sake do I rear up her boy,
> And for her sake I will not part with him.
>
> (2.1.123–37)

This votaress who has taken vows to conjoin herself to Titania has in effect intimately attached herself to her and together, if only in spirit (so to speak), produced an offspring. Traub understates the case when she argues that 'the child is the manifest *link* of a prior affection between women that is associated with their fecundity and maternal largess...Titania insists on the loyalty of female bonds' (2002, 68, emphasis added). In the world of fairydom the child is as much as can be imaginatively *conceived* or *imitated*, the product of the sexual and social union between Titania and her votaress – 'Her womb then rich with my young squire'. What Titania's narrative shares with Puck's from earlier in this scene is an erasure of the father as primogenitor. It is this erasure that Oberon wishes to erase. The boy may have been 'stolen' from the father but (at least I would argue from the viewpoint of Titania) in a sense more akin to the way a woman in our society may be said to get sperm – 'steal' sperm – from a sperm bank.

Oberon finds the boy a threat because the boy is in essence the product of female–female sexual and social relations, effectively rendering Oberon's own phallic potency obsolete, excessive. Where Hippolyta threatens castration with masculinity, Titania does so with femininity. I wish to suggest that the child is not a 'changeling' simply because he has been stolen. According to the *OED*, the changeling child would be a child left in place of a stolen child (definition 3). Most ideologically significantly, the Indian changeling child is in effect a child that has come from 'nowhere' – I put quotations around *nowhere*, heavy ones, because of the way in which the orientalizing of India functions here as a possible site for such a procreative fantasy,[36] such corporeal and physiological obscenities. I would argue too that the child is a changeling not because he has himself been stolen but because he is the product of a stolen male prerogative; he is the evidence, the *obscene* (the unseen) creation of 'one given to change; a fickle or inconstant person; a waverer, turncoat, renegade' (*OED*, definiton 1), in this instance, of a woman usurping a man's place. As a product of usurpation, the child is surplus, and, as such, his very existence works against the legality and rationality of heteronormativity and patriarchy – a legality and rationality that are always at pains to make manifest, to make biologically evidentiary, the societal imperative for heterosexual marriage.

Compulsory heterosexual marriage relies on 'compulsory reproduction' (Edelman 2004, 75) for its evidentiary validation (this partly explains the seemingly inevitable reproductive consequences dwelt upon at the end of the play), but it is precisely this narrative that Titania challenges; her queering of futurism opens up an inhabitable space between compulsory heterosexual marriage and 'compulsory reproduction'. In Titania's world, heterosexuality 'exceeds its use-value' (Edelman 2004, 65); it loses its mythical value, its romantic comedy value; in other words, to put this in Edelman's terms, 'heterosexuality, stripped of its ancient reproductive alibi, must assume at last the despiritualized burden of its status *as sexual function*' (2004, 64). Having so thoroughly moored itself to reproduction, presumptively chucking the performative for the natural, heterosexual matrimony in the hands of Titania finds itself uncomfortably yoked to both the performative and the natural, or to neither. The changeling boy is not Shakespeare's capitulation to 'compulsory reproduction' but a queer way of buying into the future. Rather, I would contend, the unseen child holds out the possibility not (only) of an alternative queer past but of an alternative queer future, where mourning the death of one's queer marriage (partner) would become a thing of the past, and where queer marriage would and could (with or without a child) sustain a natural or performative history of its own.

If Titania refuses, as she does, Oberon's request to give him the child so that he may incorporate the child (parentally, sexually, or otherwise), then Oberon can respond only by trying to show Titania how surplus is always in danger of becoming mere excess,[37] of becoming waste. When Oberon intimately yokes his queen to Bottom, he intends to punish her – *rationally, performatively* – commingling her body with scatological matter. I agree with Gail Paster's pushing further Leonard Tennenhouse's reading when she insists that 'the somatic pun on Bottom's name gives the metamorphosis an even more ambivalent social tonality ... because Bottom's relation to Titania parodies not only a transgressive social fantasy but a dangerous familial one as well' (1993, 127–28).[38] But where Paster sees Bottom as a substitution for the Indian boy and reads this substitution as also constructing 'a parodic image of adult female sexuality in which the differences between heterosexual intercourse and the anal cathexes of maternal nurture become blurred', manifesting 'cultural discomfort with the powers of maternity' (1993, 128),[39] I am offering that the substitution is not first and foremost Bottom for the boy but Bottom for the votaress, whose present death and absence can be matched only by the waste and potency of a somatic wielding Bottom.[40] As *monster*, Bottom makes visible the unnatural wasteful sexual indulgence between Titania and her votaress. To the extent that Bottom substitutes for the boy, the relationship between him and Titania becomes an intensely incestuous one, only further underscoring what I would argue is Oberon's insistence on linking same-sex coupling to narratives of monstrosity.

Bottom – who, arguably, has 'no bottom' (4.2.219–20), no demarcations – marks the site of a sexual, social, and familial indeterminacy that emerges when the strictures of heterosexual marriage are not adhered to. His presence, manifesting as it does from Titania's union of her votaress, makes corporeally visible and tangible and strangely cohesive a cathecting of scatology, incest, and bestiality onto the body engaged in same-sex coupling. In fact, Bottom emerges in the play as the most coherent demonstration of the consequences of unregulated sexual behavior, a threat that we see existing from the very opening of the play. To whatever extent we may want to link Bottom to the tradition of the *proktos lalon*, the trope of the speaking ass,[41] especially in its more coarse masculine forms, Bottom does have about him a gross and animalistic manliness. But more than this, I would argue, he is marked with a peculiarly female body as well, one characterized by orifices – here, his rather prominent ears and his mouth. As ass, ears, and mouth, Bottom is characterized by a sexual indeterminacy. His is this sexually 'mixed-up' body on which same-sex relations must ultimately play themselves out. He is also, satirically so, the horrific sodomitical center of the play, whose ass cannot stop talking, cannot stop betraying itself – cannot stop emitting those '"involuntary" asinine brays', constantly threatening 'an incontinence of noise' (Paster 1993, 130). He is the sodomitical underside, I am arguing, of both male and female queer marriage – the bodily incarnation of same-sex consummation, the 'love' (to recall the *Proposed Constitutional Amendment* [U. S. Senate Committee on the Judiciary 2005, 52]), that can go so far as to *confuse* the proper place of the child in the sexual union; that is, couples give birth to children, they do not get sexually entangled with them.[42] Paster has of course argued that Titania administering laxatives – apricots, dewberries, grapes, figs, and mulberries (3.1.1.158–59) – ties together sexual intercourse and excretion (125–33). But it is worth bringing more queer pressure to Paster's argument and stressing, as Celia Daileader has done, that Bottom becomes in Titania's bower 'the male in the receptive, "feminine" role' (2002, 326).[43] More horrific than playing the sodomite to another man is playing one to a woman, particularly a woman so thoroughly identified with women, as is Titania. Through Bottom, the sodomitical act that haunts both male and female queer marriage gets to speak.

After Oberon has had enough, he does send Bottom back to his own world and we are treated (as Smith says) to 'the happy reconciliation of a married couple who have loved each other long enough to forgive and forget' (1991, 200). All seems well. Even though the shift from female–female union to heterosexual matrimony has been more difficult to execute than that from male–male union to heterosexual matrimony, requiring a much more complex bag of tricks, Oberon seems to have achieved his goal in his newfound reunion with Titania. But just as I argued earlier that *A Midsummer Night's Dream* is not Athens's or Theseus's play, neither is it Oberon's or his fairyland's. After Oberon has finished with Bottom, Bottom has not finished with Shakespeare's play. The play, I would argue, refuses the re-inscription of Bottom into the regulatory sexual regimes demanded not only by us as witnesses but by Theseus and Oberon and by the heterosexual imperatives of Shakespeare's own culture. In *his* moment of waking, of breaking through the fourth wall, Bottom says: 'The eye of man hath not heard, the ear of man hath not seen, man's hand is not able to taste, his tongue to conceive, nor his heart to report, what my dream was' (4.2.214–17). While the ur-text of Bottom's speech may be (as critics have pointed out) 1 Corinthians 2:9, I want to push us to read it explicitly as Bottom's response to John Knox's 1558 tract, *The First Blast of the Trumpet Against the Monstrous Regiment of Women*, especially the section more than conveniently titled for us, 'The First Blast to Awake Women Degenerate'. Bottom's waking speech may be read, I think, as a mockery of Knox's text. Knox has trained his attention throughout *The First Blast* on how the 'promot[ion of a] woman to bear rule, superiority, dominion, or empire above any realm, nation, or city, is repugnant to nature…a thing most contrarious…subversion of good order, of all equity and justice' ([1558], 1999, 211).

Knox likens the relationship between the sexes to a rationality inherent and made evident in the very functions of the body itself. Says Knox, 'And the head hath he joined with the body, that from it doth life and motion flow to the rest of the members. In it hath he place the eye to see, the ear to hear, and the tongue to speak, which offices are appointed to none other member of the body' ([1558], 1999, 213). He adds:

> For the same God that hath denied power to the hand to speak, to the belly to hear, and to the feet to see, hath denied to woman power to command man.…yea, finally, he hath denied to her in any case to be a head of man, but plainly hath pronounced that man is head to woman.…no more will [God] admit, nor accept woman to be the lawful head over man. ([1558], 1999, 214)

I want to suggest that Shakespeare has Bottom pose his, Bottom's, body against Knox's more condemnatory reading of monstrosity. Knox writes and asks, 'For who would not judge that body to be a monster, where there was no head eminent above the rest, but that the eyes were in the hands, the tongue and mouth beneath the belly, and the ears in the feet' ([1558], 1999, 213). Bottom answers; he embraces what Knox abhors.

In the end Bottom does emerge as a figure of excess, of theatrical excess, who threatens to turn upside down the heteronormative marriage demands of the play. Bottom's scatology, like his body more generally, does more than 'recover the affect structure of shame and delicacy as it is reproduced in very specific theatrical settings' (Paster 1993, 116). Bottom belongs firmly to the waste, the excess that (for some of his contemporaries) would characterize the theater itself, and (as Paster has shown) most especially the genre of comedy. He is the one, the sodomitical figure, who confuses or *refuses* the proper use of body parts. He is most confidently located in what Hawkes has argued is in early modern England 'the public theatre's own involvement with the "ordure", with the actual "spittle" and "filth" of *unstructured* material existence' (2002, 92, my emphasis). He shares much with Weimann's 'body-oriented ... common player', who is 'unsure of his place in both the world of society and the world of the theatre' (Weimann 2000, 133–34),[44] and fights to remain free from the imposition of narrative structure – in this instance, of a heterosexual one – on the raw materials of the theater. I agree wholeheartedly with Hawkes's assessment of Bottom:

> It's worth grasping that Bottom's mode of acting, announced with such a flourish, would have been immediately recognised by the first audience of *A Midsummer Night's Dream*, certainly as inept, but even more crucially as 'old-fashioned'. ... In one sense, it's hardly 'acting' at all. ... Bottom is no actor. What he embodies is ... 'playing' (2002, 111).[45]

Bottom, in fact, is a theatrical whore (a point well established shortly after the audience is first introduced to him), ready to play man, woman and beast (1.2.21–74). Bottom's body is ready for whoring long before he becomes Titania's sex toy, as is evident as the 'discharging' Bottom prepares to play Pyramus:

> Bottom: I will discharge it in either your straw-color beard, your orange-tawny beard, your purple-in-grain beard, or your French-crown-color beard, your perfit yellow.
>
> Quince: Some of your French crowns have no hair at all, and then you will play barefaced. (1.2.93–8)

(The banter about the French crown refers to syphilis, a disease particularly, presumably, prominent among prostitutes.) Shakespeare stages

Bottom as a challenge to the heterosexualization of the body that is such an imperative to the ideological underpinnings of romantic comedy.

Bottom covering his head to show his ass makes him key to Shakespeare's theatricalization of desire, especially of queer desire in *A Midsummer Night's Dream*. Theater is a genre of covering and exposing, and queerness is caught in just such an elaborate ruse: it is no mere reflection of the rude mechanicals' lack of common sense when they worry over their audience mistaking an actor for a lion (3.1.25–43). Shakespeare's own audience could stand to be reminded that there are, indeed, only actors (no actual women) on Shakespeare's stage. Bottom's *waking* testimony points to the sexually unregulated bodies of the playhouse itself that continues to fashion its own elaborate and intricate narrative of trickery in order to traffic in same-sex, male–male sexual and social *play*. Indeed, our lovers are all boys and men. And nothing can supersede the theater in giving the lie to the successful regulation of heterosexual marriage than a theater that trafficks in boys and men in order to make that success evidentiary. At the level of acting, the four lovers in *A Midsummer Night's Dream* are in pursuit of heterosexual pairing, but at the level of playing, what I have been arguing throughout this essay is key to understanding Shakespeare's queer marriage theater, the actors pursue erotic engagement across gender boundaries, desiring and being desired in ways that misrecognize the patriarchalist sex-gender rules of Theseus's court. *A Midsummer Night's Dream* comes to recognize the impossibility of any kind of discrete heterosexual matrimony, finding it impossible to evacuate out the potentially sodomitical homosociality that heterosexual matrimony pushes to yield to a heterosexual imperative.

I began this essay by asking why there are so many *possible* queer marriages in Shakespeare, but I would like to suggest by way of conclusion that that question is in need of rephrasing and it would be more useful finally to ask why we resist witnessing and reading Shakespeare's queer marriages. And my proposed answer is not simply to speak to our compulsion to read (Shakespeare) heterosexually, our compulsion to subsume texts in a heterosexual singularity. At work too, I want to suggest, is our perpetuation of what Eribon calls the 'gay insult', this 'performative utterance... [that functions] to produce certain effects – notably to establish or to renew the barrier between "normal" people and... stigmatized" people and to cause the internalization of the barrier within the individual being insulted' (2004, 15). While (possible) queer marriages in Shakespeare may *yield* to heterosexual ones, we have the option of understanding this move in terms either of evolution or simultaneity. In the formal case, the bedrock of 'insult' thinking, I would argue, we create a teleology through which maturation essentially demands the evolution from queer folly to a straight deontics; and in the latter, we recognize what Eribon, using Pierre Bourdieu, sees as 'rites that produce two effects simultaneously': 'Marriage performs this same double separation: most visibly between those who are married and those who are not, but also – less visibly but just as effectively – between those who have the right to marry and those who do not' (1988, 17). I insist that we begin to recognize how our reading of history, of extending our facetious response to queerness, our 'insult' of reading the abject queer subject *back* into Shakespeare's romantic comedies, thwarts our ability to theorize the fuller significance not only of Shakespeare's queer marriages but of queerness in Shakespeare more generally. Reading queerness in Shakespeare's romantic comedies is a project of the present, but it is also a historical one, one that seeks not only to reanimate a queer past but to make more scrutable the transhistorical historicism of a heterosexual one. As Eve Kosofsky Sedgwick has rightly argued, 'The making historically visible of heterosexuality is difficult because, under its institutional pseudonyms such as Inheritance, Marriage, Dynasty, Family, Domesticity, and Population, heterosexuality has been permitted to masquerade so fully as history itself – when it has not presented itself as the totality of the Romance' (1993, 10–11).[46] Perhaps queer marriage remains at the end of Shakespeare's romantic comedies a 'rare vision' (*A Midsummer Night's Dream*, 4.1.208), but this fact makes these same plays no less substantial and serious sites for thinking through what it is *we* witness as we struggle still to claim for ourselves a local habitation and a name, a presence dictated by neither the insult nor the facetious.

Notes

I wish to thank Evelyn Gajowski and Sam See for carefully reading this essay and offering their expertise, and Patricia Parker for conversations that helped tremendously with revisions.

1. Statement made by Barney Frank, a Representative from Massachusetts in the U.S. Congress, during the congressional hearings 23 March 2004, regarding a proposed constitutional amendment to outlaw gay marriage and civil unions in the U.S. (U.S. Senate Committee on the Judiciary 2004, 15).
2. Opinion from *Bowers v. Hardwick*.
3. As commentators have already noted, this language from Shakespeare's Sonnet 116 explicitly echoes actual marriage vows in Shakespeare's England: 'If any of you know cause or just impediment why these persons should not be joined together....'

4. Allusion to *A Midsummer Night's Dream* (5.1.14–17), as well as the first part of the title of this essay: 'And as imagination bodies forth / The forms of things unknown, the poet's pen / Turns them to shapes and gives to airy nothing / A local habitation and a name'. Unless otherwise indicated, all quotations from and line references to *A Midsummer Night's Dream* are from the Signet Classic edition.
5. 'Same-Sex Marriage in the US'. *Wikipedia*. http://en.wikipedia.org/wiki/Same-sex_marriage_in_the_United_States
6. Hawkes goes on to argue that 'paying the present that degree of respect might more profitably be judged, not as a "mistake", egregious and insouciant, blandly imposing a tritely modern perspective on whatever texts confront it, but rather as the basis of a critical stance whose engagement with the text is of a particular character' (2002, 3–4).
7. Note, for example, Eve Kosofsky Sedgwick's aptly titled collection of queer essays, *Tendencies*.
8. My comment is not meant to suggest that these studies are ahistorical in their myriad approaches to these earlier literatures and cultures. Rather, I want to underscore the way the word *queer* itself announces a kind of presentist intervention. For some excellent examples of such studies, see Goldberg (1994); Pugh (2004); Blackmore and Hutcheson (1999); and Klosowka (2004).
9. The exact law being referenced here is '25 Hen. 8, c. 6'.
10. The proposal not only argues that real marriage – heterosexual marriage – is about children but that the witnessing of same-sex marriage confuses and harms children and their later matrimonial or domestic choices. See, for example, U. S. Senate Committee on the Judiciary (2005, 52).
11. Even though not the subject of this particular essay, studies such as Alan Bray's and John Boswell's, however, make clear (if not indisputable) the fact that such official readings of same-sex marriage as a thing without a history is highly inaccurate.
12. The argument I am making throughout this essay, but most particularly here, deserves comparison to that advanced by Phyllis Rackin, who in her essay on boy heroines and marriage, writes that 'the relation between reality and representation is particularly complicated because ... the issue of gender is intimately connected in the drama of the English Renaissance to the issue of theatrical representation itself' (1987, 32).
13. Weimann argues that by 1600 there was 'in the air' a perceived difference on the English stage between playing and acting, the former being 'body-oriented' and the latter 'text-oriented' (2000, 131–36). Without of course discounting the textual, understanding the exploitation of the performing body remains a central component of staging queerness.
14. While the investments of this essay are focused on Shakespeare's romantic comedies, the use of queer marriage in Shakespeare is not limited to these plays, or even to his plays (see, for example, the third epigraph to my essay and his Sonnets more generally). We may think of no better encapsulating example than the moment in *Coriolanus*, when Aufidius says to Coriolanus when first meeting him after Coriolanus has deserted Rome and offered his services to him (4.5.117–22, 126–30). In Aufidius's greeting, queer marriage works as a kind of rhetorical trope in which martial tussle and

marital passions become near equivalencies but one in which the queer marriage tussle wins out. Speaking less to any kind of erotic involvement between the two players than to Iago's intended perversion of the rites of marriage (a perversion to compete with the interracial marriage of Othello and Desdemona, the third scene of the third act of *Othello* culminates with the performance of marriage vows between Othello and Iago (3.3.461–80). *The Merchant of Venice* proves a less discrete example than those found in the two above plays. Here, Antonio's erotic attachment to Bassanio must, according to the social narratives played out in the play, be circumvented, as Portia makes ritualistically clear through the ring trick, before her marriage to Bassanio can be consummated. In her thwarting too of Antonio's willing bestowal of his flesh in the name of Bassanio, Portia prevents the literalization of the trafficking in flesh rendered only symbolically in the rites of heterosexual marriage.

15. Boswell's historical claims square well with the present-day anthropological claims of Kath Weston's *Families We Choose* (1997).
16. Rambuss's quotation is in Schwarz (2000, 225). Also see Charles: the improbable solutions that end the play 'whether explained as dramatic plot convention or a return to normalcy, expose "the failure of heterosexual regimes ever fully to legislate or contain their own ideals"' (1997, 139). See also Pequigney (1992, 206).
17. This moment is the closest in Shakespeare to what is perhaps the most explicitly dramatized same-sex marriage in early modern drama, that found in John Lyly's *Gallathea*, where Venus at the end of the play decides to change the sex of one of the two women, Gallathea and Phyllida, who have fallen in love with each other, so that the two women will be allowed to marry: 'What is to love or the mistress of love unpossible?' (5.3.171). For a kind of de-eroticization of queer marriage, see Ben Jonson's *Epicoene*.
18. For a reading of how editorial choices shape issues of sex, gender, and sexuality in *Twelfth Night*, see Laurie Osborne: 'One potential performance enabled by the Folio *Twelfe Night* allows for a much more radical exposure of the boy-actress within the role of Viola than most critics acknowledge' (1998, 219).
19. My word 'overplayed' is intended to make the argument that when something gets overplayed, repeatedly and incessantly performed, it shifts into 'acting'; that is, the (over-) formalization of playing is acting.
20. Cf. 2.3.9 and 3.14.118. The frequency of the word 'element' in this play is superseded only by the use of it in *Othello*.
21. Charles suspects that 'the homoerotic elements of the play, while troubling and disruptive in its dramatic development, may not have the power in this final scene to overcome fully the symbolic dictates of compulsory heterosexuality, at least from a perspective of formal kinship relations' (1997, 141). While there is certainly truth to Charles's argument, I would counter, however, that the role of the homoerotic in the play stretches beyond the kind of secondary position afforded it by the terms 'troubling and disruptive'. The play, I would argue, pressures the value accreted to 'formal kinship relations'.
22. Cf. 3.2.13–131.

23. Most immediately here, I am taking 'threat' from Dolan (1994, xxxvii), even though the word works as a virtual leitmotif through a lot of the rhetoric around homosexuality and particularly around same-sex marriage.
24. Unlike the bloody cloak in *A Midsummer Night's Dream*'s *Pyramus and Thisbe, As You Like It* is a play in which flesh is actually torn. It is noteworthy that a female of the species does so.
25. Orlando's words here recall for me John Boswell's work on 'the friend', a work where he specifically focuses on vows between men but whose argument, of course, as he himself acknowledges, does also pertain to women. Also, cf. Virginia Woolf's *Orlando*, where Woolf posits a different kind of social foundational myth than that provided by the mythologizing of Adam and Eve in her characterization of Orlando (now a woman) and Orlando's husband, Shel: 'No sooner had the words left her mouth than an awful suspicion rushed into both their minds simultaneously. / 'You're a woman, Shel!' she cried. / 'You're a man, Orlando!' he cried. / Never was there such a scene of protestation and demonstration as then took place since the world began' (1928, 1993, 251–52).
26. 'His hand' is almost invariably emended to 'her hand', and often defended as a necessary emendation to make the line make sense and *logically* connect it to the 'her' in the line preceding it. For a brilliant and delightful discussion of this emendation, see Jeffrey Masten (1996).
27. I use the term, 'outdoes', because I am assuming that in early modern culture the stakes would be higher for men who would engage in such social transgressions, but, more notably, because, fully exploiting the play's metatheatrical significations, Hymen does not find it necessary to change the sex of one of her characters and thereby genetically remake the couple-to-wed into a heterosexual one. Unlike Lyly's Venus, Hymen's power is theatrical and present. See note 18 for more on *Gallathea* (1976). Also, I am reading the word 'even' in Hymen's speech as meaning 'the same'. Here's a possible translation of Hymen's speech: the universe of comedy allows those who have the same biological sex to have an affinity, as these two have; it is a possibility that usually only seems possible in our mundane earthbound society between two persons of opposite sex.
28. The most popular use of this word in Shakespeare is found in this play.
29. Nagel (my emphasis on 'major location'; other emphases are in the actual text), 51. I am also in accord here with Nagel, who continues this quotation by reminding us that these two concepts, gender and sexuality, 'deserve some attention because of their usefulness in understanding social construction processes in general, for their increasingly common usage among researchers and theorists of gender and sexuality, and for their applicability to other socially constructed roles and categories ... namely race, ethnicity, and nationalism' (2003, 51).
30. Also see Bray (2003, 217), whom Traub is paraphrasing.
31. The threat of forgetting, of not remembering homoeroticism, haunts Shakespeare's play. In other words, the critical tradition around *A Midsummer Night's Dream* has replicated this erasure, has indeed sided with the dominant sexual discursive power *in* the play. The critical tradition has failed to heed Foucault's call that we form 'a different grid of historical decipherments by starting from a different theory of power .... We must at the same

time conceive of sex without the law and power without the king' (1976, 1978, 90–1). We must in fact begin to think of homoeroticism as something far more substantial than an 'alternative', and (as Alan Bray has argued) as something in the early modern era deeply embedded, commiserate with homosociality itself. To do so would constitute an act of remembering. As Valerie Traub has argued in her discussion of Bray's work, 'By excavating the remains of friendship in public sites and rituals heretofore obscured by a historical enterprise intent on recognizing only the kinship created by marriage, by locating the family within an encompassing network of friendship that kinship also created.... Bray's compelling narrative returns to the praxis of friendship a social and historical efficacy that largely has been forgotten' (2004, 341).

32. My argument here, that while the society of Shakespeare's play may find itself engrossed in the incidentals of its women, it is all finally shaped by the patriarchalist need to make non-negotiable the heteronormativity of the male body, particularly that of the father. I see my argument as being in line with that advanced by Louis A. Montrose in his now classic new historicist reading of the play, where he argues, for example, that 'Theseus represents paternity as cultural act, an art: the father is a demiurge or *homo faber*, who composes, in-forms, imprints himself upon, what is merely inchoate matter' (1986, 73).
33. Without trying to obfuscate further the difficulties of employing contemporary social categories when trying to study early modern English culture, I do mean to suggest here too that, as in our own contemporary debates about gay marriage in the U.S., conversations of gay marriage are intimately bound up in conversations about interracial ones. More conceptually, both sexuality and race participate in our myths of an originary corporeality, that is, an original body that is both heterosexual and white. A longer version of this essay would also invest in discourses of inter-racialism at work in Shakespeare's play.
34. It is worth noting, as Bruce R. Smith reminds us, that 'all the magical metamorphoses that the fairies work on the mortals in *A Midsummer Night's Dream* devolve from a single case of jealousy that has its origins in Ovid's tale of Jupiter and Ganymede' (1991, 199). I would argue that in this particular Shakespeare play in which the masculinity and cohesiveness of the male body so intricately and terrifyingly depends on his stabilizing and securing the properly feminized female body for heterosexual matrimony, the sexual indeterminacy of Hippolyta's body threatens to return us to the original (homosexual) scene of the crime.
35. I am thinking here of Homi K. Bhabha's use of the word *mimicry*: 'Mimicry is, thus, the sign of a double articulation; a complex strategy of reform, regulation and discipline, which "appropriates" the Other as it visualizes power. Mimicry is also the sign of the inappropriate, however, a difference or recalcitrance which coheres the dominant strategic function of colonial power, intensifies surveillance, and poses an immanent threat to both "normalized" knowledges and disciplinary powers' (1994, 86).
36. As Margo Hendricks has argued, even though India also became 'representable [for the early modern English] as a real geographic and cultural space, capable of being partitioned, classified, conquered, and exploited', India

'still carried with it the figuration of an imaginative site of fabulous wealth, fantastic creatures, and other rarities in the English political consciousness' (1996, 48). See also Hendricks, 1996, 51.

37. I am adopting my reading of surplus from Roderick A. Ferguson, who, in his study of race and sexuality, has argued that 'the creation of surplus is the violation of the boundaries of age, home, race, and nation', adding that 'surplus populations point to a fundamental feature of capital: It does not rely on normative prescriptions to assemble labor, even while it may use those prescriptions to establish the value of that labor' (2004, 16).
38. See Tennenhouse 1986, 42–3.
39. In addition to seeing the relationship between Bottom and Titania primarily in maternal terms, Paster sees herself in agreement with Louis A. Montrose, who sees in Bottom and Titania's relationship a 'parodic fantasy of infantile narcissism and dependency' (1986, 68). A question that could be very beneficial here is what is the relationship between this infantile narcisbesism and a Freudian understanding of homosexuality? I am not sure I am ready to sign on to the implications of Paster's and Montrose's claims with respect to Bottom and Titania.
40. The primacy of the maternal argument seems to me a difficult one, especially in light of the lovemaking that dominates the interactions between Titania and Bottom (see 3.1 and 4.1); Shakespeare does not really get more suggestively orgiastic than this.
41. See Paster (1993, 125–26) and her brief discussion of the connection between this figure and misogyny.
42. Part of what I am trying to do here is respond to Paster's argument about what Oberon accomplishes by substituting the boy for Bottom. She argues that 'the substitution ... constructs a parodic image of adult female sexuality in which the differences between heterosexual intercourse and the anal cathexes of maternal nurture become blurred' (1993, 128). Without necessarily eliding Paster's argument, I am arguing that Bottom's anality works even more so as part of the play's construction of queer (sexual) unions.
43. Celia Daileader (2002) makes an argument about 'gynosodomy' in *A Midsummer Night's Dream*, as well as in several other early modern texts.
44. Even though it may be true, as Weimann argues, that the common player 'is said to be without conviction, pride, and identity' (2000, 134), there is certainly room to argue that Bottom is deeply and *playfully* committed to his lack of these things.
45. Theseus contrasts sharply with Bottom, a fact underscored by the fact that shortly after Bottom's moment of theatrical triumph (the way I am thinking of Bottom's awakening), comes Theseus's own in the form of his 'the lunatic, the lover, and the poet' speech (5.1.2–22), the speech that includes the line I have adopted as the first part of my title (5.1.17). Bottom is as queer as Theseus is straight, and straight men do not play. Where Bottom *presents*, Theseus *impersonates* (for a discussion of the difference between these two terms, see Hawkes 2002, 111–13). And, for all Theseus's self-assurance, he is arguably the most egregious and deluded impersonator in Shakespeare's play; he is the one most thoroughly co-opted by the script, whether Shakespeare's or society's.

46. Cf. Judith Butler's argument about drag: 'As an allegory that works through the hyperbolic, drag brings into relief what is, after all, determined only in relation to the hyperbolic: the understated, taken-for-granted quality of heterosexual performativity. At its best, then, drag can be read for the way in which hyperbolic norms are dissimulated as the heterosexual mundane' (1993, 237).

Part V
Temporalities

12
'The future in the instant'

Kathleen McLuskie

Presentism, and the debates that it has generated, offer an interesting example of the discursive overkill that has affected engagement with Shakespeare's plays from the First Folio to the present day. It presents one pole of the intellectual oscillation between a sense of Shakespeare's historical existence as an early modern playwright and the view that the implications of his plays (whether or not seen as universal truths) must engage with their reproduction in our own time. Both approaches, however, posit a discursive significance for the plays, a sense that their importance requires separate articulation in commentary and interpretation. Whether that commentary derives from historical knowledge of early modern theatre and culture or from the perceived correlation (or its lack) between the plays and contemporary pre-occupations, it has played a vital role in sustaining the plays' after-lives, keeping them in the forefront of intellectual debates and developing the institutions, from the blue-stocking circle to the Royal Shakespeare Company, that re-ensured their place in the national culture.

Questions of gender have, from the beginning,[1] been an essential part of that discursive effort. In their engaged insistence that 'Shakespeare' must speak to and of them, women readers and critics opened out the ethical and aesthetic terrain within which the plays could function. They recast the plays as social worlds in which characters' motivations and actions, their past influences and their present roles, could be identified, speculated about and judged. In doing so, they shifted the emphasis from the historical Shakespeare to a Shakespeare who was eternally present in his relationship with them, and created the template for all criticism, including historicist criticism, which insists upon the significant and contemporary moment of the critical act.

Both historicist and presentist criticism, then, superimpose their own time frame onto the reproduction of Shakespeare. The discursively important relationship is between the play and the critic. The critic retells the story, shifting the time frame in which the play unrolls events to one in which the play is always already complete: the characters' motives have already resulted in actions, the structures of power or the expectations of a love affair have already been resolved for better or worse.

In critical discourse, the time past of the play and the time present of the moment of contemporary performance or reading are both drawn into the time future of articulated interpretation. The moment-by-moment present of a performance or reading is part of a connected process that is driven forward by the past and future of a narrative in which events are given significance in terms of the extent to which they prefigure the ending and are then given further, transcendent, significance by the extent to which they can be connected in interpretation to the events of the play's originating moment or its thematic connection to the pre-occupations of the moment of its reception.

This teleological critical time frame seems to me to be different from that of the plays' internal structures. The constraints of performance time create a tension between it and the time of narrative (the characters' past and future), between the immediate pleasures of performance and the form's capacity for significant meaning. It was a constant motif of commentary in the early modern theatre. Hamlet's concern that the players might speak more than was set down for them and deflect attention away from some necessary significance in the play draws attention to the potential conflict between performance and narrative. Ben Jonson theorized the issue more explicitly when, in the preface to the printed text of *Hymenaei*, he acknowledged the transience of the masque's performance and contrasted it with his desire to ensure that the footnotes and glosses of his presentation text would allow it to speak not only to present occasions but to 'more removed mysteries'.

Rather than arguing the case for or against presentism as a theoretical position in criticism of Shakespeare, I want to return the lines from which my title comes to their play. My aim will be to show how the tension between the present and the past can be mapped onto the tension between narrative and performance and their shared role in creating significance in a single play.

A particularly resonant instance of this tension and its critical effects occurs in *Macbeth*. When Lady Macbeth greets her husband after he has returned from his encounter with the witches, she says:

> Great Glamis! worthy Cawdor!
> Greater than both, by the all-hail hereafter!
> Thy letters have transported me beyond
> This ignorant present, and I feel now
> The future in the instant.
>
> (1.5.54–8)[2]

As so often in *Macbeth,* these lines have a certain eloquent familiarity that obscures the fact that we do not fully understand what they mean. There is a tension between the narrative moment – Lady Macbeth greets her husband – and the precise referent of the lines that she speaks. Her greeting brings together the past events of the witches' greetings to Macbeth and the impression that their narrative has made on her. 'Great Glamis! worthy Cawdor!' (1.5.54) glosses the completed elements of the witches' prophecy and 'Greater than both, by the all-hail hereafter' (1.5.55) refers beyond their words to a future 'all hail!' (1.3.69) that will signal his achieved greatness. But what is 'this ignorant present' (1.5.57)? And what does it mean to 'feel…/ The future in the instant' (1.5.58)? 'Ignorant present', using the flexibility with which early modern English used adjectives made from verbs, means a present in which something is not known for sure. 'Ignorant' had been used in Macbeth's letter to his Lady in which he tells her what had happened: 'This have I thought good to deliver thee, my dearest partner of greatness, that thou mightst not lose the dues of rejoicing by being ignorant of what greatness is promis'd thee' (1.5.10–13). So, 'ignorant' there does not mean knowing nothing (as in modern usage) but not knowing a particular thing: 'what greatness is promised thee'. Extrapolating from Macbeth's letter to this moment allows us to gloss 'the future in the instant' as Lady Macbeth's sense of the future fulfillment of the prophecy, her excitement at the future vision created by the instant of the witches' prophecy. Macbeth's arrival confirms for her the sense of a possible future that she had only fantasized in her fear that Macbeth will not be able to complete the prophesied future, a future that she has tried to secure independently in her invocation of the spirits that tend on mortal thoughts.

The complex compression of ideas in Lady Macbeth's lines is often ignored in the performance tradition that draws on modern critical assumptions about their relationship to sexualize the relationship between Macbeth and his Lady. The lines are often accompanied by a full-on sexual kiss that prefigures the sexual undercurrents of the scene where Lady Macbeth goads her husband into action that befits a man. It substitutes interpreted performance for attention to the precise meaning of the words. It reads the play backwards, using interpretation of moral debate over killing Duncan to read the timeless nature of their essential natures.

Attention to the words, to the references to 'the ignorant present' and 'the future in the instant', highlights the particular significance of the treatment of time and the logic of narrative in the play. The play's action depends on the implied narrative that lies behind the three repetitions of 'Hail!' (1.3.62–4) of the witches. The witches, of course, do not provide a narrative of cause and effect: they simply call out three titles. It is the events of the preceding scene – the execution of Cawdor – that connect the first two repetitions of 'all hail'. At this point in the play, the beginning of Act 1, scene 3, we know that Cawdor has been executed and that his title has been conferred on Macbeth. The events of Act 1, scene 2, are assumed as the witches confer both titles on Macbeth and that forward trajectory gives a narrative momentum to the question raised by the third title 'that shall be king hereafter'. The witches' summary movement from Cawdor to Glamis to King prefigures the movement of events, in time and in narrative that creates the action of the first part of the play. Macbeth's tormented soliloquies, his relations with his wife, the discussion with Banquo and the vision of the dagger are all held together by the fulfillment of the three all hails until the death of Duncan fulfils the prophecy that Macbeth will be king hereafter.

Macbeth is himself all too aware that the fulfillment of narratives depends upon agents. He observes 'If chance will have me king, why, chance may crown me / Without my stir' (1.3.143–44). But chance is the antithesis of narrative. The remainder of the first part of the play, though it focuses on the ethical consequences of a particular action 'whose horrid image doth unfix my hair / And make my seated heart knock at my ribs' (1.3.135–36), creates a narrative that both fulfills the knowledge created by the past and constantly considers the possibility of *in*action.

In Act 1, scene 5, Lady Macbeth's feelings of 'the future in the instant' are themselves occasioned by the narrative that Macbeth has sent her in his letter that opens the scene. That letter does not merely recount the story so far. It reorganizes the order of the events. Like a critical account of the events, Macbeth's letter begins with the proof, 'the perfect'st report' (1.5.2) of the witches' 'more ... than mortal knowledge' (1.5.3). It offers the corroboration of their prophecy *before* he tells his lady of the triple greeting. He calls that greeting 'the coming on of time' ('referr'd me to the coming on of time' [1.5.9]). He connects the fulfillment of the pattern of greeting both with the passage of time and with the fulfillment of a particular narrative trajectory, a trajectory that is eagerly seized upon by his lady and allows her to 'feel now / The future in the instant' (1.5.57–8).

The feelings that arise from narrative depend on the organization of its sequence. It reveals that the possibility of feeling 'the future in the instant' depends on access to and the forms of knowledge of the past. Macbeth's letters are able to transport her 'beyond / This ignorant present' (1.5.56–7) in which she is 'ignorant of what greatness is promis'd thee' (1.5.12–13) because of the form they take. He has given the 'perfect'st report' (1.5.2), that the witches 'have more in them than mortal knowledge' (1.5.3). He has turned around the ordering of the narrative, and by creating the connections that trigger her invocation of the 'spirits / That tend on mortal thoughts' (1.5.40–1) his letter has given her the psychic and somatic strength to take 'this night's great business into my dispatch' (1.5.68).

This process of reading (both Lady Macbeth's reading of the narrative and my reading of significant lines) will be familiar to most literary critics. It begins in an effort to explain a passage that is not in detail essential to the narrative movement of the play. The desire to do this depends upon a sense that the story has an impact of emotion or affect or philosophical significance that goes beyond its mere events, and that, in the hands of literary critics, those moments of significance can be drawn together in a chain of resonant images that implies an abstract coherent significance both for earlier times and for the present time of the reading.

The motifs I have begun to identify cry out to be read in terms of the general importance of 'time' in the play, partly because, once identified, the motif of time can be located everywhere. At the end of the exchange between Macbeth and his lady in 1.5, she advises Macbeth

> To beguile the time,
> Look like the time; bear welcome in your eye,
> Your hand, your tongue: look like th'innocent flower,
> But be the serpent under't.
>
> (1.5.63–6)

The metaphoric use of 'time', to mean both the passage of time and the conditions in which Macbeth will have to operate, opens the possibility of other, deeper, resonances for the word. At key moments in the play, the implications of time seem to lie behind Macbeth's desire that 'If it were done when 'tis done, then 'twere well / It were done quickly' (1.7.1–2) and his avowal that 'If th'assassination / Could trammel up the consequence… / We'ld jump the life to come' (1.7.2–7).

The events of the play, unfolding in time, of course, make the existential point that time never brings in its consequences without human intervention and action. The whirligig of time never just brings in its revenges; human beings have to do something in time. As Macbeth says, after the horror of the banquet scene and the terrible appearance of Banquo's ghost, 'I will to-morrow, / (And betimes I will) to the weird sisters' (3.4.131–32). The rest of the action flows on, not just in time but because of the actions that he takes. The action of the play that ends with Macbeth's head being brought on stage is concluded with Malcolm's final (again mysterious) statement: 'the time is free' (5.9.21). He then goes on to ensure the political stability of future time by transforming the thanes into earls: 'the first that ever Scotland / In such an honor nam'd' (5.9.29–30). The world of the deep time of the chaotic Scottish past is transformed into the present of the play by its sideways glance at James 6's and 1's creation of a supporting aristocracy for his new kingdom. This emphasis on 'time' in the play offers a (possibly spurious) thematic significance that transcends the more vulgar account of its key theatrical moments: the witches, the dagger, the haunted banquet and the parade of kings. It opens up instead the possibility of a reading that presents the play as an enactment of existential questions about the relationship between action and time.

Needless to say, these connections have been noted by other critics of the play. In his account of *Shakespeare's Language,* Frank Kermode offers a wonderfully persuasive route through the play that moves from one resonant speech about time to another. For those who know the play well and are attuned to the protocols of literary criticism, Kermode's reading recreates the affect – the sense that the play presents emotionally and philosophically significant meaning – that supersedes the experience of reading or seeing the play itself. The eloquence of Kermode's writing makes the connections that he makes seem the natural working out of a complex ethical proposition.

The most telling moment in Kermode's analysis comes when he clinches the universal quality of this motif by pointing to a verbal parallel between Shakespeare's most famous evocation of the passage of time – 'To-morrow, and to-morrow, and to-morrow' (5.5.19) – and a similar image in Saint Augustine's *Confessions*:

> St. Augustine wrote about such a moment, the gap between desire and act. Though he was certain of the end desires, he was 'at strife' with himself. The choices to be made were 'all meeting together in the same juncture of time'. He said to himself, 'Be it done now, be it done now', but he continued to hesitate between fair and foul, crying, 'How long? How long? Tomorrow and Tomorrow'. (*Confessions* 7, xii, quoted in Kermode 2000, 205)

Kermode weaves his own language around Shakespeare's and Saint Augustine's in a way that makes the ideas seem timeless, a recurring preoccupation of a human condition, an awareness of the transience of earthly things that is removed from its specifically Christian context in Saint Augustine or its particular narrative moment in *Macbeth* – floating free from time so that its general proposition can be recognized as true (or at least resonant) by the present-day reader.

Kermode's critical process is not explicitly presentist in that he does not connect his observations to particular present occasions. However, it offers a methodology that lies behind both presentist and historicist accounts of Shakespeare's plays. He opens the preface by declaring:

> This book is addressed to a non-professional audience with an interest in Shakespeare that has not, I believe, been well served by modern critics who on the whole seem to have little time for his language; they tend to talk past it in technicalities or down to it in arcanely expressed platitudes. (2000, vii)

He claims, in other words, that the continuing life of the play, its conduit to meaning, consists in its language rather than its narrative or historical circumstances. The route from language to significance, however, is assumed to be opaque. It requires the help of the critic, using a mix of rhetorical analysis and the assertion of general truths, to take the reader beyond its merely narrative significance to the play's universal humanist meanings.

The impact of Kermode's analysis depends for its authority on the resonant familiarity of particularly well-known passages (he does not deal, for example, with the textual and linguistic cruxes of the messenger speech from Act 1, scene 2). He does acknowledge that the familiarity of these passages depends upon their having been anthologized from the eighteenth century on. The particular suitability of these lines for anthologizing, moreover, depends upon their tenuous relationship with the narrative of the play. Macbeth's now famous speech about the inexorable movement of 'To-morrow, and to-morrow, and to-morrow, ... / To the last syllable of recorded time' (5.5.19–21) is a response to the news that 'The Queen, my lord, is dead' (5.5.16). It gains its effect from the contrast between the sudden 'cry within of women' (5.5.7) and the elongated reflection on the impossibility of there being 'time for such a word' (5.5.18). It says nothing of Macbeth's feelings or his relationship with Lady Macbeth. Instead, it takes the reader or audience beyond the immediate present of the narrative moment to a generalized statement whose rhetoric and poetic structure enacts the movement of time of which it speaks. It can therefore be extrapolated from the particular moment in the story to represent Shakespeare's capacity for articulating general truths that are not for an age but for all time.

Marshaling these truths for all time into a coherent statement about the play is a literary critical method that itself exists in time. It is particularly associated with the critical movement that Francis Mulhern has described as 'The Moment of "Scrutiny"' when a disenfranchised group of Cambridge critics sought to rescue Shakespeare studies from the sentimental reading of character that had become the dominant mode of response to Shakespeare in the nineteenth century. Its most famous example is L. C. Knights's essay, 'How Many Children Had Lady Macbeth?' That essay provided a map of the play's images to structure a claim that the play's real significance lay in its articulation of the values of a coherent, organic connection to nature, destroyed by the terrible rupture of Macbeth's insubordinate treachery. Knights's essay was influential in creating a critical methodology that placed the critic between the play and the reader. Attention to narrative and character was dismissed by Knights as the 'irrelevant moral and realistic canons that have been applied to Shakespeare's plays, for the sentimentalizing of his heroes ... and his heroines' (1946, 1)[3]. The meaning of the play now resided in its connecting strands of poetic imagery that required an abstracting critical process to give them meaning.

This process of abstraction had proved a powerful tool in the criticism of Shakespeare, not least because it echoes the relationship between poetry and narrative that is built into the plays themselves. The poetic rhetoric of the play's language always provides an excess over the narrative, a gloss on its events, a demand to consider meaning. Critical analysis of Shakespeare, since 'The Moment of "Scrutiny"', has depended on its ability to link that claimed meaning into a pattern that will stand in for the affective experience of the play. The importance of that move in the history of criticism is that it shifted attention away from the moment-by-moment experience of the play onto a wide-angle, static and abstract summation of its significance. The convoluted complexity of Macbeth's long soliloquy at the start of Act 1, scene 7, to take an example, puzzled nineteenth–century critics who wished to tie it to its narrative moment. One critic disapproves of its style but locates that disapproval in a critique of Macbeth the character rather than Shakespeare:

> This is pure rant, and intended to be so. It is the product of an unrestrained imagination which exhausts itself in the utterance. But it neither comes from the heart nor acts upon the heart. (Shakespeare 1873, 99)

Another admires the passage as a characteristic example of Shakespeare's boldness, described by invoking an elegant analogy:

> what the drama has hitherto portrayed in chiaroscuro is here unfolded in clearer treatment: it is not in the mouth of every character that the poet would put such wild, extravagant, phantasmagoric images; they are reserved for the hero, with his nervous temperament, at a moment of the highest tension, when at a glance he scans a horrible future. All of Shakespeare's images have something peculiarly sudden and emotional; they remind us of flickering torchlight illuminating a cavern of stalactites. (Shakespeare 1873, 99)

The play's language can be an effect of character, speaking from his emotions and experience, or it can be the autonomous power of Shakespeare, creating a mimetic effect that is to be admired separately from the characters' actions, or both.

These problems of performance and narrative disappear in Cleanth Brooks's famous essay on 'The Naked Babe and the Cloak of Manliness'. There the confusions of Macbeth's repeated and contradictory analogies for pity are marshaled into an elegant paradox that is linked to the ethical centre of the play:

> Pity is like the babe, the most sensitive and helpless thing; yet, almost as soon as the comparison is announced, the symbol of weakness begins to turn into a symbol of strength; for the babe, though newborn, is pictured as 'striding the blast' like an elemental force – 'like

> heaven's cherubin, horsed / Upon the sightless couriers of the air'. We can give an answer to the question put earlier: is Pity like the helpless and human babe, or powerful as the angel that rides the winds? It is both; and it is strong because of its very weakness. The paradox is inherent in the situation itself; and it is the paradox that will destroy the overbrittle rationalism on which Macbeth founds his career. (Brooks 1947, 45)

Macbeth's speech is seen not as an effect of performance in narrative but an independent articulation of the deep structures of the play's significance. Brooks's and Knights's conclusions were, of course, repudiated by new historicism, with its emphasis on particular rather than universal significance. However, their fundamental analogizing methodology, the desire for a significance that transcends narrative, remains. Faced with overturning the humanist readings of Shakespeare and their concern with 'universal' (or, as new historicists might claim, 'hegemonic') values, new historicists used the resources of history to make a case for the affect that these plays had in the early modern period by demonstrating the shared themes and language of historical and literary texts concerned with questions of gender identity and power in the construction of the early modern subject. They substituted, in other words, an assumed historical affect to replace the affect that existing readers experienced on reading *The Tempest* or *King Lear*. In some cases, this has amounted to a counterintuitive substitution of a claimed historical meaning that substitutes for the narrative significance of particular events in the play.

The now commonplace notion that *Macbeth* has some kind of symbiotic relationship to the accession of James 6 of Scotland to the English throne and the events of the Gunpowder Plot offers a critical narrative that explains away problematic events in the action such as the Porter's speech in Act 2 or the show of kings in Act 4. Both of these events involve actions that upset the balance between narrative and performance. The Porter's speech offers an immediate effect of comic commentary on events that are outside the play altogether – a classic case of a clown speaking more than is set down for him. It is too close to the present pleasure of performance and is a set piece unconnected to the narrative drive of the play. The show of kings is also a localized theatrical effect, but it too presents 'the future in the instant' and connects the play to an immediate present that has no part in the repeatable narrative as it is experienced by subsequent readers and audiences.

Neither the Porter's speech nor the show of kings was mentioned in Simon Forman's 1611 account of the play in performance. Forman's account focused almost entirely on its narrative drive: 'In the meantyme whylle Macdovee was in England, Mackbet slewe Mackdoves wife & children, and after in the battelle Mackdove slewe Mackbet'. The figures who prophecy the future to Macbeth and Banquo are not witches but '3 women feiries or Nimphes', and he makes no mention of the final witch scene, with its apparitions, prophecies and the parade of kings. Alongside this attention to the narrative, he also pays telling attention to the performance of affect in his recollection of Lady Macbeth's sleepwalking and the couple's appalled reaction to the ineradicable blood on their hands.[4] He certainly did not comment on any possible connection to contemporary politics or a larger meaning beyond the experience of the play. Of course, the critical claim that the historical significance of the play lay in its connection to the accession of James 6 and 1 did not depend on corroboration from actual readers or audiences. It could be asserted simply by coincidental historical analogies between James's alleged interest in witchcraft, the apparent reference to Banquo's place in Stuart genealogy, and the explanatory connection between the obscurities of the Porter's speech and the literature surrounding the Gunpowder Plot. Even J. Leeds Barroll's systematic argument *against* the connection between James 6 and the King's Men (1991, 133–52) cannot dislodge the critical process that laminates the significance claimed for the play to its role as a source of historical understanding and a meaning that leads back into historical themes.

Presentist readings of *Macbeth* from the twentieth century have usually taken the form of denying the historical specificity of its narrative while assuming that beyond the contingencies of narrative lies a universal understanding of significant historical themes. They have normalized the witches by presenting them as camp followers (e.g., Komisarjevsky 1933), they have presented the battlefield scenes in modern army uniforms (e.g., Sher 1998), and they have removed the supernatural elements of the dagger and Banquo's ghost by suggesting that they are the figments of Macbeth's frantic imagination (e.g., Kemble 1788). They have, nevertheless, retained the deep historicist assumption of a pre-modern culture in which conflicts of power can be resolved by the violent action of individuals rather than through the due process of political or social agencies. Whether Macbeth is a Mafia boss (*Men of Respect*) or a gang-leader in an urban slum (*Macbeth on the Estate*), the play's narrative demands that it focus on and normalize a historical understanding of the relationship between the present and the past. It assumes that the affect and significance of its events are controlled by accepting that the present of the action is determined by the past and the future of the prophecies, together with the inexorable logic of Macduff's revenge, itself made possible by the past event of his unnatural birth.

These readings are not only historicist but deeply reactionary. By modernizing the local effects but retaining the emotional affect of the narrative, they universalize rather than call into question the structures of power that the play dramatizes. Features of modernity, such as the historical development of democratic controls (however inadequate) on tyranny, the mechanized quality of modern warfare, the bureaucratized nature of modern exercises of diplomacy are all occluded in a conceptualization of power exercised through an atavistic confrontation between men. In his account of a number of postmodern film adaptations of Shakespeare, for example, Mark Burnett has shown how they depend upon creating analogies via setting between the events of the plays and a variety of other conflicts, ranging from the Balkan wars that followed the collapse of Eastern European communism to the Northern Irish troubles of the later twentieth century. He quotes Antony Sher describing how, in his production of *Macbeth*, he was aiming for a sense of 'a modern world but one you can't easily identify ... and you can't say which war this is either' (1996, 137). The profound differences in the complex historical and political circumstances of wars even in the twentieth century can thus be elided into general statements about war and the pity of war, and the even more profound differences between Shakespeare's society and our own are subsumed by the cultural capital of his narratives. The effect of that process is to emphasize direct communication of the 'essence' of Shakespeare, the encapsulation of his narrative into abstract generalizations that bear only contingent connection with the moment-by-moment experience of the relationship between poetry and narrative in the plays.

Lady Macbeth can hear Macbeth's narrative and feel (not think) the future in the instant. As we have seen, her feelings come in part from Macbeth's control of the narrative and in part from her own investment in his version of a trajectory from the past to the future. The play does provide some alternatives, however impotent, to that trajectory. In particular, the choric figures of Rosse, Lennox, the Old Man, and another unnamed 'lord' (see Act 2, Scene 4 and Act 3, scene 4) offer more varied accounts of the events that they have witnessed and make clear the possibility of a gap between experience and affect. This process from narrative and affect to significance is the trajectory that is more open in the play itself. Macbeth considers the role of agents, the choric figures explore other possible outcomes, and the action of the play offers the possibility for judgment of characters and their actions. However, by denying the complexity of a movement between narrative, performance and meaning, the critic commandeers the play's meaning for immediate use. The overloading presence of criticism, the demand that Shakespeare will have ethical or historical or present meaning flattens the moment-by-moment experience of the play into an interpretative discourse.

An alternative critical process would involve resisting the consumption of meaning offered by the explanatory critic and focusing instead on the process of the production of meaning in poetry and narrative and theatrical effect. Understanding the demands that these formal effects make on us, including the demand that we acquiesce in accepting their particular versions of the workings of power, might allow us to remain firmly in the present and from that vantage point to admire or despise, but above all, to understand the difference between the present and the past. Our presentness would not lie in the discursive analogies between our own situation and that of the plays' characters or in the satisfying sense that we are skilled in the discursive techniques of making meaning. Rather, we would be present at the play's own making of meaning and also aware of our distance from it. Rather than feeling the future in the instant or approaching the past 'only with the preconceptions and the preoccupations of the present' (Schalkwyk 2005, 2), we might stay in the present and past of the play and reflect on their difference from our own.

Notes

1. See Thompson and Roberts (1997, passim).
2. All quotations from *Macbeth* are from the Riverside edition (1974) and are cited by act, scene, and line reference in the body of the essay.
3. Cf. Carol Chillington Rutter (2004).
4. The text of Forman's notes on *Macbeth* is quoted in full in A. R. Braunmuller's Cambridge edition of the play (Shakespeare 1997b, 57–8).

Works Cited

Abbot, G. (1604) *The Reasons Which Doctour Hill Hath Brought, for the Upholding of Papistry, Which Is Falselie Termed the Catholike Religion* (Oxford: J. Barnes).

Adelman, J. (1992) *Suffocating Mothers: Fantasies of Maternal Origin in Shakespeare's Plays,* Hamlet *to* The Tempest (New York and London: Routledge).

'Agincourt' (19 February 2005) *Mysteries of Battle* (The History Channel, A&E Television Networks).

Annand, W. (1661) *Fides Catholica, or, the Doctrine of the Catholick Church in Eighteen Grand Ordinances* (London: T. R. for E. Brewster).

Apter, E. (1990) *Feminizing the Fetish: Psychoanalysis and Narrative Obsession in Turn-of-the-Century France* (Ithaca: Cornell University Press).

——, and W. Pietz (eds) (1993) *Fetishism as Cultural Discourse* (Ithaca: Cornell University Press).

Aristotle (1984) *The Complete Works of Aristotle*, J. Barnes (ed.) 2 vols. (Princeton: Princeton University Press).

Austin, W. (1637) *Haec Homo Wherein the Excellency of the Creation of Woman is Described, by Way of an Essay* (London: R. Olton for R. Mabb and C. Greene).

Aylmer, J. (1559) *An Harborowe for Faithfull and Trewe Subjectes, Agaynst the Late Blowne Blaste, Concerninge the Government of Wemen* (London: J. Daye).

Bamber, L. (1982) *Comic Women, Tragic Men: A Study of Gender and Genre in Shakespeare* (Stanford: Stanford University Press).

Barber, C. L. (1963) *Shakespeare's Festive Comedy: A Study of Dramatic Form and Its Relation to Social Custom* (Cleveland and New York: Meridian).

Barker, D., and I. Kamps (eds) (1995) *Shakespeare and Gender: A History* (London and New York: Verso).

Barker, J. (2006) *Agincourt: Henry 5 and the Battle That Made England* (London: Little, Brown).

Barroll, J. L. (1991) *Politics, Plague, and Shakespeare's Theatre* (Ithaca: Cornell University Press).

Bell, J. (dir.) (1979) *Romeo and Juliet*, by W. Shakespeare (Nimrod Theatre, Sydney, prompt copy, Nimrod Collection, Mitchell Library, State Library of New South Wales, Sydney).

——, (2002) *The Time of My Life* (London: Allen and Unwin, Crows Nest).

——, (26 March 2004) Interview by A. Kiernander, Bell Shakespeare Company Office.

Belsey, C. (1985) *The Subject of Tragedy: Identity and Difference in Renaissance Drama* (London: Methuen).

——, (2007) 'Historicizing new historicism' in H. Grady and T. Hawkes (eds) *Presentist Shakespeares* (London and New York: Routledge), pp. 27–45.

Benjamin, W. (1968) 'Theses on the philosophy of history' in H. Arendt (ed.) *Illuminations: Essays and Reflections* (New York: Schocken), pp. 253–64.

Bhabha, H. K. (1994) *The Location of Culture* (New York and London: Routledge).

Billington, M. (ed.) (1990) *Approaches to Twelfth Night* (Nick Hern Books: London).
'The Black Vera Wang', *The West Wing* (NBC Television, NBC Universal, Inc.).
Blackmore, J., and G. S. Hutcheson (1999) *Queer Iberia: Sexualities, Cultures, and Crossings from the Middle Ages to the Renaissance* (Durham: Duke University Press).
Blau, H. (1982) *Take Up the Bodies: Theater at the Vanishing Point* (Urbana: University of Illinois Press).
Bly, R. (1990) *Iron John: A Book about Men* (Reading, MA: Addison-Wesley).
Boehlert, E. (2006) *Lapdogs: How the Press Rolled Over for Bush* (New York: Free Press).
Boland, Lt. Col. J. P., USMCR (accessed 4 August 2005) Camp Fallujah, Iraq, Comment, Online Condolence Book for Jeffrey A. Boskovitch. http://obits.cleveland.com/Cleveland/GB/GuestBookView.aspx?PersonID=14731581
Boose, L. E. (1987) 'The Family in Shakespeare Studies; or—Studies in the Family of Shakespeareans; or—the Politics of Politics', *Renaissance Quarterly* 40: 707–42.
Boswell, J. (1994) *Same-Sex Unions in Premodern Europe* (New York: Vintage).
Bourdieu, P., and R. Nice (1988) 'The Work of Art as Fetish: The Production of Belief,' *Text and Context: A Journal of Interdisciplinary Studies* 2: 3–56.
Branagh, K. (dir.) (1989, 2000) *Henry 5*, by W. Shakespeare (Orion; DVD, MGM Home Entertainment).
Bray, A. (1982, 1995) *Homosexuality in Renaissance England* (London: Gay Men's Press; New York: Columbia University Press).
——, (1994) 'Homosexuality and the Signs of Male Friendship in Elizabethan England' in J. Goldberg (ed.) *Queering the Renaissance* (Durham and London: Duke University Press), pp. 40–61.
——, (2003) *The Friend* (Chicago: University of Chicago Press).
Bredbeck, G. (1991) *Sodomy and Interpretation: Marlowe to Milton* (Ithaca: Cornell University Press).
Breitenberg, M. (1996) *Anxious Masculinity in Early Modern England* (Cambridge: Cambridge University Press).
Bristol, M. D. (1996) *Big-Time Shakespeare* (New York: Routledge).
——, and K. McLuskie (eds) (2001) *Shakespeare and Modern Theatre: The Performance of Modernity* (London and New York: Routledge).
——, (2007) '…And I'm the King of France' in H. Grady and T. Hawkes (eds) *Presentist Shakespeares* (London and New York: Routledge), pp. 46–63.
Brock, D. (ed.) (accessed 26 June 2006) *Media Matters*. www.mediamatters.org
Brooks, C. (1947) 'The Naked Babe and the Cloak of Manliness' in C. Brooks (ed.), *The Well-Wrought Urn: Studies in the Structure of Poetry* (New York: Reynall and Hitchcock).
Brown, P. A., and P. Parolin (eds) (2005) *Women Players in England, 1500–1660: Beyond the All-Male Stage* (Burlington: Ashgate).
Browne, R. B. (1982) *Objects of Special Devotion: Fetishes and Fetishism in Popular Culture* (Bowling Green: Bowling Green University Popular Press).
Buckland, R. (2002) *The Witch Book: The Encyclopedia of Witchcraft, Wicca, and Neo-paganism* (Detroit: Visible Ink).
Bullough, G. (1960) 'Introduction to *1 Henry 6*' in G. Bullough (ed.) *Narrative and Dramatic Sources of Shakespeare*, vol. 3 (London: Routledge and Kegan Paul; New York: Columbia University Press), pp. 23–41.

Bullough, G. (1962) 'Introduction to *Henry 5*' in G. Bullough (ed.) *Narrative and Dramatic Sources of Shakespeare*, vol. 4 (London: Routledge and Kegan Paul; New York: Columbia University Press), pp. 347–75.

Burge, S. (dir.) (1965, 1996) *Othello*, by W. Shakespeare (National Theatre of Great Britain; VHS, Warner Home Video).

Burke, C. (2004) *Camp All-America, Hanoi Jane, and the High-and-Tight: Gender, Folklore, and Changing Military Culture* (Boston: Beacon Press).

Burnett, M. T. (2006) 'Globalization: Figuring the global/historical in filmic Shakespearean tragedy' in D. E. Henderson (ed.) *A Concise Companion to Shakespeare on Screen* (Oxford: Blackwell), pp. 133–154.

Bush, G. W. (18 December 2000) Comment during Florida recount, 2000 U.S. Presidential election.

Butler, J. (1990) *Gender Trouble: Feminism and the Subversion of Identity* (New York and London: Routledge).

——, (1993) *Bodies that Matter: The Discursive Limits of 'Sex'* (New York: Routledge).

——, (1997) *Excitable Speech: A Politics of the Performative* (New York and London: Routledge).

——, (2004) *Undoing Gender* (London and New York: Routledge).

Cagle, R. (1994) 'Auto-Eroticism: Narcissism, Fetishism, and Consumer Culture', *Cinema Journal* 33: 23–33.

Cahill, S. (2004) *Same-Sex Marriage in the United States: Focus on the Facts* (Lanham, MD: Lexington).

Caldwell, E. (13–15 April 2006) 'La France pour les Anglais', paper, *Shakespeare and the French*, 34th Annual Meeting, Shakespeare Association of America, Philadelphia, PA.

Callaghan, D. (1989) *Woman and Gender in Renaissance Tragedy: A Study of* King Lear, Othello, The Duchess of Malfi, *and* The White Devil (Atlantic Highlands, New Jersey: Humanities Press International).

——, (2000a) *Shakespeare Without Women: Representing Gender and Race on the Renaissance Stage* (New York and London: Routledge).

——, (2000b) 'Introduction' in D. Callaghan (ed.) *A Feminist Companion to Shakespeare* (Malden, Massachusetts, and Oxford: Blackwell), pp. xi–xxiv.

Cavendish, M. (1664) 'Letter 122' in *Sociable Letters* (London: W. Wilson).

CBS News Poll (27 February 2006) (CBS Television News, CBS Broadcasting, Inc.).

Charles, C. (1997) 'Gender Trouble in *Twelfth Night*', *Theatre Journal* 49: 121–41.

Charnes, L. (1993) 'Introduction' in L. Charnes (ed.), *Notorious Identity: Materializing the Subject in Shakespeare* (Cambridge, MA: Harvard University Press), pp. 1–19.

——, (2000a) 'The Hamlet Formerly Known as Prince' in H. Grady (ed.) *Shakespeare and Modernity: Early Modern to Millennium* (London and New York: Routledge), pp. 189–210.

——, (2000b) 'We Were Never Early Modern' in John J. Joughin (ed.) *Philosophical Shakespeares* (London and New York: Routledge), pp. 51–67.

——, (2006) *Hamlet's Heirs* (London and New York: Routledge).

——, (2007a) (accessed 30 July 2007) 'Reading for the Wormholes: Micro-periods from the Future', *Early Modern Culture: An Electronic Seminar* 6, Special Issue: Timely Meditations, http://emc.eserver.org/1–6/charnes.html

——, (2007b) 'Shakespeare, and belief, in the future' in H. Grady and T. Hawkes (eds) *Presentist Shakespeares* (London and New York: Routledge), pp. 64–78.
Chesterson, G. K. (2000) *Heresy/Orthodoxy* (Nashville: Thomas Nelson).
Cleaver, R. (1598) *A Godlie Forme of Hovseholde Government: for the Ordering of Private Families, according to the direction of Gods word* (London: F. Kingston for T. Man).
Countdown with Keith Olbermann (MSNBC Television, NBC Television, NBC Universal, Inc.).
Croce, B. (1941) *History as the Story of Liberty* (London: George Allen and Unwin).
——, (1960) *History: Its Theory and Practice* (New York: Russell and Russell).
Crooke, H. (1631) *Microcosmographia: A Description of the Body of Man*, 2nd edn revised(London: T. and R. Cotes for M. Sparke).
Curry, A. (2005) *Agincourt: A New History* (London: Tempus).
Daileader, C. R. (2002) 'Back Door Sex: Renaissance Gynosodomy, Aretino, and the Exotic', *English Literary Renaissance* 69: 303–34.
Daniel, S. (1595, 1962) *The Civile Wars between the Two Houses of Lancaster and Yorke*, book 4 (London: Printed by P. Short for S. Waterson) in G. Bullough (ed.) *Narrative and Dramatic Sources of Shakespeare*, vol. 4 (London: Routledge and Kegan Paul; New York: Columbia University Press), pp. 420–30.
Dash, I. (1981) *Wooing, Wedding, and Power: Women in Shakespeare's Plays* (New York: Columbia University Press).
'The Deadly Occupation' (30 July/6 August 2007) 'Editorial', *The Nation* 285: 3.
Dekker, T., and J. Webster (1607) *Westward Hoe* (London: W. Jaggard for J. Hodgets).
Deleuze, G. (1968) *Difference and Repetition*, P. Patton (translator) (London: Athlone Press).
Derrida, J. (1997) *Of Grammatology*, G. C. Spivak (translator) corrected edn (Baltimore and London: Johns Hopkins University Press).
Descartes, R. (1967) *Oeuvres* C. Adam and P. Tannery (eds) vol. 2 (Paris: J. Vrin).
——, (1985) 'The Passions of the Soul' in J. Cottingham, R. Stoothoff, and D. Murdoch (translators) *The Philosophical Writings of Descartes* (Cambridge: Cambridge University Press), pp. 325–404.
Desmet, C., and R. Sawyer (eds) (1999) *Shakespeare and Appropriation* (London and New York: Routledge).
de Torquemada, A. (1600) *The Spanish Mandevile of Miracles* (London: J. Roberts for E. Matts).
DiGangi, M. (1997) *The Homoerotics of Early Modern Drama* (Cambridge: Cambridge University Press).
DiPietro, C. (2007) 'Sex, Lies and Videotape: Representing the Past in *Shakespeare in Love*, Mapping a Future for Presentism', *Shakespeare: A Journal* 3: 40–62.
Dolan, F. E. (1994) *Dangerous Familiars: Representations of Domestic Crime in England 1550–1700* (Ithaca and London: Cornell University Press).
——, (1996) 'Reading, Writing, and Other Crimes' in V. Traub, M. L. Kaplan, and D. Callaghan (eds) *Feminist Readings of Early Modern Culture: Emerging Subjects* (Cambridge: Cambridge University Press), pp. 142–67.
——, (2000) 'Introduction' in F. Dolan (ed.) *As You Like It*, by W. Shakespeare. The Pelican Shakespeare (New York: Penguin).

Dollimore, J. (1985, 1994) 'Transgression and Surveillance in *Measure for Measure*' in J. Dollimore and A. Sinfield (eds) *Political Shakespeare: Essays in Cultural Materialism*, 2nd edn (Manchester: Manchester University Press; Ithaca and London: Cornell University Press), pp. 72–87.

——, (1991) *Sexual Dissidence: Augustine to Wilde, Freud to Foucault* (Oxford: Clarendon Press).

——, (1994) 'Shakespeare Understudies: The Sodomite, the Prostitute, the Transvestite and Their Critics' in J. Dollimore and A. Sinfield (eds) *Political Shakespeare: Essays in Cultural Materialism*, 2nd edn (Cornell University Press), pp. 129–52.

——, and A. Sinfield (1985a) 'History and Ideology: The Instance of Henry' in J. Drakakis (ed.) *Alternative Shakespeares* (London and New York: Methuen), pp. 206–27.

——, and ——, (eds) (1985b) *Political Shakespeare: Essays in Cultural Materialism* (Manchester: Manchester University Press).

Donald, A. (ed.) (1989) *Fantasy and the Cinema* (London: BFI Press).

Dowd, M. (2004) *Bushworld: Enter at Your Own Risk* (New York: G. P. Putnam's Sons).

Drakakis, J. (2007) 'Present text: Editing *The Merchant of Venice*' in H. Grady and T. Hawkes (eds) *Presentist Shakespeares* (London and New York: Routledge), pp. 79–95.

Dusinberre, J. (1975, 2003) *Shakespeare and the Nature of Women*, 3rd edn (Houndmills, Basingstoke: Palgrave Macmillan).

——, (1990) '*King John* and Embarrassing Women', *Shakespeare Survey* 42: 37–52.

Eaton, S. (1991) 'Defacing the Feminine in Renaissance Tragedy' in V. Wayne (ed.) *The Matter of Difference: Materialist Feminist Criticism of Shakespeare* (Ithaca: Cornell University Press), pp. 181–98.

——, (1996) 'A woman of letters: Lavinia in *Titus Andronicus*' in S. N. Garner and M. Sprengnether (eds) *Shakespearean Tragedy and Gender* (Bloomington: Indiana University Press), pp. 54–74.

Edelman, L. (2004) *No Future: Queer Theory and the Death Drive* (Durham: Duke University Press).

Egan, G. (2006) *Green Shakespeare: From Ecopolitics to Ecocriticism* (London and New York: Routledge).

Enterline, L. (2000) *The Rhetoric of the Body from Ovid to Shakespeare* (Cambridge: Cambridge University Press).

Eribon, D. (2004) *Insult and the Making of the Gay Self*, M. Lucey (translator) (Durham: Duke University Press).

Erickson, P. (1987) 'Rewriting the Renaissance, Rewriting Ourselves', *Shakespeare Quarterly* 38: 327–37.

Eyre, R. (dir.) (2005) *Stage Beauty*, screenplay by J. Hatcher (DVD, Lions Gate Home Entertainment).

Faludi, S. (1991) *Backlash: The Undeclared War Against American Women* (New York: Crown Publishers).

Ferguson, M. (2003) *Dido's Daughters: Literacy, Gender and Empire in Early Modern England and France* (Chicago and London: University of Chicago Press).

Ferguson, R. A. (2004) *Aberrations in Black: Toward a Queer of Color Critique* (Minneapolis: Minnesota University Press).

Fernie, E. (2005a) 'The Last Act: Presentism, Spirituality, and the Last Act of Hamlet' in E. Fernie (ed.) *Spiritual Shakespeares* (London and New York: Routledge), pp. 186–211.

——, (2005b) 'Shakespeare and the Prospect of Presentism', *Shakespeare Survey* 58: 169–84.

——, (2007) 'Action! *Henry 5*' in H. Grady and T. Hawkes (eds) *Presentist Shakespeares* (London and New York: Routledge), pp. 96–120.

Filmer, Sir R. ([1680] 1949) *Patriarcha and other Political Works*, P. Laslett (ed.) (Oxford: Oxford University Press).

Fischer, D. H. (2006) *Washington's Crossing* (Oxford and New York: Oxford University Press).

Fletcher, A. (1999) *Gender, Sex, and Subordination in England, 1500–1800* (New Haven: Yale University Press).

Foucault, M. (1976, 1978) *The History of Sexuality, vol. 1: An Introduction*, R. Hurley (translator) (New York: Pantheon, Random House).

Fradenburg, L., and C. Freccero (1996) 'Introduction: Caxton, Foucault, and the Pleasures of History' in L. Fradenburg and C. Freccero (eds) *Premodern Sexualities* (New York and London: Routledge), pp. xiii–xxiv.

Freccero, C. (2006). *Queer/Early/Modern* (Durham and London: Duke University Press).

Freud, S. ([1927] 1961, 1995) 'Fetishism' in 'Three essays on sexuality' in J. Strachey (translator) *The Standard Edition of the Complete Psychological Works of Sigmund Freud*, vol. 7 (London: Hogarth Press), pp. 152–57.

Gajowski, E. (1992) *The Art of Loving: Female Subjectivity and Male Discursive Traditions in Shakespeare's Tragedies* (Newark, DE: University of Delaware P; London and Toronto: Associated University Presses).

——, (8 March 2005) 'Responses to Doug's SAA Paper', email to Douglas Green, *Research Seminar: Shakespeare, Gender, and Sexual Orientation in the Present*, 33rd Annual Meeting, Shakespeare Association of America, Bermuda.

——, (2007) 'Lavinia as "Blank Page" and the Presence of Feminist Critical Practices' in H. Grady and T. Hawkes (eds) *Presentist Shakespeares* (London and New York: Routledge), pp. 121–40.

Gamman, L., and M. Makinen (1994) *Female Fetishism: A New Look* (London: Lawrence and Wishart).

Garber, M. (1990a) 'Fetish Envy', *October* 54: 45–56.

——, (1990b) 'Shakespeare as Fetish', *Shakespeare Quarterly* 41: 242–50.

——, (1992) *Vested Interests: Crossdressing and Cultural Anxiety* (New York and London: Routledge).

'Gays Kiss in Parliament' (29 November 1990) *The Sun*, 1.

Gercke, D. (1993) 'Ruin, Style and Fetish: The Corpus of Jean Cocteau', *Nottingham French Studies* 32: 10–18.

Girard, R. (1977) *Violence and the Sacred*, P. Gregory (translator) (Baltimore: Johns Hopkins University Press).

Goldberg, J. (1992) *Sodometries: Renaissance Texts, Modern Sexualities* (Stanford: Stanford University Press).

——, (ed.) (1994) *Queering the Renaissance* (Durham and London: Duke University Press).

——, and M. Menon (2005) 'Queering History', *PMLA* 120: 1608–17.

Gordon, M. (2000) *Joan of Arc* (New York: Penguin).

Gore, A. (2 March 2006) Comment, quoted by L. Lapham, Bush Impeachment Forum, sponsored by *Harper's Magazine* (C-SPAN 2 Television, National Cable Satellite Corp.).

Goy-Blanquet, D. (ed.) (2003a) *Joan of Arc, a Saint for All Reasons: Studies in Myth and Politics* (Burlington: Ashgate).

——, (2003b) 'Shakespeare and Voltaire Set Fire to History' in D. Goy-Blanquet (ed.) *Joan of Arc, a Saint for All Reasons: Studies in Myth and Politics* (Burlington: Ashgate), pp. 1–38.

——, (2003c) *Shakespeare's Early History Plays: From Chronicle to Stage* (London: Oxford University Press).

Grady, H. (1991) *The Modernist Shakespeare: Critical Texts in a Material World* (Oxford: Oxford University Press).

——, (1996) *Shakespeare's Universal Wolf: Studies in Early Modern Reification* (Oxford: Oxford University Press).

——, (2002) *Shakespeare, Machiavelli, and Montaigne: Power and Subjectivity from* Richard II *to* Hamlet (Oxford: Oxford University Press).

——, (July 2004) 'Where Did the Adjectives Go? Presentism, Materialism, and Historicism in the New Millennium', paper, *International Shakespeare Conference*, Shakespeare Institute, Stratford-upon-Avon.

——, (2005) 'Shakespeare Studies, 2005: A Situated Overview', *Shakespeare: A Journal* 1: 102–20.

——, (2007) 'Hamlet and the Present: Notes on the Moving Aesthetic "Now"' in H. Grady and T. Hawkes (eds) *Presentist Shakespeares* (London and New York: Routledge), pp. 141–63.

——, and T. Hawkes (eds) (2007) *Presentist Shakespeares* (London and New York: Routledge).

Green, D. E. (2002) 'Shakespeare, Branagh, and the "Queer Traitor": Close Encounters in the Shakespearean Classroom' in L. S. Starks and C. Lehmann (eds) *The Reel Shakespeare* (Madison and Teaneck: Fairleigh Dickinson University Press), pp. 191–211.

Greenblatt, S. (1980) *Renaissance Self-fashioning: From More to Shakespeare* (Chicago: University of Chicago Press).

——, (1986) 'Fiction and Friction' in T. C. Heller, M. Sosna, and D. E. Wellbery (eds) *Reconstructing Individualism: Autonomy, Individuality, and the Self in Western Thought* (Stanford: Stanford University Press), pp. 30–52.

——, (1988) *Shakespearean Negotiations: The Circulation of Social Energy in Renaissance England* (Berkeley and Los Angeles: University of California Press).

——, (1989) 'Towards a Poetics of Culture' in H. A. Veeser (ed.) *The New Historicism* (New York: Routledge), pp. 1–14.

Greenspan, A. (2007) *The Age of Turbulence: Adventures in a New World* (New York: Penguin).

Greer, G. (1979) 'Juliet's Wedding', *The Listener*, quoted in program for *Romeo and Juliet* (Nimrod).

Greif, K. E. (1982) 'The Whirligig of Time: *Twelfth Night* on the Stage, 1601–1912', PhD Thesis, Harvard University.

Grennan, E. (1987) 'The Women's Voices in *Othello*: Speech, Song, Silence', *Shakespeare Quarterly* 38: 275–92.

Gurr, A. (1992) *The Shakespearean Stage*, 3rd edn (Cambridge: Cambridge University Press).
Hall, E. ([1548] 1962) 'The Union of the Two Noble and Illustre Famelies of Lancastre and Yorke' in G. Bullough (ed.) *Narrative and Dramatic Sources of Shakespeare*, vol. 4 (London: Routledge and Kegan Paul; New York: Columbia University Press), pp. 286–88.
Halperin, D. (1990) *One Hundred Years of Sexuality* (New York: Routledge).
Halpern, R. (1997) *Shakespeare among the Moderns* (Ithaca: Cornell University Press).
Hanson, E. (2005) 'Gay Theory and Criticism: 3. Queer Theory' in M. Groden, M. Kreiswirth, and I. Sezman (eds) *The Johns Hopkins Guide to Literary Theory and Criticism*, 2nd edn (Baltimore: Johns Hopkins University Press).
Harris, J. G., and N. Korda (eds) (2002) *Staged Properties in Early Modern English Drama* (Cambridge: Cambridge University Press).
Hawkes, T. (1986) *That Shakespeherian Rag* (London: Methuen).
——, (1992) *Meaning by Shakespeare* (London: Routledge).
——, (2002) *Shakespeare in the Present* (London and New York: Routledge).
——, (2007) 'Band of Brothers' in H. Grady and T. Hawkes (eds) *Presentist Shakespeares* (London and New York: Routledge), pp. 6–26.
Hedges, C., and L. Al-Arian (30 July/6 August 2007) 'The Other War', *The Nation* 285: 11–31.
Hendricks, M. (1996) '"Obscured by Dreams": Race, Empire, and Shakespeare's *A Midsummer Night's Dream*', *Shakespeare Quarterly* 47: 37–60.
Henry, S. (25 January 2002) 'Females' Wages Still Fall Short, as Gap Widens', *The Philadelphia Inquirer*: C2.
Heywood, T. (1624) *Gynaikeion: or, Nine Bookes of Various History* (London: A. Isli Press).
Hic Mulier: Or, the Man-Woman: Being a Medicine to Cure the Coltish Desease of the Staggers in the Masculine-Feminines of Our Times, Exprest in a Briefe Declamation, Non Omnes Possumus Omnes (1620) (London: n.p.).
Hill, E (1984) *Shakespeare in Sable: A History of Black Shakespearean Actors* (Amherst: University of Massachusetts Press).
Hitt, J. (21 February 2007) 'Interview by Sam Seder', *The Sam Seder Show* (Air America Radio).
Hodgdon, B. (1991) *The End Crowns All: Closure and Contradiction in Shakespeare's History* (Princeton: Princeton University Press).
——, (1998) *The Shakespeare Trade: Performances and Appropriations* (Philadelphia: University of Pennsylvania Press).
Hoeniger, F. D. (1992) *Medicine and Shakespeare in the English Renaissance* (Newark: University of Delaware Press).
Holderness, G. (1988) *The Shakespeare Myth* (Manchester: Manchester University Press).
Holinshed, R. ([1587] 1962) 'The Chronicles of England, Scotland, and Ireland, vol. 3' in G. Bullough (ed.) *Narrative and Dramatic Sources of Shakespeare*, vol. 4 (London: Routledge and Kegan Paul; New York: Columbia University Press), pp. 376–408.
Holland, J., and G. Wihl (2005) 'Marxist Theory and Criticism: 2. Structuralist Marxism' in M. Groden, M. Kreiswirth, and I. Sezman (eds) *The Johns Hopkins*

Guide to Literary Theory and Criticism, 2nd edn (Baltimore: Johns Hopkins University Press), pp. 633–38.

Homily of the State of Matrimony, An ([1563] 1996) in R. McDonald (ed.) *The Bedford Companion to Shakespeare: An Introduction with Documents* (Boston and New York: Bedford/St. Martin's), pp. 278–87.

Howard, J. E. (1986) 'The New Historicism in Renaissance Studies', *English Literary Renaissance* 16: 13–43.

——, (1988) 'Crossdressing, the Theatre, and Gender Struggle in Early Modern England', *Shakespeare Quarterly* 39: 418–40.

——, (1994) *The Stage and Social Struggle in Early Modern England* (New York: Routledge).

——, and P. Rackin (1997) *Engendering a Nation: A Feminist Account of Shakespeare's English Histories* (London and New York: Routledge).

International Committee of the Red Cross (12 August 1949a) (accessed date: 25 February 2008) 'Convention 3: Relative to the Treatment of Prisoners of War' in Geneva Conventions, http://www.icrc.org/ihl.nsf/7c4d08d9b287a421 41256739003e636b/6fef854a3517b75ac125641e004a9e68

——, (12 August 1949b) (accessed date: 25 February 2008) 'Convention 4: Relative to the Protection of Civilian Persons in Time of War' in Geneva Conventions, http://www.icrc.org/ihl.nsf/7c4d08d9b287a42141256739003e636b/6756482d 86146898c125641e004aa3c5

Ivins, M. (2004) *Bushwhacked: Life in George W. Bush's America* (New York: Vintage).

Jackson, G. B. (1988) 'Topical Ideology: Witches, Amazons, and Shakespeare's Joan of Arc', *English Literary Renaissance* 18: 40–65. [Reprinted R. J. C. Watt (ed.) (2002) *Shakespeare's History Plays* (London: Longman), pp. 20–41].

Jardine, L. (1983, 1989) *Still Harping on Daughters: Women and Drama in the Age of Shakespeare* (Sussex: Harvester Press; New York: Columbia University Press).

——, (1996) *Reading Shakespeare Historically* (New York and London: Routledge).

Jehlen, M. (1995) 'Gender' in F. Lentricchia and T. McLaughlin (eds) *Critical Terms for Literary Study*, 2nd edn (Chicago: University of Chicago Press).

Jones, N. R. (2002) 'Trevor Nunn's *Twelfth Night*: Contemporary Film and Classic British Theatre', *Early Modern Literary Studies*, Electronic Publication 8: 1–38.

Jonson, B. (1969) 'Preface to *Hymenaei*: or The Solemnities of Masque, and Barriers' in S. Orgel (ed.) *Ben Jonson: The Complete Masques* (New Haven: Yale University Press), pp. 75–6.

Kahn, C. (1981) *Man's Estate: Masculine Identity in Shakespeare* (Berkeley: University of California Press).

——, (1997) *Roman Shakespeare: Warriors, Wounds, and Women* (London and New York: Routledge).

Kamen, A. (14 October 2005) 'In the Loop: George W. Bush and the G-Word', *The Washington Post*: A17.

Kastan, D. S. (1999) *Shakespeare After Theory* (London and New York: Routledge).

Keeble, N. H. (ed.) (1994) *The Cultural Identity of Seventeenth-Century Woman: A Reader* (London: Routledge).

Keegan, J. (1983) *The Face of Battle: The Story of Agincourt, Waterloo, and the Somme* (London: Penguin).

Kelly, J. (1984) 'Did Women Have a Renaissance?' in J. Kelly (ed.), *Women, History, and Theory: The Essays of Joan Kelly* (Chicago and London: University of Chicago Press), pp. 19–50.

Kemble, J. P. (dir.) (1788) *Macbeth*, by W. Shakespeare (Drury Lane Theatre).

Kennedy, Sen. E. (D-MA) (27 July 2004) Speech, Democratic National Convention.

Kennedy, Jr, R. F. (2006) (accessed 3 December 2006) 'Was the 2004 Election Stolen?', *Rolling Stone* www.rollingstone.com/news/story/10432334/was_the_2004_election_stolen

Kermode, F. (2000) *Shakespeare's Language* (London: Allen Lane).

Kiernander, A. (1998) 'Cupid's bow burn'd; or, Difference Endangered in John Lyly's *Gallathea* and Shakespeare's Cross-dress Comedies', *Australasian Drama Studies* 33: 54–64.

Kippax, H. G. (24 March 1979) 'Comedy into Tragedy—Almost', *Sydney Morning Herald*, p. 21.

Klosowka, A. (2004) *Queer Love in the Middle Ages* (New York: Palgrave Macmillan).

Knights, L. C. (1946) 'How Many Children Had Lady Macbeth? An Essay on the Theory and Practice of Shakespeare Criticism' in *Explorations: Essays in Criticism Mainly on the Art of Literature of the Seventeenth Century* (London: Chatto and Windus), pp. 1–39.

Knox, J. ([1558] 1999) 'The First Blast of the Trumpet Against the Monstrous Regiment of Women' in G. K. Paster and S. Howard (eds) *A Midsummer Night's Dream: Texts and Contexts*, by W. Shakespeare (Boston and New York: Bedford/St. Martin's), pp. 210–14.

Kolodny, A. (4 May 1988) 'Respectability is Eroding the Revolutionary Potential of Feminist Criticism', *The Chronicle of Higher Education* 34: A 52.

Komisarjevsky, T. (dir.) (1933) *Macbeth*, by W. Shakespeare (Shakespeare Memorial Theatre, Stratford-upon-Avon).

Korda, N. (2002) *Shakespeare's Domestic Economies: Gender and Property in Early Modern England* (Philadelphia: University of Pennsylvania Press).

Kunzle, D. (1982) *Fashion and Fetishism* (Towota, NJ: Rowman and Littlefield).

Lacan, J. (2005) *Écrits*, B. Fink (translator) (New York: Norton).

Lakoff, G. (2004) *Don't Think of an Elephant: Know Your Values and Frame the Debate* (White River Junction, VT: Chelsea Green Publishing).

Lapham, L. (2 March 2006) Comment, *Bush Impeachment Forum, sponsored by Harper's Magazine* (C-SPAN 2 Television, National Cable Satellite Corp.).

Laqueur, T. (1990) *Making Sex: Body and Gender from the Greeks to Freud* (Cambridge, MA: Harvard University Press).

Leggatt, A. (1988) *Shakespeare's Political Drama: The History Plays and the Roman Plays* (London: Routledge).

Lemnius, L. (1658) *The Secret Miracles of Nature*, Anonymous (translator) (London: J. Streater for H. Mosley, J. Sweeting, J. Clark, and G. Sawbridge).

Lenz, C. R. S., G. Greene, and C. T. Neely (eds) (1980) *The Woman's Part: Feminist Criticism of Shakespeare* (Urbana and Chicago: University of Illinois Press).

Levin, C. (1987) '"I Trust I May Not Trust Thee": Women's Visions of the World in Shakespeare's *King John*' in C. Levin and J. Watson (eds) *Ambiguous*

Realities: Women in the Middle Ages and Renaissance (Detroit: Wayne State University Press), pp. 219–34.

Levin, J. (2002) 'Lady Macbeth and the Daemonologie of Hysteria', *ELH* 69: 21–55.

Levine, L. (1994) *Men in Women's Clothing: Anti-theatricality and Effeminization 1579–1642* (Cambridge: Cambridge University Press).

Levine, N. S. (1998) *Women's Matters: Politics, Gender, and Nation in Shakespeare's Early History Plays* (Newark: University of Delaware Press).

Liebler, N. (ed.) (2002) *The Female Tragic Hero in English Renaissance Drama* (New York and Houndmills: Palgrave).

Loomba, A. (1992) *Gender, Race, Renaissance Drama* (Oxford: Oxford University Press).

——, and M. Orkin (eds) (1998) *Post-Colonial Shakespeares* (London and New York: Routledge).

Luhrmann, B. (dir.) (1996) *William Shakespeare's Romeo + Juliet* (Twentieth Century Fox/Bazmark Production; Fox Home Video).

Lukacs, G. (1923, 1971) *History and Class Consciousness* (Boston: MIT Press).

Lyly, J. (1976) *Gallathea* in R. A. Fraser and N. Rabkin (eds) *Drama of the English Renaissance* vol. 1 (New York: Macmillan), pp. 125–43.

Lyotard, J.-F. (1991) *Phenomenology*, B. Beakley (translator) (Albany: State University of New York Press).

MacDonald, J. (2002) *Women and Race in Early Modern Texts* (Cambridge: Cambridge University Press).

Mack, J. (1995) 'Fetish? Magic Figures in Africa' in A. Shelton (ed.) *Fetishism: Visualising Power and Desire* (London: South Bank Centre/Lund Humphreys), pp. 52–65.

Magnus, L. (2007) 'Michael Radford's *The Merchant of Venice* and the Vexed Question of Performance', *Literature/Film Quarterly* 35: 108–20.

Maher, B. (3 March 2006) Comment, *Real Time with Bill Maher* (HBO Television, Home Box Office, Inc.).

Marcus, L. S. (1986) 'Shakespeare's Comic Heroines: Elizabeth I and the Political Uses of Androgyny' in M. B. Rose (ed.) *Women in the Middle Ages and the Renaissance: Literary and Historical Perspectives* (Syracuse: Syracuse University Press), pp. 135–53.

——, (1988) *Puzzling Shakespeare: Local Reading and Its Discontents* (Berkeley: University of California Press).

Marr, D. (ed.) (1994) *Patrick White Letters* (Sydney: Random House, Australia).

Massinger, P. (1632) *The Maid of Honour* (London: J. Beale for R. Allot).

Masten, J. (1996) 'Textual Deviance: Ganymede's Hand in *As You Like It*' in M. Garber, P. B. Franklin, and R. L. Walkowitz (eds) *Field Work: Sites in Literary and Cultural Studies* (New York: Routledge), pp. 153–63.

——, (1997) *Textual Intercourse: Collaboration, Authorship, and Sexualities in Renaissance Drama* (Cambridge: Cambridge University Press).

Mazzio, C. (1997) 'Sins of the Tongue' in D. Hillman and C. Mazzio (eds) *The Body in Parts: Fantasies of Corporeality in Early Modern Europe* (New York and London: Routledge), pp. 53–79.

McLaverty, J. (1981) 'Comtean Fetishism in Silas Marner', *Nineteenth-Century Literature* 36: 318–36.

McLuskie, K. (1994) 'The Patriarchal Bard: Feminist Criticism and Shakespeare: *King Lear* and *Measure for Measure*' in J. Dollimore and A. Sinfield (eds) *Political Shakespeare: Essays in Cultural Materialism*, 2nd edn (Ithaca and London: Cornell University Press), pp. 88–108.

Mello, M. (2004) *Legalizing Gay Marriage* (Philadelphia: Temple University Press).

Michaelis, S. (1613) 'To the Reader' in *The Admirable History of the Possession and Conuersion of a Penitent Woman*, W. B. (translator) (London: F. Kingston for W.Aspley).

Michaud-Fréjaville, F. (2003) 'Person vs. Personage: Joan of Arc in 17th-Century France' in D. Goy-Blanquet (ed.) *Joan of Arc, a Saint for All Reasons: Studies in Myth and Politics* (Burlington: Ashgate), pp. 39–58.

Milhous, J., and R. D. Hume (1985) *Producible Interpretations: Eight English Plays* (Carbondale: Southern Illinois University Press).

Miller, J. (dir.) (1981, 2000) *Othello*, by W. Shakespeare (BBC-TV; VHS, Ambrose Video).

Miller, M. C. (2005) *Fooled Again: How the Right Stole the 2004 Election and Why They'll Steal the Next One Too (Unless We Stop Them)* (New York: Basic Books).

——, (Posted 16 June 2006) (accessed 29 September 2006) 'Some Might Call It Treason: An Open Letter to Salon', www.huffingtonpost.com/mark-crispin-miller/some-might-call-it-treaso-b_23187.html

Milton, J. (2003) *The Complete Poems and Major Prose*, M. Y. Hughes (ed.) (Indianapolis: Hackett Publishing Company).

Miner, M. M. (1980) '"Neither mother, wife, nor England's queen": The Roles of Women in *Richard 3*' in C. R. S. Lenz, G. Greene, and C. T. Neely (eds) *The Woman's Part: Feminist Criticism of Shakespeare* (Urbana: University of Illinois Press), pp. 35–55.

Montrose, L. A. (1981) 'The Place of a Brother in *As You Like It*: Social Process and Comic Form', *Shakespeare Quarterly* 32: 28–54.

——, (1986) '*A Midsummer Night's Dream* and the Shaping Fantasies of Elizabethan Culture: Gender, Power, Form' in M. W. Ferguson, M. Quilligan, and N. J. Vickers (eds) *Rewriting the Renaissance: The Discourses of Sexual Difference in Early Modern Europe* (Chicago: University of Chicago Press), pp. 65–87.

Moore, H. (15 August 2003) 'Present and Correct', *TLS: Times Literary Supplement*: 22.

Morris, B. (1989) 'Introduction' in B. Morris (ed.) *The Taming of the Shrew*, by W. Shakespeare. Arden 2nd ed. (London: Methuen), pp. 1–150.

Muir, K. (1978) *The Sources of Shakespeare's Plays* (New Haven: Yale University Press).

Mulhern, F. (1979) *The Moment of 'Scrutiny'* (London: New Left Books).

Mulvey, L. (1993) 'Some Thoughts on Theories of Fetishism in the Context of Contemporary Culture', *October* 65: 3–20.

Murray, M. A. (1921) *The Witch-Cult in Western Europe* (London: Oxford University Press).

Nagel, J. (2003) *Race, Ethnicity, and Sexuality: Intimate Intersections, Forbidden Frontiers* (Oxford: Oxford University Press).

Neely, C. T. (1985a) 'Feminist Criticism in Motion' in P. A. Treichler, C. Kramarae, and B. Stafford (eds) *For Alma Mater: Theory and Practice in Feminist Scholarship* (Urbana: University of Illinois Press).
——, (1985b) *Broken Nuptials in Shakespeare's Plays* (New Haven: Yale University Press).
——, (1988) 'Constructing the Subject: Feminist Practice and the New Renaissance Discourses', *English Literary Renaissance* 18: 5–18.
New Formations: A Journal of Culture/Theory/Politics (1993): 19.
Neuschäfer, A., and F. Serror (1984) *Le Théâtre du Soleil: Shakespeare* (Köln: Prometh Verlag).
Newman, K. (1987) ' "And Wash the Ethiop White": Femininity and the Monstrous in *Othello*' in J. E. Howard and M. F. O'Connor (eds) *Shakespeare Reproduced: The Text in History and Ideology* (New York: Methuen), pp. 143–162.
——, (1991) *Fashioning Femininity and English Renaissance Drama* (Chicago: University of Chicago Press).
Nickel, T. (1992) 'Pamela as Fetish: Masculine Anxiety in Henry Fielding's *Shamela* and James Parry's *The True Anti-Pamel*', *Studies in Eighteenth-Century Culture* 22: 37–49.
Novy, M. (1984) *Love's Argument: Gender Relations in Shakespeare* (Chapel Hill and London: University of North Carolina Press).
Nunn, T. (dir.) (1995) *Othello,* by W. Shakespeare (RSC, BBC-TV; VHS, Films for the Humanities and Sciences).
——, (dir.) (1996) *Twelfth Night,* by W. Shakespeare (Image Entertainment).
Olivier, Sir L. (dir.) (1946) *Henry 5,* by W. Shakespeare (Two Cities Films).
——, (dir.) (1948, 2000) *Hamlet,* by W. Shakespeare (DVD, Criterion Collection).
Orgel, S. (1996) *Impersonations: The Performance of Gender in Shakespeare's England* (Cambridge: Cambridge University Press).
——, (1999) 'Why Did the English Stage Take Boys for Women?' in M. Riggio (ed.) *Teaching Shakespeare through Performance* (New York: MLA), pp. 102–13.
Orkin, M. (1987) '*Othello* and the "Plain Face" of Racism', *Shakespeare Quarterly* 38: 166–88.
Orlin, L. C. (1994) *Private Matters and Public Culture in Post-Reformation England* (Ithaca: Cornell University Press).
——, (1998) 'The Witness Who Spoke When the Cock Crowed', unpublished paper.
Ornstein, R. (1972) *A Kingdom for a Stage: The Achievement of Shakespeare's History Plays* (Cambridge: Harvard University Press).
Osborne, L. E. (1996) *The Trick of Singularity: Twelfth Night and the Performance Editions* (Iowa City: University of Iowa Press).
——, (1998) 'Editing frailty in *Twelfth Night*' in J. Gondris (ed.) *Reading Readings: Essays on Shakespeare Editing in the Eighteenth Century* (Madison: Fairleigh Dickinson University Press; London: Associated University Presses), pp. 209–23.
——, (2002) 'Clip Art: Theorizing the Shakespeare Film Clip', *Shakespeare Quarterly* 53: 227–40.
Ovid (1929) *Metamorphoses*, F. J. Miller (translator) Loeb Library (London: Heinemann).

——, (1963) *Heroides* and *Amores*, G. Showerman (translator) Loeb Library (London: Heinemann).
——, (1970) *Ovid's Metamorphosis* [sic], G. Sandys (translator), K. K. Hulley and S. L. Vandersall (eds) (Lincoln: University of Nebraska Press).
Park, K. (1988) 'The Organic Soul' in C. B. Schmitt (general ed.) *The Cambridge History of Renaissance Philosophy* (Cambridge: Cambridge University Press), pp. 633–38.
Parker, A., and E. K. Sedgwick (1995) 'Introduction: Performativity and Performance' in A. Parker and E. K. Sedgwick (eds) *Performativity and Performance: Essays from the English Institute* (New York: Routledge), pp. 1–17.
Parker, O. (dir.) (1995, 2000) *Othello,* by W. Shakespeare (Columbia, DVD).
Parker, P. (1996) 'Virile Style' in L. Fradenburg and C. Freccero (eds) *Premodern Sexualities* (New York and London: Routledge), pp. 201–22.
Paster, G. K. (1993) *The Body Embarrassed: Drama and the Disciplines of Shame in Early Modern England* (Ithaca: Cornell University Press).
——, (2004) *Humoring the Body: Emotions and the Shakespearean Stage* (Chicago: University of Chicago Press).
——, K. Rowe, and M. Floyd-Wilson (eds) (2004) *Reading the Early Modern Passions: Essays in the Cultural History of Emotion* (Philadelphia: University of Pennsylvania Press).
Pequigney, J. (1985) *Such Is My Love: A Study of Shakespeare's Sonnets* (Chicago and London: University of Chicago Press).
——, (1992) 'The Two Antonios and Same-Sex Love in *Twelfth Night* and *The Merchant of Venice*', *English Literary Renaissance* 22: 201–21.
Pike, J. (1992) 'Exquisite Corpses: The Fetish of the Female Dead Body in Late Eighteenth- and Nineteenth-Century Literature', *Dissertation Abstracts International* 52: 12.
Pipon, J. K. (1861) *Manual of Military Law: For All Ranks of the Army, Militia, and Volunteer Services*, 2nd edn, Adjutant General's Office, Great Britain (London: W.H. Allen).
Plato (1997) *Complete Works,* J. M. Cooper (ed.) (Indianapolis: Hackett).
Polanski, R. (dir.) (1971, 2001) *Macbeth,* by W. Shakespeare (Columbia Tristar, DVD).
Porter, C. (1988) 'Are we being historical yet?', *South Atlantic Quarterly* 87: 743–87.
——, (1990) 'History and Literature: "After the New Historicism"', *New Literary History* 21: 253–81.
Pugh, T. (ed.) (2004) *Queering Medieval Genres* (New York: Palgrave Macmillan).
Rabkin, N. (1977) 'Rabbits, Ducks, and *Henry 5*', *Shakespeare Quarterly* 28: 279–96.
——, (1981) 'Either/Or: Responding to *Henry 5*' in N. Rabkin (ed.), *Shakespeare and the Problem of Meaning* (Chicago: University of Chicago Press), pp. 223–40.
Rackin, P. (1985) 'Anti-Historians: Women's Roles in Shakespeare's Histories', *Theatre Journal* 37: 329–44.
——, (1987) 'Androgyny, Mimesis, and the Marriage of the Boy Heroine on the English Renaissance Stage', *PMLA* 102: 29–41.

Rackin, P. (1989) 'Patriarchal History and Female Subversion in *King John*' in D. Curren-Aquino (ed.) *King John: New Perspectives* (Newark: University of Delaware Press), pp. 65–82.

Rackin, P. (1990) *Stages of History: Shakespeare's English Chronicles* (Ithaca: Cornell University Press).

——, (1991) 'Genealogical Anxiety and Female Authority: The Return of the Repressed in Shakespeare's Histories' in M.-R. Logan and P. L. Rudnytsky (eds) *Contending Kingdoms: Historical, Psychological, and Feminist Approaches to the Literature of Sixteenth-Century England and France* (Detroit: Wayne State University Press), pp. 323–45.

——, (1999) 'Staging the Female Body: Maternal Breastfeeding and Lady Macbeth's "Unsex Me Here"' in C. Nesci and G. van Slyke (eds) *Corps/Décors: Femmes, Orgie, Parodie* (Amsterdam: Rodopi), pp. 17–29.

——, (2000) 'Misogyny Is Everywhere' in D. Callaghan (ed.) *A Feminist Companion to Shakespeare* (Malden, MA, and Oxford: Blackwell), pp. 42–56.

——, (2002) 'Women's Roles in the Elizabethan History Plays' in M. Hattaway (ed.) *The Cambridge Companion to Shakespeare's History Plays* (Cambridge: Cambridge University Press) pp. 71–86.

——, (2005) *Shakespeare and Women* (Oxford: Oxford University Press).

Radford, M. (dir.) (2004) *The Merchant of Venice,* by W. Shakespeare (Sony Pictures).

Rambuss, R. (1998) *Closet Devotions* (Durham, NC: Duke University Press).

Reilly, W. (dir.) (1991) *Men of Respect* (Arthur Goldblatt Productions/Columbia Pictures).

Reynolds, E. (1640) *A Treatise of the Passions and Faculties of the Soule of Man* (London: R. H. for R. Bostock).

Rich, A. (1993) 'Compulsory Heterosexuality and Lesbian Existence' in H. Abelove, M. A. Barale, and D. M. Halperin (eds) *The Lesbian and Gay Studies Reader* (New York: Routledge), pp. 227–54.

Roach, J. (1985) *The Player's Passion: Scenes in the Science of Acting* (Newark: University of Delaware Press).

Romero, A. (20 February 2006) Comment, Town Hall on Presidential Authority and NSA Surveillance, George Washington University, Washington, DC (C-SPAN Television, National Cable Satellite Corp.).

Rothschild, M. (March 2005) Editor's Note: 'Hidden Passages', *The Progressive* 69: 4.

Rove, K. (15 August 2007) Interview, The Rush Limbough Show (Premiere Radio Networks).

Rutter, C. C. (2004) 'Remind Me: How Many Children Had Lady Macbeth?', *Shakespeare Survey* 57: 38–53.

Ryan, K. (2007) '*Troilus and Cressida*: The Perils of Presentism' in H. Grady and T. Hawkes (eds) *Presentist Shakespeares* (London and New York: Routledge), pp. 164–83.

Saccio, P. (1977) *Shakespeare's English Kings: History, Chronicle, and Drama* (London: Oxford University Press).

'Same-Sex Marriage in the United States' (Accessed 15 June 2006) http://en.wikipedia.org/wiki/Same-sex_marriage_in _the_United_States

Schalkwyk, D. (2005) 'Between Historicism and Presentism: Love and Service in *Antony and Cleopatra* and *The Tempest*', *Shakespeare in Southern Africa* 17: 1–17.

Schoenfeldt, M. C. (1999) *Bodies and Selves in Early Modern England: Physiology and Inwardness in Spenser, Shakespeare, Herbert, and Milton* (Cambridge: Cambridge University Press).

Schor, N. (1988) 'Fetishism and Its Ironies', *Nineteenth-Century French Studies* 17: 89–97.

Schwarz, K. (2000) *Tough Love: Amazon Encounters in the English Renaissance* (Durham: Duke University Press).

——, (2003) 'A Tragedy of Good Intentions: Maternal Agency in *3 Henry 6* and *King John*', *Renaissance Drama* 32: 225–54.

Scot, R. (1651) *Scot's Discovery of Witchcraft Proving the Common Opinions of Witches Contracting with Divels, Spirits, or Familiars* (London: R. C. for G. Calvert).

Sedgwick, E. K. (1985) *Between Men: English Literature and Male Homosocial Desire* (New York: Columbia University Press).

——, (1993) *Tendencies* (Durham: Duke University Press).

Shakespeare, W. (1873) *A New Variorum Edition of Shakespeare* H. H. Furness (ed.) vol. 2 (Philadelphia and London: J. W. Lippincott).

——, (1969) *The Complete Pelican Shakespeare*, by William Shakespeare, A. Harbage (ed.), revised edn (Baltimore: Penguin).

——, (1974) *The Riverside Shakespeare*, G. B. Evans *et al.* (ed.) (Boston: Houghton Mifflin).

——, (1989) *The Taming of the Shrew*, Brian Morris (ed.) Arden 2nd edn (London: Methuen) [Reprinted London: Routledge].

——, (1997a) *The Complete Works of Shakespeare*, D. Bevington (ed.) 4th edn (New York: Longman).

——, (1997b) *Macbeth*, A. R. Braunmuller (ed.) (Cambridge: Cambridge University Press).

——, (1997c) *The Norton Shakespeare Based on the Oxford Edition*, S. Greenblatt *et al.* (ed.) (New York: Norton).

——, (1997d) *The Riverside Shakespeare*, G. B. Evans and J. J. M. Tobin (eds.) 2nd edn (Boston: Houghton Mifflin).

——, (1998a) *The Complete Works*, S. Wells, G. Taylor, J. Jowett, and W. Montgomery (eds) 2nd edn (Oxford: Clarendon Press).

——, (1998b) *A Midsummer Night's Dream*, W. Clemen (ed.) 2nd revised edn (New York: New American Library).

——, (2000a) *As You Like It*, F. Dolan (ed.) The Pelican Shakespeare (New York: Penguin).

——, (2000b) *Twelfth Night*, J. Crewe (ed.) Pelican Shakespeare (New York: Penguin).

——, (2001) *Twelfth Night: Text and Contexts*, B. R. Smith (ed.) (Boston and New York: Bedford/St. Martin's).

——, (2002) *The Merchant of Venice: Texts and Contexts*, M. L. Kaplan (ed.) (Boston and New York: Bedford/St. Martin's).

——, (2007) *Othello: Texts and Contexts*, K. F. Hall (ed.) (Boston and New York: Bedford/St. Martin's).

Shapiro, M. (1987) 'Lady Mary Wroth Describes a "Boy Actress"', *Medieval and Renaissance Drama in England* 4: 187–94.

Sher, A. (dir.) (1998) *Macbeth*, by W. Shakespeare (Royal Shakespeare Company, Swan Theatre, Stratford-upon-Avon).

Shiels, M., with D. Camper (17 March 1975) 'Hiring Muddle', *Newsweek.*

Shulevitz, J. (26 January 2003) 'The Close Reader', *The New York Times Book Review.*

Shulevitz, J. (20 February 2005) 'The Mommy Track', review of *Perfect Madness: Motherhood in the Age of Anxiety,* by J. Warner, *The New York Times Book Review.*

Simpson, D. (1982) *Fetishism and Imagination* (Baltimore: Johns Hopkins University Press).

Sinfield, A. (1992) *Faultlines: Cultural Materialism and the Politics of Dissident Reading* (Berkeley: University of California Press).

——, (1994) 'Introduction: Reproductions, Interventions' in J. Dollimore and A. Sinfield (eds) *Political Shakespeare: Essays in Cultural Materialism,* 2nd edn (Ithaca and London: Cornell University Press), pp. 154–57.

——, (1996) 'How to Read *The Merchant of Venice* Without Being Heterosexist', in T. Hawkes (ed.) *Alternative Shakespeares,* vol. 2 (London and New York: Routledge), pp. 122–39.

——, (2002) 'Lesbian and Gay Taxonomies', *Critical Inquiry* 29: 120–38.

——, (2006a) 'How to Read *The Merchant of Venice* without Being Heterosexist' in A. Sinfield (ed.), *Shakespeare, Authority, Sexuality: Unfinished Business in Cultural Materialism* (London and New York: Routledge), pp. 53–67.

——, (2006b) *Shakespeare, Authority, Sexuality: Unfinished Business in Cultural Materialism* (London and New York: Routledge).

Singh, J. (1994) 'Othello's Identity, Postcolonial Theory, and Contemporary African Rewritings of *Othello*' in M. Hendricks and P. Parker (eds) *Women, 'Race,' and Writing in the Early Modern Period* (New York: Routledge), pp. 287–99.

Siraisi, N. G. (1990) *Medieval and Early Renaissance Medicine: An Introduction to Knowledge and Practice* (Chicago: University of Chicago Press).

Sloterdijk, P. (1987) *A Critique of Cynical Reason* (Minneapolis: University of Minnesota Press).

Smith, B. R. (1991) *Homosexual Desire in Shakespeare's England: A Cultural Poetics* (Chicago: University of Chicago Press).

Smith, G. (5 September 2006)) (accessed 16 January 2007) 'Remember His Name' http://sportsillustrated.cnn.com/2006/magazine/09/05/tillman0911/2.html

Sprengnether, M. (1996) 'The Gendered Subject of Shakespearean Tragedy' in S. N. Garner and M. Sprengnether (eds) *Shakespearean Tragedy and Gender* (Bloomington: Indiana University Press), pp. 1–27.

Stallybrass, P. (1991a) 'Boy Actors, Female Roles, and Elizabethan Eroticism' in D. S. Kastan and P. Stallybrass (eds) *Staging the Renaissance: Reinterpretations of Elizabethan and Jacobean Drama* (New York and London: Routledge), pp. 57–67.

——, (1991b) 'Reading the Body and the Jacobean Theater of Consumption' in D. S Kastan and P. Stallybrass (eds) *Staging the Renaissance: Reinterpretations of Elizabethan and Jacobean Drama* (New York and London: Routledge), pp. 209–20.

——, (1992) 'Transvestism and the "Body Beneath": Speculating on the Boy Actor' in S. Zimmerman (ed.) *Erotic Politics: The Dynamics of Desire on the Renaissance Stage* (London: Routledge), pp. 64–83.

Stanton, K. (2000) '"Made to write 'whore' upon?": Male and Female Use of the Word 'Whore' in Shakespeare's Canon' in D. Callaghan (ed.) *A Feminist Companion to Shakespeare* (Oxford: Blackwell), pp. 80–102.

Sullivan, K. (1999) *The Interrogation of Joan of Arc* (Minneapolis: University of Minnesota Press).

Suskind, R. (2004a) *The Price of Loyalty: George W. Bush, the White House, and the Education of Paul O'Neill* (New York: Simon and Schuster).

——, (17 October 2004b) 'Without a Doubt', *The New York Times*. http://cscs.umich.edu/~crshalizi/sloth/2004-10-16b.html

Sutcliffe, M. (1629) *A True Relation of Englands Happinesse, Under the Raigne of Queene Elizabeth* (London: n. p.).

Sutherland, J., and C. Watts (2000) *Henry 5, War Criminal? and Other Shakespeare Puzzles* (Oxford and New York: Oxford University Press).

Suzman, J. (dir.) (1988) *Othello*, by W. Shakespeare, Market Theatre, Johannesburg (VHS, Films for the Humanities).

T. S. (30 March 1979) 'Australian Touch to Shakespeare', *Manly Daily*, p. 11.

Taunton, N. (1994) 'The Turn of the Shrew', *Skin Two* 15: 90–4.

——, (1996) 'Patterns of Sadomasochism and Fashion-Fetishism in *Taming of the Shrew*', *Erfurt Electronic Studies in English* 8, accessed 6 May 2008, http://webdoc.gwdg.de/edoc/ia/eese/eese.html

Taylor, G. (1982) 'Introduction' in G. Taylor (ed.) *Henry 5*, by W. Shakespeare (Oxford: Oxford University Press), pp. 1–74.

Tennenhouse, L. (1986) *Power on Display: The Politics of Shakespeare's Genres* (London: Methuen).

Thompson, A. (1991) 'Are there any women in *King Lear?*' in V. Wayne (ed.) *The Matter of Difference: Materialist Feminist Criticism of Shakespeare* (Ithaca: Cornell University Press), pp. 117–28.

——, and S. Roberts (eds) (1997) *Women Reading Shakespeare, 1660–1900* (Manchester: Manchester University Press).

Thompson, B. (18 May 2004) 'The King and We: Henry 5's War Cabinet Mock Debate at Shakespeare Theatre Has Familiar Ring', *The Washington Post* C01.

Thurn, D. (1990) 'Sovereignty, Disorder, and Fetishism in Marlowe's *Edward 2*', *Renaissance Drama* 21: 115–41.

Traub, V. (1992) *Desire and Anxiety: Circulations of Sexuality in Shakespearean Drama* (New York: Routledge).

——, (2002) *The Renaissance of Lesbianism in Early Modern England* (Cambridge: Cambridge University Press).

——, (2004) 'Friendship's Loss: Alan Bray's Making of History', *GLQ* 10: 339–65.

Tribe, L. (20 February 2006) Comment, Town Hall on Presidential Authority and NSA Surveillance, George Washington University, Washington, DC (C-SPAN Television, National Cable Satellite Corp.).

Trumbach, R. (1998) *Sex and the Gender Revolution, vol. 1, Heterosexuality and the Third Gender in Enlightenment London* (Chicago and London: University of Chicago Press).

Tulchin, A. (2007) 'Same-Sex Couples Creating Households in Old Regime France: The Uses of the Affrèrement', *Journal of Modern History* 79: 613–47.

U.S. Senate Committee on the Judiciary (2004) *A Proposed Constitutional Amendment to Preserve Traditional Marriage*. Serial No. J-108–61 (Washington, DC: U. S. Government Printing Office).

U.S. Supreme Court (1986) Bowers v. Hardwick, 478 US 186, accessed on 1 August 2006. http://www.law.cornell.edu/supct/html/historics/USSC_CR_0478_0186_ZS.html

Vaughan, V. M. (1989) '*King John*: A Study in Subversion and Containment' in D. T. Curren-Aquino (ed.) *King John: New Perspectives* (Newark, DE: University of Delaware Press), pp. 62–75.

Walker, J. M. (ed.) (1998) *Dissing Elizabeth: Negative Representations of Gloriana* (Durham and London: Duke University Press).

Wall, W. (1998) '"Household Stuff": The Sexual Politics of Domesticity and the Advent of English Comedy', *ELH* 65: 1–45.

Waller, M. (1987) 'Academic Tootsie: The Denial of Difference and the Difference It Makes', *Diacritics* 17: 2–20.

Warner, M. (1981) *Joan of Arc: The Image of Female Heroism* (New York: Knopf).

Wayne, D. E. (1990) 'New Historicism' in M. Coyle, P. Garside, M. Kelsall, and J. Peck (eds) *Encyclopaedia of Literature and Criticism* (London and New York: Routledge), pp. 802–03.

Wayne, V. (1991a) 'Historical Differences: Misogyny and *Othello*' in V. Wayne (ed.) *The Matter of Difference: Materialist Feminist Criticism of Shakespeare* (Ithaca: Cornell University Press), pp. 153–79.

——, (1991b) 'Introduction' in V. Wayne (ed.) *The Matter of Difference: Materialist Feminist Criticism of Shakespeare* (Ithaca: Cornell University Press), pp. 1–26.

Weimann, R. (2000) *Author's Pen and Actor's Voice: Playing and Writing in Shakespeare's Theatre*, H. Higbee and W. West (eds.) (Cambridge: Cambridge University Press).

Wells, R. H. (2000) 'Historicism and 'Presentism' in Early Modern Studies', *Cambridge Quarterly* 29: 37–60.

Weston, K. (1997) *Families We Choose* (New York: Columbia University Press).

Whitbread, O. (dir.) (17 October 1967) *Romeo and Juliet*, by W. Shakespeare, television program (ABC-TV, Australia)

White, J. S. (Winter 2005) 'Pipeline to Pathways: New Directions for Improving the Status of Women on Campus', *Liberal Education* 91: 22–7.

Wiles, D. (1987) *Shakespeare's Clown: Actor and Text in the Elizabethan Playhouse* (Cambridge: Cambridge University Press).

Williams, R. (1983) *Keywords: A Vocabulary of Culture and Society*, revised edn (New York: Oxford University Press).

'Women in Banks' (1 November 1975) *The Economist*.

Woodbridge, L. (1984) *Women and the English Renaissance: Literature and the Nature of Womankind* (Urbana: University of Illinois Press).

Woodward, B. (2004) *Plan of Attack* (New York: Simon and Schuster).

Woolcock, P. (dir.) (1997) *Macbeth on the Estate* (BBC-TV).

Woolf, V. (1928, 1993) *Orlando: A Biography* (San Diego: Harcourt Brace).

Wright, T. (1604) *The Passions of the Minde in Generall* (London: V. Simmes for W. Burre).

Zeffirelli F. (dir.) (1968) *Romeo and Juliet*, by W. Shakespeare (BHE-London, Verona Productions, D. de Laurentiis).

Zeikowitz, R. E. (2003) *Homoeroticism and Chivalry: Discourses of Male Same-Sex Desire in the Fourteenth Century* (New York: Palgrave Macmillan).
Ziegler, G. (1997) *Shakespeare's Unruly Women* (Washington, DC: Folger Shakespeare Library).
Zizek, S. (1989) *The Sublime Object of Ideology* (London: Verso).
——, (2002) *On Belief* (London and New York: Routledge).

Index

PTO